THE ANCIENT ABBEYS AND PRIORIES OF WALES

J. Richard Williams

First published in 2015

© J. Richard Williams

© Gwasg Carreg Gwalch 2015

ISBN: 978-1-84524-229-9

Cover design: Lynwen Jones

Published by Gwasg Carreg Gwalch,
12 Iard yr Orsaf, Llanrwst, Wales LL26 0EH
tel: 01492 642031
fax: 01492 641502
email: books@carreg-gwalch.com
internet: www.carreg-gwalch.com

Contents

1. Introduction

In so far as beauty of structure is beauty of line and curve, balance and harmony of masses and dimensions, I have seldom relished it as deeply as on the grassy nave of some crumbling church, before lonely columns and empty windows where wild flowers were a cornice and the sailing clouds a roof.

English Hours. Henry James. Heinemann. 1905

Wales *'is a country with relatively few great churches and abbeys'*, from the Middle Ages, so says Adrian Pettifer. If anyone is asked which of its ancient buildings typifies Wales, few would suggest a cathedral as there are only five in existence:

- Bangor Cathedral – the second to be built in Britain and the oldest in Wales
- Brecon Cathedral – one of the newest cathedrals in Britain and is a medieval church raised to cathedral status in 1923.
- Llandaff Cathedral – founded in 1107 but best known for its modern bridge bearing 'Christ aloft', the work of Sir Jacob Epstein
- St Aspah Cathedral – known for its connections with the Welsh Bible translators
- St David's Cathedral – a popular pilgrimage site in the Middle Ages; two trips here were equal to one trip to Rome; three equalled a pilgrimage to Jerusalem. It contains a shrine to St David, patron saint of Wales.

Possibly the most readily offered answer would be 'castles' as there are 49 castles owned by CADW – *the official guardian of the built heritage of Wales*. Another list has over 150 castles but is still beaten into second place by the one that lists over 350 Welsh castles!

But there are a number of abbeys and priories, buildings *'where glory reigned'* that are also part of the history of Wales. Most were built in places of relative solitude where peace was plentiful, in quiet, out of the way positions; others were not so but wherever they are they have been continually seen and appreciated by scholars and ordinary worshipers alike. Poets have lauded and magnified their names. Over fifty medieval poets have sung the praises of the abbots and abbeys of Wales in one hundred and twenty four poems.

More contemporary poets have written about our national treasures and if any of those poems and if any of these buildings were to be ignored our Christian heritage and social history would be incomplete.

It was Saunders Lewis who wrote:

Wales, my country, is a vineyard given to us to care for,
to be delivered to my children, and my children's children,
as an eternal heritage…
so the glories of the past can be kept for the future.

(*a translation*)
Buchedd Garmon. S. Lewis. Gwasg Aberystwyth. 1937

Further Reading

Ancient Cathedrals of Wales: Their Story and Music. Meurig Owen. Gwasg Carreg Gwalch. 2013.
Library of Wales Journal. C. Davies. Summer. 1974.
Welsh Castles. A. Pettifer. Boydell Press. 2000.

2. Same calling – different order

The concept of giving up one's life to live in a monastery might seem rather strange and not at all appealing to many members of the human race of the twenty first century as a life of prayer and service is not recognised as being of value by many who have turned their back on religion. Their knowledge of monks who might live such a life is almost entirely gleaned from films and television advertisements. Mine was from the same source, mostly from the middle years of the twentieth century, but religion then had more appeal and had a more secure hold on members of the community who were able to differentiate between facts and the fiction of *The Adventures of Robin Hood* and his companion – the fat and jolly Friar Tuck.

During the early years of the Middle Ages, to be a monk was a more familiar calling but it did not necessarily mean being attached to any particular family or order of monks. It was enough for them to be considered Christians who happened to be members of a particular abbey or monastery which followed the Rule of St Benedict and who were dedicated to following and serving Christ.

Monasticism (from the Greek *monos* meaning 'single' or 'alone') usually refers to the way of life adopted by individuals, whose ideal of perfection or a higher level of religious experience was through living together in a community. Monastic orders have been organized around a rule or teacher, the activities of the members being closely regulated by the rule adopted. Such a life originated in India in the first millennium BC, and exists in many of the world's leading religions including Buddhism, Christianity, Jainism and Daoism (Taoism). In the western world, monasticism was a strong influence in the shaping of political, social and artistic events for about 1,200 years, from the sixth through to the eighteenth century.

Monasticism always includes a disciplined self-denial which included fasting, silence, being against personal ownership, an acceptance of bodily discomfort, poverty, celibacy and obedience to a spiritual leader. Their hope was and still is a more intense relationship with God or the service of God through prayer, meditation and good works.

Though not the founder of Christian monastic life, that had begun two and a half to three centuries before his birth, in Egypt, Palestine, and Asia Minor, St Benedict became a monk as a young man, having learned of the tradition by being with monks and reading monastic literature. The organization of western monasticism is due primarily to him and the Benedictine Rule which formed the basis of monastic community life until the twelfth century.

St Benedict lived from 480 to 547. His biography was written by St Gregory the Great, pope from 590 to 604. Benedict was born in Nursia, a village northeast of Rome. He was sent to Rome to be educated but he fled to a place southeast of Rome called Subiaco where he lived as a hermit for three years tended by the monk Romanus and was discovered by a group of monks who persuaded him to be their spiritual leader but his regime was not one the monks could adhere to so they plotted to poison him. Benedict blessed a pitcher of poisoned wine given to him by the monks and it broke into pieces. After the attempt on his life, he left to establish twelve monasteries with twelve monks each to the south of Rome. Later, possibly in 529, he moved to Monte Cassino, about eighty miles south-east of Rome; where he destroyed a pagan temple to Apollo and built his monastery. It was there that he wrote The Rule for the Monastery of Monte

Cassino which came to be used and adhered to by every monk, whatever order they belonged to. Benedict was more of a monastic leader than a scholar but he read the works of Cassian and other monastic writings, which contained many rules and sayings used by him. The Rule is the only example of Benedict's writing.

Among the leading monastic orders that evolved in the early Middle Ages were the Carthusians in the eleventh century and the Cistercians in the twelfth. The mendicant begging orders – Dominican, Franciscan and Carmelite friars arose in the thirteenth century.

Matters changed in the tenth century when monks from the Abbey of Cluny travelled further afield and founded other churches and monasteries. These were not considered independent institutions but rather an extension of the original Cluny house. Wherever a Cluniac monk settled, he swore obedience to the abbot of Cluny.

The concept of a religious order was further established by some of the first Cistercian monks of Citeaux Abbey. When they moved from the 'mother house' they founded the abbey at Clairvaux and from there monks moved on to Rivelaux but even though they had left the 'mother abbey', they were beholden to the abbot of the 'mother abbey' and it was his duty to inspect and oversee standards in each new 'daughter house'. Cistercian abbots of every abbey were also expected to attend an annual meeting at Citeaux. This meant that every Cistercian abbey in Europe kept to the same disciplined order.

The ideal of being committed to an order rather than one particular abbey was expanded by St Francis and St Dominic, the founding fathers of the friars.

Friars were monks who travelled from place to place to preach and rather than work for a living would beg food and shelter. They were members of an international organisation who still retained

3. Do as I say – the rule of Saint Benedict

Every monastery lived by The Rule or *Reglua* and if any of the rules were broken, a punishment, some of which were very severe, was recorded for each transgression in a Punishment Book or *Libri Posnitentiales*.

All monasteries were founded with the same purpose in mind and were originally linked by their adherence to The Rule of Saint Benedict (*Regula Benedicti*), a book written by Benedict at Monte Cassino, Italy as a guide for the spiritual and administrative life of monks living under the authority of an abbot. The over-riding theme of St Benedict's Rule is *pax* (peace) and *ora et labora* (prayer and work). The Rule provides a moderate guideline to monastic life but because of different emphasis and interpretations of the rules, it led to the formation of other, different, monastic orders.

After the Morning Mass, the monks would gather in the Chapter House for their daily meeting which included the reading of a chapter of The Rule of Saint Benedict. This practice gave the Chapter House its name. Presiding over the meeting was the abbot, who was in absolute control of the abbey. He was regarded as Christ's representative in the building. When the abbot entered a room, all stood up; when he passed, a monk would stop and bow his head. In a large or wealthy abbey, the abbot could be unavoidably absent for long periods, the meeting would then be chaired by his deputy, the prior. Like the abbot, he would also have a separate house and would not sleep in the dormitory with the other monks. This, though, was not in keeping with The Rule of Saint Benedict.

The Rule of Saint Benedict has been used by Benedictines and others for 1,500 years and opens with a preface which sets the main principles of a religious life:

> The renunciation of one's own will and arming oneself with the strong and noble weapons of obedience under the banner of the true King, Christ the Lord.

The Rule's seventy three chapters then follow with rules and instructions on every aspect of a monk's daily life, on the qualifications of an abbot, on the moderation in the use of speech. Chapter 7 divides humility into twelve degrees, or steps on the ladder that leads to Heaven: (1) Fear God; (2) Substitute one's will to the will of God; (3) Be obedient to one's superior; (4) Be patient amid hardships; (5) Confess one's sins; (6) Accept oneself as a worthless workman; (7) Consider oneself inferior to all; (8) Follow examples set by superiors; (9) Do not speak until spoken to; (10) Do not laugh; (11) Speak simply and modestly; (12) Be humble in bodily posture.

Chapters 8–19 regulate the Divine Office, the Godly work to which nothing is to be preferred, namely the eight canonical hours. Detailed arrangements are made for the number of Psalms, etc., to be recited in Winter and Summer, on Sundays, weekdays, Holy Days, and at other times. Other rules included regulations regarding the appointment of a Dean over every ten monks, dormitory rules stipulating that each monk should have a separate bed and should sleep in his habit so as to be ready to rise without delay [for early Vigils]; a light was burnt in the dormitory throughout the night.

Chapters 23 to 29 have a scale of punishments for disobedience, pride, and other faults: beginning with private admonition; next, public reproof; then separation from the brothers at meals and elsewhere and finally excommunication or corporal punishment instead.

corporal punishment instead.

Chapters 39 and 40 regulate the quantity and quality of the food. Two meals a day were allowed, with two cooked dishes at each. Each monk was allowed a pound of bread and a *hemina* (probably about half a pint) of wine. The flesh of four-footed animals was prohibited except for the sick and the weak.

Chapters 48 to 51 emphasize the importance of daily manual work appropriate to the ability of the monk. The hours of work varied with the seasons but were never less than five hours a day. Rules for monks working in the fields or travelling were also included. Chapter 54 forbade the monks to receive letters or gifts without the abbot's permission. Chapter 55 says clothing was to be adequate and suited to the climate and locality, at the discretion of the abbot. Chapter 68 ordered that all cheerfully try to do whatever was commanded, however hard it would seem. Chapter 70 prohibited them from striking one another. Chapter 71 encouraged the brothers to be obedient not only to the abbot and his officials, but also to one another. Chapter 73 is the Epilogue, declaring that the Rule was not offered as an ideal of perfection, but merely as a means towards godliness.

Some of the Rules might appear to be very condescending to twenty first century readers but others have made their way into our language as sayings and proverbs giving us wealth of a different kind:

- *Listen and attend with the ear of your heart.*
- *The first degree of humility is prompt obedience.*
- *Idleness is the enemy of the soul; and therefore the brethren ought to be employed in manual labour at certain times, at others, in devout reading.*
- *And let them first pray together, that so they may associate in peace.*
- *He should first show them in deeds rather than words all that*

is good and holy.
- *The prophet shows that, for the sake of silence, we are to abstain even from good talk. If this be so, how much more needful is it that we refrain from evil words, on account of the penalty of the sin!*
- *The sleepy like to make excuses.*

Benedict's Rule stressed the importance of manual labour but not for financial gain but to endorse and sanctify a moral discipline.

Nunc lege, nunc ora,
Multoque labore labora;
Sic erit hors brevis,
Sic labor ille levis.

(Now read, now pray,
Now work hard;
So the hour will appear to be short,
And the work will be effortless.)
(a translation)

Their motto in life seemed to be *'Cruce et aratro'* meaning 'with the Cross and the plough.' If nothing else, the Rules of St Benedict gave a sensible guide to living be we monks, nuns or just ordinary members of the public.

Further Reading

Life in a Medieval Abbey. T. McAleavy. English Heritage. 1996.
Life in a Monastery. S. Hebron. Pitkin Publishing. 2004.
Rule of St Benedict. Catholic Encyclopaedia. Ed. C. Herbermann. Robert Appleton Company. 1913.

4. Builders and Craftsmen – *'He who creates true beauty ever lives'*

The Craftsman

I ply with all the cunning of my art
This little thing, and with consummate care
I fashion it – so that when I depart
Those who come after me shall find it fair
And beautiful. It must be free of flaws –
Pointing no laborings of weary hands;
And there must be no flouting of the laws
Of beauty – as the artist understands.

Through passion, yearnings infinite – yet dumb –
I lift you from the depths of my own mind
And glid you with my soul's white heat to plumb
The souls of future men. I have behind
This thing that in return this solace gives:
"He who creates true beauty ever lives."

Most abbeys and monasteries were built to a similar plan on a site with access to an adequate supply of fresh, flowing water. The most important part was the church which would have been built to a design favourable to whoever paid the bill. It was normally an east/west church with north/south transepts. All the other domestic buildings were built around a cloister on the southern side.

Much work had to be done after a sponsor or founder had agreed to his role. A suitable site had to be chosen before any building could be started even though most medieval monasteries were laid out to much the same plan. All religious orders wanted solitude for their abbeys so places well away from centres of habitation were best suited. Cwmhir and Strata Florida are two examples of abbeys in very remote mountainous or marshy areas. Not all sites though were remote and some such as Valle Crucis, Margam, Llantarnam and Grace Dieu were built on sites of earlier foundations. The most important building was always the church. On one side of the church would be the four covered walls of the cloister around a square courtyard. The dormitory, dining hall, kitchen and other buildings normally opened off the cloisters in a set pattern. The chapter house was built onto the southern transept. The common room and dorter were built next to the west of the cloister, with a stairway leading to the church. Near to the stairs was situated the treasury. On the southern side of the cloister would be a kitchen and refectory. Built apart from the cloister would be the infirmary and guest house.

Skilled craftsmen were some of the most important people in medieval society and without them, day-to-day life could not function. Millers or bakers made bread; blacksmiths made horseshoes or tools and stonemasons and carpenters built the cathedrals and churches. Their skills were in such demand, that medieval craftsmen could make a good living and provide for their families, but only after serving a long apprenticeship. If he wanted to be apprenticed in any trade a boy went to work for a master craftsman at twelve years of age. He lived in his master's house and learned the trade. Apprenticeships were for a period of seven years. During that time the learning boy was not paid but was clothed and fed by his master. After seven years, an apprentice became a Journeyman. Now he was paid for his work and if he wished, he could leave his master to work for someone else or start out on his own. Some journeymen travelled from town to town looking for work.

The next step on the ladder to success was to be called a Master Craftsman. For the journeyman to become a master, he had to make a Masterpiece to show the guild that he was a good craftsman. If the guild thought his work was good enough, he was allowed to call himself a Master Craftsman and to have a workshop in which he made his work pieces and from which he could sell his goods. All craftsmen belonged to a guild, the modern version of which might be called a trade union. There were guilds for every sort of craft. It set examinations to see who could become a craftsman; it made sure that goods were properly made; it fixed wages and looked after old or sick members.

Early abbeys tended to be of a similar design but the design for a new abbey was made by a layman adding his own variations on a theme. Before their monasteries were compeleted the monks would have lived in wooden dwelling houses and even their first church and other monastic buildings would be built of wood. Plans would be drawn on parchment by an architect, who in reality was a master mason with more experience in the field than any of the monks or clergy in this specialised work. Due to a lack of scientific knowledge about how some materials would react, accidents did sometimes happen if the building in question was more complicated in design than the plainer, simpler design of some Cistercian abbeys as occurred in Abingdon in 1091, Winchester in 1107, Gloucester in 1170 and Worcester in 1175.

The master mason was a very important member of the team

in the building of an abbey. He was the lynch pin of the whole operation. It was he who was in charge of a large team of workers including carpenters (woodworkers), cart men, glaziers (whose trade it is to glass windows), masons (who work with stone), metalworkers, painters, plasterers and tilers. Masons and carpenters would travel the country looking for work. When Vale Royal Abbey, Cheshire was being built in 1278–1280, masons from as far as Lincoln, Oxford and Salisbury were employed on the project with local labourers employed for the unskilled work.

Building was not a year round occupation. The building season was from early spring to late autumn – from the Feast of the Purification of the Virgin Mary on February 2nd to All Saint's Day on November 1st, with the work day starting at 5 a.m. and finishing at about 7 p.m. The pay was usually good while it lasted, which made the travelling worthwhile but at the onset of winter the unfinished work would be covered with bracken or straw to protect it from frost, ice or snow damage. Cold, damp weather affected the lime mortar used and it would be completely useless in freezing weather. Most workers would be laid off with only a small number being retained. These would be amongst the most skilled and would spend their time in the Mason's Lodge or workshops working on more specialised aspects of the work such as detailed carving, cleaning and sharpening the tools.

Despite there being so many remains of their work, few of the craftsmen who built abbeys and priories are known by their names. It is a case of heeding the words of Sir Christopher Wren's epitaph: '*Lector, si monumentum requiris, circumspice*' (If you seek his memorial, look about you.) In Penmon Priory is a carving of a mason and a masonic axe but we know not his name. Master Ralph Gogun of London is one of the very few names that can be associated with building work. His 'memorial' is Tintern Abbey. Master Ralph, being a master mason, was a designer, engineer and contractor. He was a builder of renown who was, most probably, trained at a local quarry and gained experience on building sites. He was a man who had worked his way up from an inexperienced apprentice to become a 'superman' of the building site. During his apprenticeship and years of work, he would have had experience of laying out wall patterns and foundations; using a straight edge, rule, or staked lines; shaping, trimming, facing and cutting marble or stone in preparation for setting; using cutting equipment and hand tools; using plumb bob, gauge line, compass, straight edge, L-shaped square and level. He needed to know how to mix mortar or grout and pour or spread mortar or grout on marble slabs, stone, or foundations; remove wedges; fill joints between stones; finish joints between stones, using a trowel and smooth the mortar to an attractive finish; set stone or marble in place, according to layout or pattern; clean excess mortar or grout from surface of marble, stone, or monument, using sponge, brush and water; lay bricks to build shells of chimneys and smokestacks; replace broken or missing masonry units in walls or floors; smooth, polish and bevel surfaces using hand tools. To manage all the tasks he would have used cold chisels, brick hammers, claw hammers, sledge hammers, stone mason's hammers, trowel, buttering trowels, margin trowels and pointing trowels. He would need to have knowledge of Mathematics, especially arithmetic and geometry; knowledge of materials, methods, and the tools involved in the construction or repair of houses, buildings, or other structures together with a knowledge of design techniques, plans, drawings, and models. The skills that he would have mastered would be using logic and reasoning to identify the strengths and weaknesses of alternative solutions, conclusions or approaches to problems; managing his own time and the time of others; complex problem solving; judgment and decision making; giving full attention to what other people were saying, taking time to understand the points being made and asking appropriate questions. He was responsible for the management of his workers by motivating, developing, and directing them to work; identifying the best people for the job; monitoring and assessing the performance of himself and other individuals to make improvements or take corrective action. Such a man needed:

- muscle force to lift, push, pull, or carry objects
- to keep his hands and arms steady
- dexterity to grasp, manipulate, or assemble objects
- the ability to tell when something was wrong or likely to go wrong.

Work activities would include handling and moving objects; climbing, lifting, balancing, walking, stooping and handling materials; providing information to supervisors, co-workers and subordinates; getting members of a group to work together to accomplish tasks; training and teaching others; estimating sizes, distances, and quantities; determining time, costs, resources and materials needed; observing, receiving and obtaining information; inspecting equipment, structures and materials to identify the cause of defects, errors and problems; making decisions and solving problems.

He would be in charge of the whole team and the success or failure of the job lay in his hands and no one else. Other members of the team included:

- labourers – who dug foundations, ditches, trenches and carried away unwanted earth.
- rough masons – the most unskilled of all the workers.
- freemasons – who were skilled in cutting and dressing stone. After the foundations had been completed, the walls were built from an east to west direction and up to a height of three feet so the presbytery or chapel could be

finished before any other parts of the building and used as a place of worship. The very wide walls would then be completed with blocks of stone and the centre filled with rubble.

- smith – who was responsible for the sharpening and general upkeep of tools such as axes, chisels and saws.

- glaziers – who were the glass workers designing and making plain and coloured glass windows including the strips of lead needed to hold the many parts of a stained glass window together.

- carpenters – who doubled up as scaffolders erecting wooden scaffolding, usually conifer, wooden poles. The putlog holes, where the poles were fixed in the walls, can still be seen on many ancient buildings. They were also responsible for the centering of arches, ladder making and fine carvings on the inside furniture.

- roofers – who built a wooden roof so as to protect the builders and the building. When the main roof was completed, they would work on the inside arches and vaults.
  Carpenters and roofers used few nails. Instead they would use wooden pegs or a simple mortice and tennon or the more complicated, decorative dovetail joint.

- sculptors – who worked on the fine details on pillars and tombs.

- tilers – who worked on the outside of the roof and laid the floor tiles. The clay would be dug in autumn and left in the winter rains to wash away impurities. There would be a kiln on site and the tiles made especially for a particular project.

- painters – to protect the building materials from the elements the outside and inside walls were lime washed. Artists were called upon to paint on the inside walls scenes from the Bible or the lives of saints. All the paint was prepared by the artists themselves and bound together with egg white.

It was these un-named, forgotten craftsmen that left their treasured 'memorials' for us to appreciate today.

Another highly skilled craftsman but rarely seen in a monastery, due to pressure of work, would be the scribe. Monasteries flourished before the printing press was invented and all documents were written or copied by hand by monks or scribes (*someone whose job was to copy documents and books before printing was invented*) onto parchment (*the skin of a sheep or goat prepared for writing on. Preparation was a lengthy process: once the wool had been removed, the skin was soaked in lime to remove the flesh, then stretched on a frame, scraped with a lunellum, and treated with chalk to whiten the surface*). Parchment was quite expensive to buy – 150 sheets cost 3/4d circa 1300 (£384.44 in 2013). Depending on their importance, they would have been written on vellum (*treated calf skin which had two different sides – one on which the hair grew was matt or unglossy and the other was smooth and glossy*). Some of the most important work carried on during the Dark Ages was done by humble monks copying ancient manuscripts in cold, dark monasteries. Scribes copied thousands of manuscripts, Bibles and classical works.

Viking invasions were a constant danger for many peaceful monastic communities. The scriptorium was the most important room in a monastery next to the chapel itself and for this reason these writing rooms were often built at the top of an attack-proof fortress tower with curved walls. The towers were separate buildings enclosed within the walls of the compound. The monks climbed 15 to 20 feet up a ladder to the scriptorium and then pulled the ladder up after them. This made it almost impossible for the attacking warriors to reach them.

A scribe's day would begin after Lauds, the Morning Prayer,

when he entered the scriptorium and worked hunched over a tiny table while seated on a backless stool. Due to the many calls to prayer and services during his day, the monk would work for a period of two hours at the most but the time spent at work was very intense and all done for no payment but solely for the glory of God and honour to his monastery. The desk was placed in front of a small window that provided the only available light in the room. No candles for light or fires for warmth were allowed because the parchment material they used was highly flammable. Whatever the conditions, the work had to be done with only a few simple tools. He kept his quill (*a feather, usually of a goose, formed into a pen for writing*) in his hand and dipped it in an inkpot nearby. His other hand held a lunellum (*a small crescent-shaped knife used for scraping a sheet of parchment in its preparation or for scraping off mistakes or sharpening the quill*). A devout monk always began his work by writing a prayer in the upper left hand corner of his first sheet. Then he practiced his letters in an abecedarian sentence which contained every letter of the alphabet.

The work involved in copying fragile, ancient manuscripts was a tedious task which demanded the scribe's full attention. It was easy to make mistakes, misspelled words might be incorrectly placed in the sentences, and such errors might be copied over again into different manuscripts and change the entire meaning of a phrase. A scribe's life was not an easy one.

Because of the worry about making mistakes a little, imaginary demon named Titivillus was born. The scribes used Titivillus' humour to make a point about the problem. He slipped around peeking over their shoulders in search of mistakes. Upon finding a blunder, he seized it and threw it into a sack on his back. The little devil was required to fill his pack a thousand times a day. He also recorded every mistake in a ledger book and tallied them to be used against each monk on Judgment Day.

One of the scribes' many complaints was about the ink they used. It was difficult to get the correct consistency when making their own or the parchment might not have such a smooth surface as they desired. Blots and spills could ruin many months or even years' work.

A twelfth century ink recipe manual by the monk/scribe Theophilus instructs: *'When you are going to make ink, cut some pieces of (haw)thorn wood in April or May, before they grow blossoms or leaves. Make little bundles of them and let them lie in the shade for two, three, or four weeks, until they are dried out a little. Then you should have wooden mallets with which you should pound the thorn on another hard piece of wood, until you have completely removed the bark. Put this immediately into a barrel full of water. Fill two, three, four or five barrels with bark and water and so let them stand for eight days, until the water absorbs all the sap of the bark into itself. Next, pour this water into a very clean pan or cauldron, put fire under it and boil it. From time to time also put some of the bark itself into the pan, so that if any of the sap has remained in it, it will be boiled out. After boiling it a little, take out the bark and again put some more in. After this is done, boil the remaining water down to a third, take it out of that pan and put it into a smaller one. Boil it until it grows black and is beginning to thicken, being absolutely careful not to add any water except that which is mixed with the sap. When you see it begin to thicken, add a third part of pure wine, put it into two or three new pots, and continue boiling until you see that it forms a sort of skin on top.*

Then take the pots off the fire and put them in the sun until the black ink purges itself from the red dregs. Next, take some small, carefully sewn parchment bags with bladders inside, pour the pure ink into them, and hang them in the sun until the ink is completely dry. Whenever you want, take some of the dry material, temper it with wine over the fire, add a little green vitriol (iron sulphate) and write.

write. If it happens through carelessness that the ink is not black enough, take a piece of iron a finger thick, put it into the fire, let it get red hot, and immediately throw it into the ink.' The ink could also be made blacker by adding iron or iron oxide (added as metallic filings).

A simpler, more traditional ink recipe was to take a quantity of albumen (egg white) and mix thoroughly with soot. Then add honey and mix into a smooth paste. The ink was then ready to use. Another traditional ink recipe was to gather a quantity of lawyer's wig mushrooms also known as Shaggy Ink Cap (*Corprinus comatus*) and place them in a glazed pot or small cauldron. If left for several days in a warm place, the mushrooms will liquefy. The liquid can either be used as it is or boiled until it is about half its original volume it will make a blacker ink.

In medieval England and Wales liquid ink was kept in inkwells made of horn or lead.

One copy of the Bible took up to five years to copy and the monastic scribes protected their work with zeal. Stealing a manuscript was a serious crime and often a scribe might write a warning at the beginning of the volume. One which was found in a twelfth century Bible warned:

'If anyone steal this book, let him die the death; let him be fried in the pan; let the falling sickness and fever seize him; let him be broken on the wheel and hanged. Amen.'

The illuminated manuscript (*a handwritten book with pictures and decoration painted or drawn in bright colours, illuminating the page*) was a major form of artistic expression in medieval times. Few people could read during this period so that almost all knowledge and literature, as well as the Bible and the great texts of Christian religion were produced by monks and preserved in monasteries.

The colours used were mainly black for the actual text, gold and silver leaf, blue which was the most costly pigment but also the most durable, green obtained from verdigris (carbonate of copper) or vegetables, red obtained from sulphured mercury or red lead, yellow from lead oxide and white obtained from lime white. The scribe or illuminator's toolbox contained a mixture of implements such as pens, pencils, chalk, brushes of badger hair, grinding slabs, penknife, palette knife, ruler, dividers to prick out the guide lines, burnishers for the gold/silver leaf, colour box, pigments, sponge and pumice stone erasures and leather bindings for the work – usually of deer skin.

By the thirteenth century universities began to take on the role of preserving the intellectual heritage of western Europe. More people learnt to read and many more books were needed. This led to the development of faster printing methods and the appearance of a printing press which eventually led to the monastic scribes being made redundant.

Anglo-Saxon book decoration in the tenth and eleventh centuries is often called the Winchester School because Winchester was its first centre. From the late tenth century onwards, however, Canterbury became equally important. A variety of different books were copied and illuminated including the Gospels and liturgical books, books of the Old Testament and works of ancient authors.

As monastic life spread throughout Europe in the later eleventh and twelfth centuries an increase in the production of manuscripts by and for monasteries had to be catered for. The most popular illuminated books were large bibles, illustrated with elaborate initials or miniature paintings, and psalters (psalm books), frequently accompanied by biblical scenes.

Further Reading
Builders & Decorators. Medieval Craftsmen in Wales. N. Coldstream. Cadw. 2008.

Illuminated Manuscripts in Classical and Medieaval Time. J. H. Middleton. Cambridge University Press. 1892.

Life in a Medieval Abbey. T. McAleavy. English Heritage. 1996.

The Craftsman – from The Poetry of the Negro. M. B. Christian. Doubleday. 1970.

Tintern Abbey. O. E. Craster. HMSO. 1964.

5. Valuable Welsh Manuscripts

In the twenty first century, printed material of all kinds can be accessed from books, in libraries or from the Internet but in earlier times most of the poets' work was copied onto parchment to be kept in manuscript form. The National Library of Wales in Aberystwyth houses the most important collection of Welsh manuscripts some of which are part of a collection such as The Cwrtmawr Collection whilst others are single manuscripts such as The B(V)icar of Woking Manuscript. Many others have been lost but in those remaining are possibly the oldest and best of Welsh literature. Others contain ecclesiastical works, legal documents such as the laws of Hywel Dda (Hywel the Good) or Hywel ap Cadell (c.880–950) who was a King of *Deheubarth* (the South Lands) and who eventually came to rule most of Wales, examples of early Welsh prose in the form of fables and tales. The languages in which they were written include Welsh, Latin, French and English.

- **The Cwrtmawr Manuscripts** – were collected by John Humphreys Davies of Cwrtmawr, Llangeitho, Cardiganshire and were donated to the National Library of Wales by the collector. The collection contains 1,549 various volumes of work dating from the late Middle Ages to the eighteenth century. As well as historical documents, they contain very early Welsh literature.
- **The Llansteffan Manuscripts** – much of the work contained in this collection was copied by the Reverend Samuel Williams (c.1660–1722) of Llandyfrïog and Llangynllo, Cardiganshire and his son the historian Moses Williams (1685–1742). Later, manuscripts belonging to

Walter Davies (Gwallter Mechain (1761–1849) clergyman, poet, editor and translator; Lewis Morris (1701–1765), poet and scholar; Edward Breese (1835–1881) and E. G. B. Philimore were added to the collection. The works of some of the most important Poets of the Nobility are included in the collection including Dafydd ap Gwilym, Guto'r Glyn, Lewys Glyn Cothi, Tudur Aled, Gutun Owain, Siôn Brwynog, Morgan Elfael and Llywelyn Siôn.

Sir John Williams presented the collection, named after his native village, to the National Library of Wales in 1909.

- **The Peniarth Manuscripts** – are a collection of Welsh manuscripts from the Middle Ages collected by Sir Robert Vaughan (1592–1667) of Hengwrt, Merionethshire. The manuscripts were kept at Peniarth, Llanegryn, Merionethshire in the nineteenth century and contain some of the oldest and most important manuscripts in the history of Welsh literature e.g. The Black Book of Carmarthen, The Book of Taliesin, The White Book of Rhydderch as well as early versions of the Laws of Hywel Dda together with examples of the works of many of the Poets of the Nobility.

The collection was sold by William Wynne VII of Peniarth to Sir John Williams in 1898. Williams was a staunch supporter of the National Library of Wales and presented the collection to the library on condition that it was displayed there.

Some of the other manuscripts which contain important examples of Welsh literature include:

- **The Hendregadredd Manuscript** – is a 126 page manuscript, containing more than two hundred poems, written on parchment at Strata Florida Abbey, Cardiganshire. It contains some of the earliest and most important works of the *Gogynfeirdd* (Early Welsh Poets). Part 1 contains at least eighteen poems by *Beirdd y Tywysogion* (the Princes' Poets); Part 2 is the hand work of nineteen different copiers; Part 3 contains the handwork of twenty different copiers using poor quality ink. It disappeared in the nineteenth century only to be discovered in a wardrobe at Hendregadredd, near Criccieth, Gwynedd in 1910 and bought at a London auction by the Davies Sisters (Margaret and Gwendoline, both philanthropists) of Gregynog, Powys in 1923 and presented to the National Library of Wales.

The manuscript dates from 1282–1350, with later additions including the works of Dafydd ap Gwilym (c.1315–c.1350) who is considered amongst Europe's best who is remembered not for his deep and thoughtful themes but for his almost light-hearted attitude to life and composing to his girlfriends, nature and other subjects, and Gruffudd Gryg, an Anglesey poet of the second half of the fourteenth century, a contemporary of Dafydd ap Gwilym and involved in a bardic 'controversy' between the two, done more in jest than in earnest.

One poem, of his own work, was probably written by the hand of Dafydd ap Gwilym himself. Other poets whose works are included in the manuscript make it almost a 'Who's Who' of early Welsh poets – Bleddyn Fardd, Casnodyn, Cynddelw Brydydd Mawr, Daniel ap Llosgwrn Mew, Dafydd Benfras, Einion ap Gwalchmai, Elidir Sais, Gwalchmai ap Meilyr, Gwilym Ryfel, Gwynfardd Brycheiniog, Hywel ab Owain Gwynedd, Llygad Gŵr, Llywarch Brydydd y Moch, Llywelyn Fardd, Meilyr Brydydd, Owain Cyfeiliog and Seisyll Bryffwrch.

This particular manuscript has had a very exciting

existence being, at different times, the property of Ieuan Llwyd ap Ieuan ap Gruffudd Foel of Parcryddgoch, Llangeitho; Gruffudd Dwnn (1500–1570) and by 1580 was the property of Wiliam Llŷn (1534/5–1580). Later it was the property of Robert Vaughan of Hengwrt and copied by John Davies of Mallwyd (c.1567–1644) scholar of the late Renaissance, author, editor, and clergyman in 1617. After being lost in nineteenth century, it was found by John Jones (Myrddin Fardd. 1836–1921), writer and collector of old letters and manuscripts and Edward Breese in 1940 at Hendregadredd. Now it is kept at the National Library of Wales, Aberystwyth.

- **The Book of Aneirin** – this manuscript was copied at about 1265 making it one of the earliest manuscripts in Welsh at either Aberconwy Abbey or at Strata Marcella, Powys. It contains a very early copy of *Y Gododdin* and other poems and a total of 132 poems. It contains the handwork of at least two different copiers which can be deduced by the different style of handwriting or calligraphy. It has, at different times, been the property of Dafydd Nanmor (c.1450–1490) a poet born at Nanmor (or Nantmor), near Beddgelert in Gwynedd,) and Gwilym Tew (c.1460–1480) a poet and manuscript copyist from Tir Iarll, Glamorgan. It was seen by Edward Lhuyd (1660–1709) naturalist, botanist, linguist, geographer and antiquary in the seventeenth century before it was housed in Aberdâr and later possessed by the historian Theophilus Jones (1758–1812) lawyer and historian of Brecknockshire and Carhuanawc (Reverend Thomas Price 1787–1848), historian and a literary figure of the early 19th century. It was presented by Sir Thomas Philipps to the City of Cardiff Library.

- **The B(V)icar of Woking's Book** – a 963 page manuscript from the sixteenth century containing a great deal of the works of the Poets of the Nobility and almost a hundred poems by Dafydd ap Gwilym.

   The manuscript was written in Bangor, Gwynedd at the Court of Bishop Rowland Meyrick (1505–1566) and is dated 3 February 1565. Its owner was Sir Richard Gruffudd, vicar of Woking. It is kept at the City of Cardiff Library.
- **The Red Book of Talgarth** – written in 1400 by more than one scribe. The manuscript contains a collection of early Welsh poetry and prose. So named after the colour of its covers. The manuscript was kept at Talgarth, Brecknockshire for many centuries but when it became the property of Sir John Williams, he presented it to the National Library of Wales in 1909.
- **The Black Book of Carmarthen** – a small sized manuscript of 108 pages written in the thirteenth century circa 1250, containing 39 poems and one short piece of prose of differing styles. The copier changed the size of his font on the vellum on at least fourteen different times so as to accommodate as many poems as possible. The works within contain examples of praise poetry, prophecy poems, religious poems and fables, some of which were composed by Cynddelw Brydydd Mawr. It was most probably written and kept in the Priory of St John the Evangelist and Teulyddog in Carmarthen. During the second quarter of the sixteenth century it belonged to Sir John Price (1502–1555) and was later kept at Hengwrt for almost three hundred years. The Hengwrt Library was bequeathed to William Watkin Edward Wynne of Peniarth in 1859 and sold to Sir John Williams who presented it to the National Library of Wales.

- **Taliesin's Book** – an early fourteenth century manuscript of sixty one poems and some Latin work written on eighty pages of vellum, written circa. 1300–1350 at Cwmhir Abbey. The unknown copier used a *textualis formata* font in his work and this can be seen in at least four other manuscripts of his work. Taliesin's Book contains the early works of Taliesin (sixth century Brythonic poet who was a court poet of at least three kings); it is kept at the National Library of Wales.
- **Peniarth 20** – a thirteenth century manuscript containing, amongst other treasures, some of the works of the Early Poets and a Grammar for Chief Poets. It was possibly written at Basingwerk Abbey or at Aberconwy.
- **The Book of Saint Chad** – a Latin manuscript containing the Gospels of Saint Matthew, Mark and portions of the Gospel of Saint Luke. It is decorated in the style of the Lindisfarne Gospels (a richly decorated Christian manuscript from eighth century with a mixture of Celtic and Christian influences).

  It was originally known as the Book of Saint Teilo but renamed on its arrival in the tenth century at the cathedral of Saint Mary and Saint Chad at Lichfield, Staffordshire where it has been exhibited since 1982.
- **The White Book of Hergest** (a well-known Herefordshire family) – the manuscript was copied by Lewys Glyn Cothi (c.1420–1490) poet, sometime before 1490 and was lost in a fire at Mostyn Mansion in the early nineteenth century. Fortunately, it had been available and copied previously and its contents are known to be the works of Lewys Glyn Cothi (1447–1486), an early version of the Welsh Bible and a book of heraldry and ancient genealogy.
- **The Red Book of Hergest** – a major source of the work of

the Early Poets and the Princes' Poets from the twelfth and thirteenth century. The first part of the manuscript contains prose, including the Mabinogion. This is one of the manuscript sources (the other being the White Book of Rhydderch), other tales, historical texts including a Welsh translation of Geoffrey of Monmouth's *Historia Regum Britanniae*. The manuscript also contains a collection of herbal remedies associated with Rhiwallon Feddyg, founder of a medical family that lasted over 500 years – *The Physicians of Myddfai* from the Llandovery area. It is kept at the Bodleian Library, Oxford.

- **The White Book of Rhydderch** – written circa. 1350 at Strata Florida Abbey during the incumbency of Llywelyn Fychan ap Llywelyn as abbot. It was named after its sponsor – Rhydderch ap Ieuan Llwyd. Five different persons worked on the manuscript of 476 pages of good quality vellum containing the earliest examples of Welsh prose such as the four tales of The Mabiniogi – Pwyll, Branwen, Manawydan and Math.

POETS AND POETRY

Long known as The Land of Song, Wales can also, justifiably, be called The Land of Poets. Poets and poetry have been a feature of the Welsh way of life for many centuries and the bardic heritage can be traced back to the sixth century when the oldest Welsh literature belonged not to the geographical Wales as it is known today but to when it encompassed parts of southern Scotland, northern England, from Glasgow and Edinburgh and southwards to the Cornwall, Devon and Somerset of the twenty first century. Remarkably, poems written fifteen centuries ago can be read and understood today providing not only a literary heritage but a geography and history lesson at the same time. From that early period has grown a tradition of poets and poetry from the very early poets or *Gogynfeirdd* such as Taliesin and Aneirin, two of the earliest poets to write in Welsh.

> *'Gwŷr a aeth Gatraeth oedd ffraeth eu llu;*
> *Glasfedd eu hancwyn, a gwenwyn fu.*
> *Trichant trwy beiriant yn catâu –*
> *A gwedi elwch tawelwch fu. '*
> (Aneirin)

> (A group of willing warriors went to Catterick.
> They drank mead which proved a costly mistake.
> Three hundred were ordered to fight
> but after their carousing, a deathly silence fell upon them.)
> (*a translation of Aneirin's work*)

On moving to the present day Wales and after many battles and skirmishes with the English and the Danes in particular and also amongst themselves, peace reigned and different schools of poets developed:

- *Beirdd y Tywysogion* (The Poets of the Princes) c.1100–c.1300 such as Talhaearn tad (father of) Awen, Morfran, Myrddin, Selyf ap (son of) Cynan, etc. Their names live on but unfortunately most of their work has been lost.
- *Beirdd yr Uchelwyr* (The Poets of the Nobility) c.1300–c.1600, which included the likes of Gwalchmai, Einion, Cynddelw Brydydd Mawr (the most prolific), Llywarch ap Llywelyn, Gruffudd ab yr Ynad Coch (*Gruffudd son of the Red Justice*), Gwynfardd Brycheiniog (*the White bard of Brecon*), Phylip Brydydd (*prydydd=poet*), Gwilym Ddu o Arfon, Dafydd y Coed and Gruffudd ap Maredudd and others. Also in this group was Dafydd ap Gwilym.

The Poets of the Nobility, like the Poets of the Princes before them, benefitted from much patronage and support and their work, in general, is full of praise to their wealthy and generous patrons.

In researching '*Poems to Religious Houses as a Historical Source*', Cartin T. Beynon has identified over fifty poets who sang in praise of abbeys and abbots and their support. This body of work amounts to one hundred and twenty four poems. Thirty six were written in praise of Valle Crucis Abbey; twenty were written in praise of Aberconwy despite its short life but Cymer Abbey and Lewis ap Thomas, its last abbot, is mentioned only once in four short lines of a poem asking neighbours for four oxen. Iolo Goch mentions, almost in passing, the Friary of Llanfaes, Anglesey despite it being considered an important establishment at the time of Llywelyn Fawr.

Lewys Glyn Cothi tells of how all the St John's Houses were considered as hospitals for everyone and seen as places of sanctuary:

'A phob tŷ yn ysbyty i'r byd,
A'i rhifo yn santwari hefyd.'

Other places were seen as places of pilgrimage, such as Bardsey Island and Slebends – 'Like Bardsey, one path is often trod to Slebends; pardons for the purification of men can be obtained there.'

'Mal Enlli, amla unllwybr,
Yw Slebends, islaw wybr;
Pardynau'n puro dynion
Sy yno swrn i Sain Siôn.'

Lewys Glyn Cothi

Much can be gleaned from such poems of praise but Tintern Abbey, the largest of Welsh abbeys, does not feature in any poet's catalogue due, possibly, to its Norman (French) and English connections. Guto'r Glyn (1440–1493) and Tudur Aled (c.1465–1525), on the other hand, do praise the abbeys at Chester and Welshpool because the abbots of both were Welshmen. Gutun Owain (c.1460–1503) was also pleased to receive the support of Siôn ap Rhisiart at Valle Crucis Abbey. Siôn's court and his heart were filled with happiness. Abbot Dafydd ab Owain was the subject of twenty five poems of praise from which we learn that he was a wise and strong ruler and a good administrator. Dafydd ap Tomas ap Hywel is described as being a happy and glorious personality as abbot of Margam and Rhys, abbot of Strata Florida, was almost too generous as he found himself in the Debtor's Prison in Carmarthen.

'He gave to thousands –
But God will repay him.'

Thomas ap Dafydd Pennant at Basingwerk was also described as being pleasant and generous by Tudur Aled, who was quite prepared to forgive him his faults (but the compiler of official documents was not so inclined). Lewys Glyn Cothi compares Siôn ap Rhosier, abbot of Llantarnam, and his monks as swans, so graceful were they in their movements. Lewis Morgannwg (fl.1520–1565) stresses that Lleision Tomas, of Neath Abbey was a very learned scholar, fully conversant in the Seven Sciences of Arithmetic, Music, Sophistry, Rhetoric, Civil and Canon Law and Logic. Sion ap Dafydd Lluyd was able to speak three languages and nowhere could such cultured Latin be heard as that emanating from his lips.

'Siôn – speaker of three languages,
Your teachings will live long after you.'

At Basingwerk, it was the abbot Thomas ap Dafydd Pennant who was praised for bringing success to the abbey. He filled the mills on every hill and in every valley.

'Ef a lanwodd felinau
Ymhob glyn a phen y bryn bau.'

When Strata Florida was in a very dilapidated condition following the Glyndŵr Rebellion, it was Dafydd ab Owain who worked hardest to renovate the abbey. He had brought joy to a saddened place:

'Daeth llawenydd a dydd da
I'r deml oedd drist yma.'

Ieuan Deulwyn (fl.1460)

His successor, Abbot Morgan also made many repairs according to Dafydd Nanmor:

'Y côr, efe a'i cweiriawdd,
A dorau teg o wydr tawdd.
Toau, a phlwm trwm tramawr,
Tŷ deri maint Tewdwr Mawr.
Tô ar wŷdd, nid a trwyddaw
Rew na gwlyb, nac eira nag law.'

(He repaired the choir with panes of glass.
The roof was covered with huge sheets of lead
to keep out the ice, damp, snow and rain.)

(a translation of Dafydd Nanmor's work)

Neath Abbey was praised by Lewis Morgannwg and Llewelyn Goch (fl.1360–1390) for the *mynachlys* (monk's apartments) and Abbot John's Court:

'Neuadd beirdd a'u nawdd a'u bwyd
O newyddiaeth a naddwyd.'

(A brand new hall for the poets
to eat and compose in was built.)

(*a translation of Llewelyn Goch's work*)

When an abbot, as in the case of Dafydd ab Owain, moved from one post to another, it was always a matter of someone's loss and another's gain.

(He was the patriarch of Strata Marcella
and at Strata Florida his better could not be found
but it was at Aberconwy, where he gave freely to his court,
that he really blossomed.)

(*a translation of Hywel Rheinallt's work*)

'Padriarch Ystrad Marchell,
A Fflur heb gaffael ei well;
Abad, cwrt, rhoddiad rhydd
Aberconwy brig gwinwydd.'

Hywel Rheinallt

Tudur Aled wrote asking Sir Lewis Sytun (Sutton) for a workhorse for Abbot Dafydd but Ieuan Llwyd Brydydd on the other hand says that he squandered a lot of money by giving freely to Henry VII and aslo asked God's blessing on the Tudor cause. He was a wizard at praying and all his prayers were answered by God:

'Dewin oeddit dan weddi,
Duw deg a'th wrandawai di.'

Others saw a new abbot as the saviour of the Welsh language. Siôn ap Dafydd Lluyd's appointment to St Asaph was the wish of many for it would mean a revival to the language in that part of north Wales.

'Ceir bedydd newydd o'n hiaith
Ceir Siôn in croesi unwaith.'

It was the wish of Lewis Môn but sadly the appointment was not made.

For a wandering poet, a warm welcome was longed for where ever they went and at Valle Crucis, abbot Dafydd ab Ieuan's welcome was always well received:

'I neuadd Ddafydd siwrneais – pob dyn
A'I law a dderbyn wledd ddiarbed.'

(I journeyed to Dafydd's hall and there
all men are warmly received with a wonderful feast).
(a translation)

But not all were as welcoming and one abbot offered only ale, bread and cheese.

'Drink al', meddai mab Alis,
'Brwder, sit, eat bread a'r sis.'

When such generous men died, the poets were at a complete loss as to what to do.

'Duw'r ŵyl i ba wlad yr af?
Ar Basg odid awr y bwyf,
A Nadolig, nad wylwyf.

Gutun Owain

(Oh God, where will I go to?
I will live for an hour at Easter
and I'll try not to cry at Christmas.)
(a translation of Gutun Owain's work)

Life, even for a poet, was never easy but when it was time to leave, Guto'r Glyn knew where and who to turn to despite being old and infirm:

> *'Mi a wn lle mae enaint*
> *A dynn hwn a doniau haint*
> *Aed i nef i fod yn iach –*
> *Llyn Egwystl, lle enwogach.'*

(I know where to find balm to cure my ills.
I will go to the haven of Valle Crucis. Where better?)
(a translationof Guto'r Glyn's work)

Victorian Poets

As well as attracting 'home grown' poets, the abbeys and religious houses of Wales have attracted visiting poets. William Wordsworth's (1770–1850) Romantic English poet, work titled **COMPOSED A FEW MILES ABOVE TINTERN ABBEY, ON REVISITING THE BANKS OF THE WYE DURING A TOUR. JULY 13, 1798** is possibly the most well-known. It was written five years after his summer of 1793 visit. He wrote:

> *'No poem of mine was composed under circumstances more pleasant for me to remember than this. I began it upon leaving Tintern, after crossing the Wye, and concluded it just as I was entering Bristol in evening, after a ramble of four or five days (10–13 July) with my sister. Not a line of it was altered, and not any the part of it written down till I reached Bristol.'*

> *Once again*
> *Do I behold these steep and lofty cliffs,*
> *That on a wild secluded scene impress*
> *Thoughts of more deep seclusion; and connect*
> *The landscape with the quiet of the sky.*

The day is come when I again repose
Here, under this dark sycamore, and view
These plots of cottage-ground, these orchard-tufts,
Which at this season, with their unripe fruits,
Are clad in one green hue, and lose themselves
'Mid groves and copses.

Alfred, Lord Tennyson (1809–1892) Victorian poet and writer, formed his ideas for the poem **'TEARS, IDLE TEARS'** at Tintern:

Tears, idle tears, I know not what they mean,
Tears from the depth of some divine despair
Rise in the heart, and gather to the eyes,
In looking on the happy autumn-fields,
And thinking of the days that are no more.

'Beat poet' Allen Ginsberg's '(1926–1997) **Wales Visitation**' was also written after his visit there.

Welsh poets were also inspired by Tintern Abbey:

ABATY TINTERN (TINTERN ABBEY)

How many hearts stopped beating here?
How many eyes closed forever?
How many who are buried here
have been forgotten?
How often, at dawn or evensong,
did the sound of the bell ring through the valley?
How many Aves, Creed and prayers
have been intoned between these walls?

On the stone opposite
eroded by the weather
I thought I saw, before his idol,
 a pilgrim at prayer.

Was it a column of white smoke
from a thurible that I saw?
Or did I hear the sound of the organ
reverberating to the Heavens?

But there is only silence here
Where anthems were sung;
There is, from chancel to choir,
nothing but the sound of a moaning wind.
                              (a translation of Alun's work)
                              John Blackwell (1797–1841), (Alun)

Another abbey, not quite as imposing as Tintern but as well known, inspired Arthur Simon Thomas (Anellydd (1865–1935) cleric and writer, wrote:

TALLEY ABBEY

I have never seen on any journey such a lovely place as Talley
with its myriad of flower and two lakes.
All kinds of beauty can bewitch you and make you sing their
praise.

Is that a monastery I see reflected in the waters of the lake?
Its rich history, from the olden days
is full of chants, prayers and fables of church miracles.

At dusk, it is so peaceful in these sweet surroundings.
The sound of the silver abbey bells call the faithfull to prayer,
to worship and follow the Lord.

You can imagine seeing the White Monks like angels, slowly making their way
in a slow procession each evening
towards Jesus, Saviour of their church.

(a translation of Anellydd's work)

Because of its connections with Dafydd ap Gwilym, possibly Wales' best known medieval bard, the abbey has inspired many. In 1916, the Chair at the Aberystwyth National Eisteddfod of Wales was offered for a long poem in strict meter on the title *Ystrad Fflur* (Strata Florida).

In 1947 Valle Crucis became the focus of attention as the topic for the Crown competition in the Colwyn Bay National Eisteddfod of Wales. The winning poet was the thirty eight year old Reverend Griffith John Roberts, rector of Nantglyn, Denbighshire and much was made in the Press of how he had written his poem whilst snow bound on the Denbighshire moors as his home had been cut off by blizzards and frost for two months at the beginning of the year.

Hence this sad ruin in Llangollen's Vale,
Whose music now is whistling in the gale;
The organ's notes are changed to notes of woe,
And hallow'd robes for robes of winter's snow.

(Anonymous. *from Salisbury and Winchester Journal*–
Monday, 24 February 1840)

Other, much earlier, poets were of the same desire. Meilyr (fl.1100–37), the court poet of Gruffudd ap Cynan, wrote on his deathbed.

> *When it is time to resurrect those that are in the grave,*
> *I hope that I will be ready to meet my Maker*
> *Who will welcome me with the good people of Enlli.*
> > (*a translation of Meilyr's work*)

Many other saints are said to have been buried on Bardsey including Henwyn the son of Gwyndaf Hen, Beuno, Cadfan, Derfel, Dyrdan, Dochwy, Eithras, Elgar, Mael, Llywen, Llyfab, Sulien, Tanwg and Tecwyn; so many that the island became known as Insula Sanctorum.

> *I will go to my grave*
> *On an island, off Gwynedd.*
> > (*a translation of Elgar's work*)

Many of the poets throughout the ages have only echoed our own desires and feelings about the religious houses that we have come to know of and that is why so much of their work remains so popular.

Further Reading

Barddoniaeth y Plant. Hughes & Son.

Buarth beirdd. Eurig Salisbury. Cyhoeddiadau Barddas. 2014.

Caniadau. T. Gwynn Jones. Hughes & Son. 1934.

Enlli. Gol: R. G. Jones & C. J. Arnold. University of Wales Press. 1996.

Gwae Fi Fy Myw: Cofiant Hedd Wyn, Alan Llwyd. 1991.

Gwelaf Afon. Gwyn Thomas. Gwasg Gee. 1990.

Hanes Llenyddiaeth Gymraeg. Thomas Parry. Gwasg Prifysgol Cymru. 1944.

Lyrical Ballads. Wordsworth Illustrated. 1798.

The Oxford Book of Welsh Verse. Ed. Thomas Parry. Clarendon Press. 1962.

Y cerddi i'r tai crefyddol fel ffynhonnell hanesyddol. Catrin T. B. Davies. Cylchgrawn Llyfrgell Genedlaethol Cymru. Gaeaf 1974.

6. *'I vow to thee'* – A life of prayer and service

Most of the abbeys of Wales were built in isolated, out of the way places. Today, a journey from north Wales to Strata Florida involves crossing the counties of Clwyd or Gwynedd and many miles of the Ceredigion country side by car to reach the sacred spot. In its heyday, a journey there on foot or on horseback would involve many hours of planning and a number of days travelling.

Such places gave monks the isolation they craved so as to lead their lives in contemplation, thinking of God and spending most of the twenty four hours of every day in prayer and worshiping in the eight daily services. The word 'monk' derives from the Greek for living alone. It was an escape from the tedium and dangers of everyday life, from famine, disease, warfare and violence.

On entering a monastery all devout, Christian candidates took a vow of obedience. The first month was a period of postulancy, after which a period of novitiate lasted for a year. On successfully completing this period monks took simple vows and after four more years would be allowed to take their solemn vows and become full members of the order.

Whilst different orders had their own rules and regulations to keep, they all kept three main vows:

- A Vow of Poverty
- A Vow of Chastity
- A Vow of Obedience

and to a fairly similar pattern of day to day existence of hard work, scholarship, prayer and worship in addition to which they spent most of the remaining hours in church, reading from the Bible, in private prayer and meditation. An order of lay brethren

The Abbey of St Mary, Bardsey
and below, early inscribed stones now located in the island's chapel

Basingwerk Abbey
in Greenfield Valley Heritage Park,
Holywell

Cymer Abbey, near Dolgellau

Valle Crucis Abbey near Llangollen

The tombs of the princes of Powys at Valle Crucis abbey

Strata Florida Abbey in Ceredigion

Yma dan ywen ger mur Ystrad F
I chwe chanrif yn ôl y claddwy
DAFYDD AP GWILYM
"prydydd â'i gywydd fel gwin

Dafydd gwiw awenydd gwrdd
Ai yma'th roed dan goed gwyr
Dan lasbren hoyw ywen hardd
Lle'th gladdwyd y cuddiwyd c

Hun

The graves of Dafydd ap Gwilym (under the yew tree) and the princes of Deheubarth at Ystrad Fflur

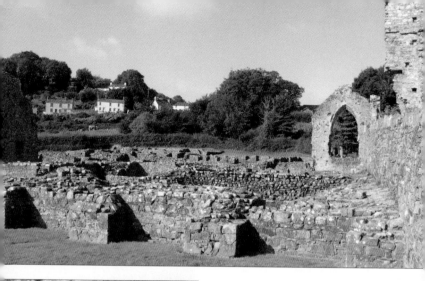

*Llandudoch
(St Dogmael's) Abbey
– of the Tironensian order –
in Pembrokeshire*

Talyllychau – the only Premonstratensian abbey in Wales

Whitland Abbey ('Yr Hen Dŷ Gwyn ar Daf'), the first Cistercian Abbey in Wales. A Cistercian community was sent to Wales from Clairvaux in September 1140.

Neath Abbey

Llywelyn ap Gruffudd remembered at Abaty Cwm Hir

Llanddewi Nant Honddu Abbey

The hotel situated within the historical archecture

Margam Abbey

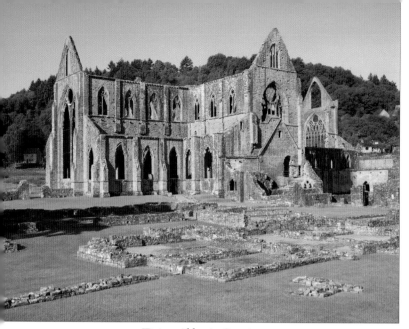

Tintern Abbey in Gwent

Bangor Is-coed's early 6th century monastery lies under the Dee river when it changed its course. 1,200 of its monks were slaughtered by Northumbrian Saxons during the Battle of Chester c.616.

The stone coffin of Llywelyn Fawr, moved from Aberconwy Abbey to Maenan Abbey when Edward I cleared the site to build his coloniad town and castle at Conwy. The coffin now rests in Gwydir Chapel, Llanrwst parish church, after the dissolution of Maenan Abbey.

Penmon Priory, founded by St Seiriol

might well be organised to take responsibility for the hard, physical work in the fields and gardens or in workshops so that the fully-fledged members of the abbey could devote their time to prayer and learning. Whatever their occupation, all the monk's labours would be interrupted or regulated by the services to which they were called by the ringing of a bell every three hours – all day and all night. Such regular interruptions meant that it was difficult to concentrate on the task in hand but it was not for monks to complain. Their lives were dedicated to live and work for God and they gave all their tasks their undivided attention.

Much of their work was educationally or learning based. They were the most educated members of the medieval society as they spent their time reading, copying and illuminating sacred texts and manuscripts in the scriptorium. All abbeys and monasteries had libraries where new and old manuscripts were kept.

A day in the life of a monk varied very little from one day to another except for some seasonal changes. It consisted of church services or offices, meals, work, study and a daily meeting. Most days followed a pattern laid down in The Book of Hours which included the round of daily prayers (*Opus Dei*):

1.30 a.m. – Prayers to be followed by a sung service – *Nocturns*. A bell would be rung to wake the monks and after putting on their hoods or cowls and night shoes on (they slept in their habits), they would make their way down the night stairs from the dormitory to the church.

Being clothed thus they will always be ready, and rising at the signal without any delay may hasten to forestall one another in the Work of God. When they rise for the Work of God, let them gently encourage one another, on account of the excuses to which the sleepy are addicted.

During the services, sleepy or not, they would stand in the choir stalls having only a small carved ledge or misericord to lean on. The circator would walk up and down the choir with a lamp to shine in the monk's faces to ensure that they were all wide awake!

3.30 a.m. – *Matins* (also known as *Vigils*) – prayers and then back to bed.

6.00 a.m. – *Prime Prayers* and the first mass of the day followed by the daily meeting in the Chapter House and a session of spiritual work.

8.00 a.m. – *Terce* – prayers and a sung mass.

9.00 a.m. – Reading.

11.30 a.m. – *Sext* prayers.

12.00 – main meal of the day followed by rest and private prayer.

2.30 p.m. – *None* prayers followed by at least two hours of physical work.

5.30 p.m. – supper.

6.00 p.m. – *Vespers*.

7.30 p.m. – a light supper followed by *Compline* service.

8.15 p.m. – bed time.

The pattern of such services was based on two quotations from the Book of Psalms:

1. *At midnight I rose to give praise to thee.*
2. *Seven times a day have I given praise to thee.*

All prayers were sung unaccompanied in plainsong or Gregorian chant. Few abbeys had musical instruments apart from bells or a small portable organ. Everyone would attend the services and all were expected to spend time in daily, private prayer for which small aisle or transept chapels were provided.

The daily meeting was an early morning affair in the Chapter House when important abbey business would be discussed and the reading aloud of a chapter of St Benedict's Rule – sixth century guidelines set by Benedict himself for monastic life. Before the meeting closed, confessions would be heard, the day's work discussed and all disciplinary matters would be attended to.

Study included reading and learning religious texts and manuscripts and silent thought or contemplation. Despite the loneliness of a monk's life and his withdrawal from the world at large, he was more educated and well informed than most of the population.

If elderly or unable to manage physical work because of illness or infirmity, monks were expected to spend only part of their day at work. Some worked in the scriptorium copying and illustrating religious manuscripts. Amongst the most famous work of this type was:

- The Book of Kells which was created at the abbey of Iona, Scotland and taken to Kells, Ireland for safety.
- The Lindisfarne Gospels is thought to be the work of Eadfrith, who became Bishop of Lindisfarne in 698 and died in 721. It is believed that they were produced in honour of St Cuthbert.

All abbeys were centres of learning with the abbot being a very intelligent and literate leader of the community who was often entrusted with secretarial work for bishops, kings and queens.Those that were more able and physically stronger would be found working outside in the cloister garden or out on the grange. Some abbeys carried out specialised farming and became very wealthy through sheep rearing and the woollen industry.

Abbey life had a very strong element of 'all for one and one for all' and in such a close knit community everything was done together. Monks slept in the dormitory; ate side by side in the refectory; prayed, worked and studied together. The most un-natural aspect of abbey life was that it was carried out in silence and conversation was very, very limited. Meals were eaten in silence. After washing their hands outside the refectory, the monks would walk in silence to the tables; grace would be said and a gong struck to signal that the meal could begin. While all else were eating, one monk would read a religious text. The food was mainly vegetarian consisting of bread, vegetables and eggs, washed down with weak ale. Fish would be served on Fridays and meat offered only to important visitors on other days.

Daily life in an abbey had to be well organised so as to run smoothly and efficiently. The heads of the management team were the abbot and prior with the abbot in overall charge of all matters. The abbot would have been elected and given a vote of confidence by the monks though many appointments were political, made by the king and confirmed by the Pope. Most abbots ran a 'tight ship' and led by proper example but not all as it is recorded that Abbot Beaton of Arbroath in Scotland gave a poor example as he had a mistress to keep, seven children to support and another post – Archbishop of St Andrew's to fill.

An abbey was a closed community; the abbot was seen as a link-pin between his abbey and the outside world. He had his own house on site, where he lived, entertained and met with important guests and visitors. He was also frequently called from the abbey to deal with affairs of state and the diocese and matters of political and spiritual importance. Some abbots were even military leaders. Unless an abbot had a reliable prior as his deputy, matters would soon become unstuck and day to day life would become very haphazard. Both abbot and prior were dependent on others such as obientaries, precentor, sacrist, cellarer, infirmarion, roundsmen or circatores, almoner, chamberlain, faterer, novice master, kitchener and guest master to ensure the smooth running of the abbey. (See Glossary.)

Further Reading
Investing Abbeys and Priories in Scotland. Heritage Scotland.
Life in a Medieval Abbey. T. McAleavy. English Heritage. 1996.
Life in a Monastery. S. Hebron. Pitkin Publishing. 2004.

CLEANLINESS

Washing before meals was something all monks did but taking a bath was not quite so popular. Lanfranc, in the eleventh century, laid down rules which stipulated that a bath was to be taken five times a year!

The brethren shall, when shaved, take their change of clothes and go to the place where the baths are prepared, and there, taking off their clothes in due order as they do in the dormitory, they shall enter the bathing place as directed, and letting down the curtain that hangs down before them they shall sit in silence in the bath. If anyone needs anything let him signal for it quietly, and a servant lifting the veil shall quickly take to him what he wants and return at once. When he has finished washing himself, he shall not stay longer for pleasure but shall rise and dress and put on his shoes as he does in the dormitory, and having washed his hands shall return to the cloister.

Should a healthy monk ask for a bath which would take him over the number stipulated by Lanfranc,

his desire was not to be gratified, for sometimes, what gives pleasure is thought to do good, even though it may do harm.

But,

A bath should be by no means refused to a body when compelled there to by the needs of ill health.

Attached to the dormitory was the necessarium, a large latrine block. Such facilities were unknown in most homes and houses and Lanfranc insisted that a new monk, on arrival at the start of his postulancy be shown the conveniences that were to be used.

And he shall be taken beyond the dormitory, and the cells shown him to which he is to repair when nature's way demand it, and he shall be told how to bear himself seemly in there in sitting and departing and how to satisfy the demands of nature with modesty.

Shaving was done in the cloister. For the tonsured monk, this meant shaving the head and face and was done every three weeks. Everyone lined up and shaved one another in order of seniority with the most senior monks being shaved first. By the time the novices were to be shaved, the razor was quite blunt, the water in the shaving bowl cold and the towels used to dry the face and head dripping wet. A weekly activity was the Maundy, in which the monks washed each other's feet. Hands were also washed at the lavatorium before entering the refectory. At a time when cutlery was almost unknown except to the most wealthy, food was eaten mainly with the fingers.

Monks were taught to look after their bodies and keep them hygienic and so lived fairly healthy lives. Medical knowledge was one field of study and practice which was of great value not only to the abbey community of monks but to the local community as well. Abbot Baldwin of Bury St Edmunds was physician to William the Conqueror as was Faricius, abbot of Abingdon, to Henry I and his queen-Matilda. Some monks went as far as the European continent to study medicine.

One interesting facet of medieval medicine and used by monks was the study of a person's urine. Its colour was thought to be good indicator of a person's health. Not only did Gutun Owain (historian of Basingwerk and Strata Florida Abbeys) copy a chart showing the parts of the body to be bled for different diseases into the Black Book of Basingwerk but he also copied a chart showing urine colours and their meaning. Abbot John of St Albans examined his own urine and was able to work out how many days he had left to live.

Although he inspected it diligently he was unable, because the keenness of his eyesight had been blunted, to observe to his liking the subtle and secret signs of death, which he knew. So he said to one of our monks, Master William the Physician, 'What do you

see here, brother?' He indicated what he saw and the abbot said,
'Ah! Praise be to God! He has allowed me three more days for
penance, but after the three days I shall die.' Those who heard this
believed it, for he was most experienced in the art of medicine
and had often infallibly foretold similar things concerning others
in such circumstances.

Monks gained valuable knowledge and learnt useful practices
in the field of medicine which they used and shared in their lives
of service.

The solitary life has but one aim, the service of the individual. But
this is plainly in conflict with the law of love. Whose feet then wilt
thou wash? Whom wilt thou care for?

Further Reading
Investing Abbeys and Priories in Scotland. Heritage Scotland.
Life in a Medieval Abbey. T. McAleavy. English Heritage. 1996.
Life in a Monastery. S. Hebron. Pitkin Publishing. 2004.

ABBEY BELLS AND BELLRINGING – A CALL TO PRAYER
Bells have been a very important feature of everyday life for
almost eight centuries. Pealing bells have signalled the hours of
the day and times for prayers; they have brought warnings of
storms and enemy armies; they heralded masses, funerals, and
deaths. They have brought all manner of people together. Bells
have been the voice of God, calling out His message.

On 4 January 1216 Pope Innocent III wrote of the need to have
bells [*campanas*] *to distinguish the hours, and to summon the*
people to church.

Bells have always been central to the Christian faith, fulfilling
the practical and material needs of the church in marking the
hours in the daily routine of monastic prayer and to summon the

faithful to church. If they were not able to get to the service in time they could make a gesture that they had heard the bells and knew the significance of their sound.

Whether they are involved in business or detained by illness, bowing their heads toward the church where the body of the Lord is being sacrificed, they should adore and say some prayer, at the very least saying 'Lord Jesus Christ, have mercy on us' or say the Paternoster.

Medieval men rang the bells with many purposes in mind. By the ringing of the hours and notifying the people of prayer times, church bells helped to create communities. During funerals, bells gave notice of private moments. Listeners and ringers of bells as well as the bells themselves had and still have a special significance in the Christian's life and work.

Bells were rung at special times or for a special purpose:
- The Curfew bell – associated with the laws of William the Conqueror.
- The Pancake Bell was originally associated with the preparations for the Lenten Fast.
- Sunday Uses – the Matins and Mass bells.
- The Sanctus bell was rung just before the sermon.
- For Matins and Evensong the bell would be ringing or chiming for a period varying from 15 to 45 minutes.
- Week Day Uses (for services).
- Festivals – the Great Festivals at Christmas or Easter morning, at Whitsuntide, on Ascension Eve, on Ascension Day, on All Saints Day, on Trinity Sunday, on the Harvest Festival.
- On Christmas Eve in connection with the distribution of charities.
- On Good Friday.
- On New Year's Eve.

- Secular and Social Festivals. Weddings, Royal Anniversaries.
- Funeral Uses – the Passing Bell or Death Knell would be rung immediately after a death was announced.
- Tolling at funerals – continued for between forty-five minutes and two hours and quickened when the funeral procession arrived.

The Morning Bell and the Curfew were survivals of the old Ave Peals. The Pancake Bell was rung on Shrove Tuesday. The Gleaning Bell was rung during harvest. In cases of fire the bells were chimed quickly as a warning. In stormy weather the bells would be rung to call the people together for Special prayers. During a storm of thunder and lightning, it was best to keep clear of the belfry and church. During the Middle Ages, the ringing of the bells was believed to diffuse lightning, and many medieval bells were engraved with *Fulgura frango* ('I break up the lightning'). This theory was discredited by a medieval scholar who observed that over a 33-year period, there were 386 lightning strikes on church towers and 103 fatalities among bell ringers!

One would expect large, wealthy abbeys to have a peal of bells. Smaller ones would not have so many but the presence of some bells in the tower was very important. Llangennith Priory for instance was only small but had a peal of four bells in the north east tower. The Treble bell had a diameter of 23½ inches. It was cast by Thomas and David Davies of Oystermouth, Swansea. The parishioners who had paid for the casting had their initials inscribed onto the bell:

E: I. G: B.D.T.W.B.P.: H. (bell)
T.D. (bell) D. (bell) (1722)
L. (coin) France.

The second bell had a diameter of 24 inches and a Latin inscription meaning 'To the Glory of God Alone':

inscription meaning 'To the Glory of God Alone':
   SOLI DEO GLORIA: C. (bell) P:H.L.NC:
   IR:IF:TR:1675

The third and fourth (Tenor) bells were cast by William Evans at Chepstow Bell Foundry. Bell Number Three had a diameter of 28 inches and was inscribed:
   PROSPERITY TO THIS PARISH W. (bell) 1758

The Tenor bell had a diameter of 30 inches and was inscribed:
   Wm. TUCKER & JOHN CULLIN
   CHURCH W'NS W. (bell) E. 1758

The word 'Cullin' is a mistake for it was John Hullin, a member of a well-known Gower family, who was churchwarden.

After the Dissolution of the Monasteries many of the bells were seen as a real bargain by some of the scrap metal dealers of the time. Dealers from English cities bargained with the Crown for the bells. Most of the south Wales bells went to Bristol. The three bells of the Grace Dieu Abbey were taken to Monmouth and from there to Bristol as were the four bells of Neath, the six bells of Margam and the one bell from the Friary House at Haverfordwest and the Black Friary, Cardiff. Bells, being made of an alloy of iron and copper were very valuable for the manufacture of cannons. The three bells of Brecon, one of which was originally from Cwmhir Abbey, went to Caerleon. Whether it was taken from there to Bristol like so many of the others is not known. The Friars' House at Newport had only one bell which was sold for thirty shillings to Morrice Vaughan but one of the Carmarthen Friars' House was sold for only twenty shillings and another followed so many of its kind to Bristol.

   The bells from Friars' Houses were of a small size compared to the bells from an abbey. Strata Florida's three bells were sold for £10 13s 4d to the parish of Caron and those of Whitland Abbey went for £13 6s 8d. Legal action was taken in Brecon and Abergavenny to try and keep the bells locally. William Thomas and William Walter of Brecon argued that the bells should stay in the locality as the inhabitants of Brecon owned three of the bells in the steeple of St John's, Brecon and they paid the Prior four pence whenever they wished the two bigger bells in the steeple to be rung at a funeral. The Court of Augmentations found in the King's favour and informed the people of Brecon that the bells were to be sold. An appeal against the decision was made but the sale went through with three bells – one from Cwmhir and the other two from the Priory of St John's, Brecon were taken to Caerleon. The king permitted the three smaller bells from Brecon to be kept there but made up for his loss by selling the priory land and '*the silver of two relics set with crystal stones and the silver of two tablets of wood, with relics garnished with crystal stones.*' A long struggle followed to keep the bells in Brecon and eventually the parishioners were allowed to keep the bells as they had no others in the town. Abergavenny also put up a fight to keep the four bells of the Priory of St Mary. Fortunately, they had written proof of ownership and many elderly witnesses came forward to testify and swear that they had paid a portion of the cost of buying them. There is no documentation to state that the bells of Abergavenny were sold to Bristol.

Llantarnam Abbey had four bells, weighing more than 38 cwt. The four bells were acquired by a William Jones of Caerleon, who paid the sum of £15 to have them taken down; the lead removed and melted down. It was reported that the lead weighed over 4 fothers. (1 fother = 2,000 lbs.)

Nicholas Purcell, the Crown tenant, sold the three bells of Strata Marcella Abbey to Chirk parish church.

Haverfordwest churchwardens in 1589, includes purchasing a baldron for the bells and oiling the bells. They also met the cost of mending the clapper to one of the bells, obtaining horse hide to make baldrons for the bells, mending the Fourth bell's clapper and supplying gloves to the ringers

The precise origins of Monmouth Priory are unknown but before 1678 there were five bells in the tower. The sixth bell was cast on 19 January 1678 by John Pennington, a local bell maker. At least two of the bells were removed and recast on the 23 June 1685 by Rudhall's Bell Foundry in Gloucester. All the bells were rehung by Evan Evans of Chepstow in 1704 at a cost of £3.00. The existing ring of eight was recast in 1706 by Abraham Rudhall at a cost of £60. Oil for the new bells was 10d a half pint in 1706.

In 1883 the bell frame was replaced at a cost of £200 by a new timber frame inscribed 'George Day & Son, Church Bell Hangers, Eye, Suffolk, 1883'. All eight bells were overhauled in 1953 by Gillett & Johnson of Croydon. The bells fell silent in 1972 for repairs to the steeple which was seen to sway when the bells were rung. A new bell frame was installed in 1982 and the bells retuned by the Whitechapel Bell Foundry at a cost of £22,000. The bells are now pealed from a platform above the new entrance to the church.

The first recorded peal of five thousand and forty changes was mentioned in Pugh's Hereford Journal on Wednesday, 21 December 1791. Local tradition has it that at least one of the bells was presented to the church by Henry V who took issue with having bells rung as he left Calais.

THE OLD ABBEY BELL

Full many a spell hath the old abbey bell,
in the tones of its iron tongue.
And many a day has passed fleeting away
since it first in the belfry was hung.

In the ages of old when it sounded, it told
the hour of the monkish prayer,
and it sounded a knell for the martyrs, who fell
in the faith of their fathers there.

Though centuries have passed since the metal was cast,
it high in the old tower swings,
it hath sounded for clay that unknown passed away
and tolled for the death of kings!

Of the strangers who've fled from the kings that are dead,
there is now but a name to tell
for time levels all, 'neath its funeral pall
when his voice is a passing knell.

But the old abbey bell though it sounded to tell
of forms that have passed away,
its tunes have rung out 'mid the song and the shout
of many a festival day.

                              Harry Cowles

Further Reading

Acta Innocentii Pope Innocent III. (1198–1216).
Les sermons et la visite pastorale de Federico Visconti. Archbishop of
    Pisa. Ed. N. Bériou Rome. 2001.

Pisa. Ed. N. Bériou Rome. 2001.

'*Margam Abbey*'. Glanmor Williams. Morgannwg Transactions of the Glamorgan Local History Society Vol. 42. 1998.

The Old Abbey Bell. Harry Cowles. A. P. Schmidt. Boston.

'*The Church Bells of Gower*' G. R. Orrin. Gower (journal of the Gower Society). 1988.

The History of St Mary's Church, Haverfordwest. Pat Barker. 2009.

'*Welsh Monastic Bells*' – Wales. J. Conway Davies. Wales. Autumn 1946.

VISITORS

Despite being in remote places, many official and some not quite so official visitors would visit abbeys. Whatever their reason for calling, all were welcomed.

Once the French founding fathers (usually a group of at least thirteen monks) had been replaced with native monks and officials, regular contact with the mother house was maintained. This meant that visitors from abroad such as the abbot of L'Aumône, who was called to investigate a dispute between Tintern Abbey and its daughter house of Kingswood in 1192, would visit. The prior of L'Aumône had the pleasanter duty in 1321 of being present at the installation of Abbot Walter at Tintern. In 1330 the abbot of L'Aumône was again in Wales, visiting *diverse houses subject to the Cistercian order.*

Other groups of regular visitors were pilgrims or travellers in need of hospitality; the poor and sick in need of shelter or a hospital to convalesce in. Strata Florida had a hospice at Ysbyty Ystrad Meurig, about two miles away which, in 1294, had many lepers staying there.

Others to be seen at an abbey would be those who had taken holy orders in their last weeks or months of life as a form of spiritual insurance. In return for their stay, they would will their wealth to the order. Owain Cyfeiliog, founder of Strata Marcella, (c.1130–1197) a prince of the southern part of Powys, died and was buried there in 1197. Gruffudd ap Rhys (died 25 July 1201) was a prince of Deheubarth (the South Lands), his wife Matilda (1209) and son Rhys (1222) stayed in and were buried at Strata Florida.

Corrodians were wealthy members of society who could afford to pay to spend their retirement years at an abbey, which included *retired superiors, superannuated servants and lay folk who had purchased annuities and board and lodging as an insurance against old age.* One such person was a blinded hostage named Canaythen who gave land in Resolven to Margam Abbey in about 1290 so he, as a lay brother, could spend the rest of his life there. Geoffrey Sturmi also gave the abbey land in return for twelve marks to clear his debts, and a clock and four gold pieces to each of his sons and a promise that when the time came, he would be accepted into the abbey. In 1245 Roger Gramus forfeited a yearly rent of half a silver mark in return for a promise of support to Agnes, his wife. The deal was that she would receive seven loaves and five gallons of beer weekly and at Michaelmas (29 September) a Crannock (an old (Irish) measure of corn equivalent to a quarter of gruel), a crannock of beans and a bushel of salt. In 1325, John Nichol gave lands at Kenfig (*Cynffig*, near Bridgend, Glamorganshire) to Margam Abbey in return for support in later life. He was given three daily loaves and a gallon of strong beer for the rest of his life. Yearly, he was to receive half a silver mark (in 1066 worth 160 pence, or 13 shillings and 4 pence, i.e. ⅔ of a Pound Sterling), four pairs of shoes, a quart of oats and pasture for two animals whilst John would work inside or outside the abbey, as long as his health held out. A good bargain if ever there was one.

Valle Crucis Abbey gave John Puleston, a gentleman, *for his good counsel and aid spent on us* an annual income together with a room for John and two servants, three horses, two hare hounds

In an agreement with Whitland Abbey a tennant, in 1540, exchanged his land and holdings for *food, a good room for his own use, a meadow, and a yearly sum of twenty shillings for the term of his natural life*.

Edward I, in 1304, wanted a room for Geoffrey de Lastessen to live in at Tintern Abbey. In ten years' time, Edward II sent one of his servants to live at Tintern for the rest of his life. In 1319, William de Bromfeld from Holm Cultran Abbey, Cumberland was sent to Tintern in search of living quarters as his abbey had been destroyed. Another of the king's servants, the Sergeant of the King's Chamber, was housed in Tintern from 1412 onwards.

Not all abbeys were able to afford the hospitality demanded by the king. Aberconwy Abbey was asked in 1315 to take in Dafydd Goch (the illegitimate and only surviving son of Dafydd III, last free Welsh Prince of Wales) and supply him with food and clothing for the rest of his life but as the abbey faced hard times, the request was refused.

Roger, retiring abbot of Grace Dieu Abbey, in 1341, was given a place to live, one or two servants according to his needs and a pension of twenty pounds, food for his table to include bread, drinks, meat and fish (raw or cooked), as much as for two or three monks. Abbot Gruffudd of Grace Dieu Abbey, in 1543, gave Hywel ap John ap Ievan and his wife, for a sum of money paid in advance, a home, supply of food including half a trug (a shallow, usually oval gardening basket made with wide strips of wood. In Middle English, *a shallow wooden tray, measure of corn*, perhaps from Old Norse) of wheat, oaten malt and a quarter of beef at Christmas, a pig at Michaelmas, wood for his fire, a horse and a garden. This must have involved some really hard bargaining.

Abbeys were also known to sponsor poets as in the case of Gwilym Tew (fl. 1460–1480) poet and manuscript copier, who was at the Pen-Rhys hospital of Llantarnam Abbey in 1460.

at the Pen-Rhys hospital of Llantarnam Abbey in 1460.

> *I will go to Pen-Rhys in my one shirt for fear of ague, upon my knee a taper a fathom (long) and the prayer of the labourers, where at Pen Rhys is ever a host for them.*

Gutun Owain (c.1460–1503) was at Strata Florida in 1480 but he spent much of his later years at Basingwek with Tudur Aled. Guto'r Glyn, when lame and deaf, was welcomed at Valle Crucis as was Lewis Morgannwg at Neath Abbey in the early sixteenth century.

Not unknown were royal and regal visitors. King John visited Margam Abbey twice and Tintern in 1210, as did Richard II in 1399. Edward I visited Aberconwy Abbey in 1283 and Neath Abbey in 1284. The Bishop of Worcester visited Tintern in 1289 with a retinue of men and thirty horses.

The poor knew when to call at Tintern Abbey. A sum of £1 10s was shared every Maundy Thursday. It was a case of necessity when they called at Margam Abbey in 1188 as they were in dire need of food at the time and the abbot sent a ship to Bristol to obtain a load of oats for their benefit.

Most of the abbeys' visitors were thankful for what they received but Hugh de Hereford may well have been more thankful than most. He borrowed nine silver marks from Margam Abbey to pay for his release from prison. Abbot Ralph of Tintern lent money to one of King John's daughters.

Most abbey doors were open and many made use of their hospitality.

Further Reading

The Welsh Cistercians. D. H. Williams. Hughes & Son, Ltd., Griffin Press. 1969.

MONKS AND MEDICINE

As monasteries were regarded as centres of learning and monks regarded as being more educated than most of the population it was perhaps natural that it was monks and monasteries that were responsible for establishing a tradition of medical knowledge. When ordinary people were in need of help, it was to the Church that they turned for assistance. Even royalty turned to the Church when in need of medical advice. William the Conqueror's doctor was Baldwin, abbot of Bury St Edmunds. Henry I and Matilda, his wife, were patients of Faricius, abbot of Abbingdon. Other abbots, who were richer than ordinary monks, could afford to study in continental medical schools. Warin, abbot of St Albans was one who travelled as far as Salerno in Italy to study and on his return was able to filter medical knowledge to some of his contemporaries. If a large abbey was fortunate enough to have a monk or physician residing there who could administer cures, he could charge for his services and the money used to enhance the building. Others, such as most in Wales, had no such luck but as disease and poor health were part of daily life and medicines were both basic and often useless, ordinary people had to rely on what services the monks could offer.

Not all monks were conversant with herbal or natural remedies. Some did not want the work; others were prohibited or at the least not supported in their quest to heal as it could bring them into contact with members of the opposite sex which in turn could lead to improper relations, if they were unable to resist such temptations. Because of this, in the later Middle Ages doctors and physicians tended to be university educated and trained and monks in medical practice became a much less common occurrence.

The monastery garden was known in Latin as the *herbularius*. Medicinal herbs were grown in the physic garden, close to the infirmary so that the herbs could be harvested as and when needed. They were often grown in raised beds with pathways between the beds. Only one type of herb was grown per bed. The herbs grown in the physic garden were in great demand throughout the monastery. They were grown for their healing properties to help in the treatment of any monks that had been taken ill and to help heal the sick and poor people that took shelter in the monasteries. Many of them also had religious significance. The monastery infirmary often doubled as the local hospital in areas that didn't have separate hospitals for travellers and local peasants who couldn't afford the services of a physician.

Those monks who had the knowledge knew when herbs and plants should be gathered (when in full flower and perfectly dry) and at the correct time of the astrological calendar (when the planet governing them was rising or facing south at sunrise) when pulling the herbs made them more potent. Tree barks were gathered in Spring when the sap was rising and the bark peeled off easily. It was best to wait until the plant had finished growing if the roots were needed.

Agrimony (*Agrimonia eupatoria*) – a cure for eye complaints. An all-purpose plant added to wine as a cure for stomach complaints. It was also used as a poultice to clean wounds. Its dried flowers and leaves was claimed to help sleep. The plant also contained tannin and was used in the dyeing of linen and in the manufacture of leather.

Alecost Costmary (*Tanacetum balsamita*) – used to treat indigestion and bowel disorders and in the brewing of ale. Nicholas Culpeper (*Physician of the 17th century*) – recommended that the seed be given to children for worms.

Apothecary Rose (*Rosa gallica/officinalis*) – emblem of Royal House of Lancaster. Rose water was used as a lotion to soothe sore eyes. **Applemint** (*Mentha suaveolens*) – used to add flavour to drinks to aid digestion and bowel complaints.

Bay (*Laurus nobilis*) – bay leaves were sprinkled on the floors to disguise bad smells.

Betony (*Betonica officinalis*) (*Stachys officinalis*) – a cure-all herb used in syrup or as an ointment to cure complaints ranging from palsy to headaches and shortness of breath. A drink made from honey and Betony would aid digestion.

Blackberry (*Rubus fruticosus*) – used to treat gout. Would be used in a syrup to treat dysentery. The leaves and bark were chewed to relieve bleeding gums and placed on burns and scalds to soothe them.

Black Henbane seeds (*Hyosyamus*) – used as an anaesthetic.

Blackthorn (*Prunus spinosa*) – used to make a mouthwash for throat infections. Drinks made from the berries were good for stomach and bowel pain.

Borage (*Borago officinalis*) – added to wine and considered good for strengthening the heart. Used to soothe sore throats and excellent in curing bronchial and chest complaints.

Bugle (*Ajuga reptans*) – the flowers and leaves mixed with wine were used to treat bruises and wounds. When mixed with honey and alum it was also used as a treatment for mouth ulcers.

Burdock (*Arctium lappa*) – used as a treatment for leprosy and the roots were used to treat fevers, ringworm and skin infections.

Catmint (*Nepeta cataria*) – when mixed in ointments it was used to relieve piles.

Celery (*Apium graveolens*) – also known as Small Ache because of its medicinal properties.

Chervil (*Anthriscus cerefolium*) – a diuretic. As an infusion it would aid the circulation, or as a poultice it would ease rheumatism.

Chicory (*Cichorium intybus*) – together with Endive, this herb was known as 'Succory' and was used as a laxative. The juice was taken in milk and water to help the digestion and to treat gallstones. The

leaves were boiled and wrapped in poultices to reduce inflammation.
Chives (*Allium schoenoprasum*) – a medicinal herb used mainly to aid digestion.

Coloured cloths – draping coloured cloths from the bed and around a person was considered a suitable treatment for someone infected with smallpox!

Cowslip (*Primula veris*) – used to treat palsy. It was also a cure for cramp and administered during childbirth.

Creeping Thyme (*Thymus serpyllum*) – a cure for snake-bites and headaches. Oil of Thyme was added to Oil of Lavender to treat muscle pains.

Daisy (*Bellis perennis*) – the juice was drunk to relieve chest wounds and cure mouth ulcers. Applied as an ointment it was believed to reduce inflammation and improve complexion.

Dill (*Anethum graveolens*) – dill water was given to babies to help them sleep.

Elecampane (*Inula helenium*) – contains an antiseptic which makes it useful in the application of surgical dressings. All parts of the plant were used to make powders, syrups and infusions. The roots were used in cakes and sweets to tempt monks who were too sick to eat.

Fennel (*Foeniculum vulgare*) – was used as a laxative, for easing stomach aches, and, when mixed with the seeds of other herbs and plants such as Rose, Vervain, Rue and Celandine, would be an effective eye-wash.

Feverfew (*Tanacetum parthenium*) – used to reduce fevers, and when made into syrup with honey eased winter coughs. It was also used in midwifery.

Foxglove (*Digitalis purpurea*) – used it as treatment for Scrofula. Foxgloves contain substances which are used in the treatment of heart disease but the plant is highly toxic!

Good King Henry (*Chenopodium bonus henricus*) – also known as

'All-Good', it was supposed to cure all ills. Its leaves were boiled and eaten like spinach or applied as a poultice for the treatment for ulcers.

Greater Celandine (*Chelidonium maior*) – used to heal eye complaints, and when mixed with honey and ale drunk as a cure for jaundice.

Greater Plantain (*Plantago maior*) – its flowers were used in ointments to treat wounds and sores. The juice would ease pain from bruises; the leaves cooked with Mallow would assist healing; also used to reduce swollen glands.

Heartsease (*Viola tricolor*) – a member of the pansy family, was used as a medicine and syrup to treat coughs and fevers.

Hemp Agrimony (*Eupatorium cannabinum*) – used by Anglo-Saxons to treat wounds and also to treat indigestion and diarrhoea, or in a mouthwash for treating sore throats and coughs.

Herb Robert (*Geranium robertianum*) – used to treat victims of the plague. It was also used to staunch bleeding and to treat kidney disorders.

Holly Thistle (*Cnicus (cardous) benedictus*) – an ingredient of plague medicines.

Horsemint (*Mentha longifolia*) – Culpeper suggested it for treating 'wind in the stomach' and other complaints.

Houseleek (*Sempervivum tectorum*) – used to treat St Anthony's Fire, and the juice was said to ease headaches.

Hyssop (*Hyssopus officinalis*) – was used to cleanse leper hospitals. As a medicine it was used as a purgative. It was also mixed with wine and syrup and drunk as a remedy for catarrh or chest complaints.

Iris (*Iris versicolor*) – used to treat respiratory disorders.

Jacob's Ladder (*Polemonium caeruleum*) – used in the treatment of toothache and dysentery.

Lady's Bedstraw (*Galium verum*) – used as a coagulant or to repel vermin.

Lady's Mantle (*Alchemilla vulgaris/xanthochlora*) – used to stop bleeding and as an antiseptic. Widely used on battlefields.

Lavender (*Lavendula angustifolia/officinalis*) – lavender water was a good tonic for heart disease and as an antiseptic. Its fragrance was also believed to prevent the spread of plague.

Lemon Balm (*Melissa officinalis*) – its aroma was said to drive away all sadness. The dried leaves could be added to cordials and wines to add flavour. The juice of Lemon Balm was also used as a coating for surgical dressings and it had a calming effect on the heart.

Lesser Periwinkle (*Vinca minor*) – reputed to stop bleeding.

Lungwort (*Pulmonaria officinalis*) – used to treat diseases of the lung.

Maple/Field Maple (*Acer campestre*) – a concoction made from the leaves and bark was said to strengthen the liver.

Marigold (*Calendula officinalis*) – considered to offer protection against the plague. Mixed with grease or fat it was used to dress cuts and wounds.

Mint (*Mentha*) – used to add flavour to cordials to aid digestion and bowel complaints.

Motherwort (*Leonurus cardiaca*) – a treatment for heart trembling and convulsions. It was mixed with wine and given to women in labour to reduce cramps.

Mullein (*Verbascum thapsus*) – the leaves, when dried, produced an oil which was rubbed onto poultices to reduce inflammation. It was also used a diuretic and a treatment for gout.

Nettle-leaved Bellflower (*Campanula trachelium*) – believed to have beneficial properties in treating sore throats.

Parsley (*Petroselinum crispum*) – often mixed with wine, vinegar and honey as a diuretic. Mixed with Rue and oil it was used to treat gout. Mixed with Fennel, Sage and rose-tinted olive oil it was applied to limbs to relieve paralysis.

Penicillum funghi – used to treat bacterial infections.

Penicillum funghi – used to treat bacterial infections.

Pennyroyal (*Mentha pulegium*) – as an ointment this was believed to cure eye complaints. Taken with honey and vinegar or oil it was used as a cure for stomach disorders and to cure constipation. It was also used as a valuable insect repellent, and was frequently strewn over beds and clothes to repel fleas.

Poppy (*Papaver Ranunculus latifolius*) – used to make a pain killing ointment.

Primrose (*Primula vulgaris*) – used as an ointment to heal wounds and added to wine as a cure for palsy.

Roman Chamomile (*Chamaemelum nobile*) – the flowers were used to make sedatives, and chamomile oil was used to perfume baths.

Rosemary (*Rosmarinus officinalis*) – rubbed into the scalp or used in a paste to clean the teeth. Rosemary leaves dipped in wine made a soothing treatment for sore eyes.

Sage (*Salvia officinalis*) – mixed with vinegar to cleanse the body of pestilence. Mixed with Rosemary, Plantain and wine as a gargle. It was also used to treat fevers and coughs.

St John's Wort (*Hypericum perforatum*) – its healing properties were mainly in treating wounds and bleeding.

Salad Burnet (*Sanguisorba officinalis*) – an aid in the treatment of wounds and digestive disorders.

Sorrel (*Rumex acetosa*) – a tonic for the heart and a diuretic and treatment for bowel complaints.

Southernwood (*Artemisia abrotanum*) – the leaves were used as a dressing for wounds and to treat fevers.

Spearmint (*Mentha spicata*) – Spearmint oil was taken to loosen the bowels.

Sweet Cicely (*Myrris odorata*) – supposed to offer protection against the plague or pestilence.

Sweet Violets (*Viola odorata*) – petals of the flower were considered to be an emetic and purgative.

Sweet Woodruff (*Galium odoratum*) – used in cordials to cure liver complaints.

Tansy (*Tanacetum parthenium*) – used as an insect repellent. As a gargle it was used to relieve mouth ulcers and treat other sores.

Thyme (*Thymus vulgaris*) – believed to have antiseptic properties.

Treacle (*theriac*) – considered a cure-all. It was said to prevent internal swellings, cure fevers, unblock internal stoppages, alleviate heart problems, epilepsy, and palsy, get rid of blemishes, induce sleep, improve digestion, strengthen limbs, heal wounds, remedy snake bites, cure prolapsed uteruses, and cure the plague.

Valerian (*Valeriana officinalis*) – a treatment for pleurisy. Also known as 'Heal-All' and used to treat bruises and convulsions.

Vervain (*Verbena officinalis*) – a treatment for ulcers.

Wallflower (*Cheiranthus cheiri*) – known as 'Heartsease' because of their association with curing heart complaints.

Wall Germander (*Teucrium chamaedrys*) – used to treat fevers and ailments of the digestive system. If taken with honey it would relieve coughs, or if applied with oil would relieve eye complaints.

White Deadnettle (*Lamium album*) – older leaves would be applied to wounds to stop bleeding.

Nettles were also added to wines for general medicinal purposes.

White Horehound (*Marrubium vulgare*) – taken with honey as a cure for asthma and colds. Its leaves were used to treat and heal sores.

Wild Marjoram (*Oreganum vulgare*) – to ease rheumatic pain, also regarded as a preventative against sickness. When added to honey as a drink it was used to treat headaches, while as an infusion it was used to treat sore throats.

Willow (*Salix fragillis*) – in hot vinegar would be used to dissolve warts.

Winter Savory (*Satureja Montana*) – cooked with Pears, Fennel

Woad (*Isatis tinctoria*) – used in the treatment of St Anthony's Fire and for ointments used to treat sores and ulcers.

Wormwood (*Artemisia absinthium*) – used as a treatment for worms, and was often given to relieve constipation.

Yarrow (*Achillea ptarmica*) – used to stem the flow of blood from an injury and also known as Carpenter's Herb.

Many folk remedies were used in the hope of finding a cure. These were a relic from the days of the Druids and had been passed on to wise women, who had learned the secrets of which herbs, flowers, trees and plants had the power to heal and ward off evil influences.

Some of the folk remedies applied were effective because of the medicinal qualities and beneficial substances contained within the plants. Many failed. Some of the most unusual remedies included:

Buttercups worn in a bag around the neck to cure insanity.

An amulet of senna, mint, and rue worn as a bracelet to avert evil, as did primrose and convolvulus picked on the First of May and twined into wreaths.

Woodbine cut on the waxing moon was made into hoops which were preserved until the following March. When children were ill they were passed through a hoop three times to cure them.

St John's Wort was most effective for curing fever if found by accident, especially on Midsummer's Eve.

Mustard and garlic warded off the plague.

Eating nettles mixed with the white of an egg cured insomnia.

Heather boiled in water and applied warm to the top of the head cured a headache.

To cure cataracts draw fresh water from a well, taking care not to rest the basin on earth or stone, only wood. Add a gold or silver coin to the water, then blades of grass and let seep. Pass the blades of grass across the eye, then pour water from the basin into the eyes.

To cure ague swallow a spider wrapped in a raisin.

To cure baldness rub goose droppings over the affected area.

Tie an eel skin around the knee to alleviate cramps.

To cure a toothache, touch a dead man's tooth.

To make freckles disappear, cover them with blood from a bull or hare, or use water distilled from crushed walnuts.

Large bouquets of herbs and flowers would be strategically placed to avoid breathing noxious smells.

Another technique used by monks was the study of urine. The Black Book of Basingwerk Abbey contains a chart showing urine colours and their meaning. It was believed that the colour of urine was an important indicator of a person's health and Abbot John of St Albans is said to have predicted how long he had to live by studying the colour of his own urine.

Few operations were carried out due to lack of training and facilities and those that were were barbarous by modern day standards.

The treatment for toothache was to take a candle and burn it close to the tooth. The worms that gnawed the tooth would fall out into a cup of water held by the mouth.

For evil spirits in the head a surgeon used trepanning. This called for a surgeon cut a hole into the skull to release evil spirits trapped in the brain. The operation might also include cutting out the part of the brain that had been 'infected' with these evil spirits. Incredibly, people are known to have survived operations such as these as skulls have been found which show bone growth around the hole cut by a surgeon – a sign that someone did survive such an operation if only for a short time.

an operation if only for a short time.

Blood letting was a much used process when blood was drained from a certain spot in the body. The idea behind this was similar to trepanning in that it released bad blood from the body. The use of leeches was also common for this but dirty knives were used, only to increase the risk to the patient.

Cauterisation was where a physician identified that a certain part of the body was ill and the cure was having red hot pokers put on it.

Few monasteries had cottage hospitals attached to them. The monks who worked there had only a basic medical knowledge but were amongst the few qualified people in the country to help the poor and those who could not afford their own physician.

Western medicine advanced very little during the Middle Ages. Scholarship was not considered that important and curing the soul became more important than curing the body. Disease and injury were thought to be the result of supernatural intervention and many insisted that cures were only possible through prayer. No new medical research was conducted, and no new practices were created. The earliest known herbal of British origin is the Saxon Leech Book of Bald, written in the tenth century. Around 950, a nobleman named Bald persuaded King Alfred to commission the book, which combined all aspects of herbalism-Anglo-Saxon, Celtic, Greco-Roman and Arab. Containing a mixture of sacred ritual and herbal remedies, it discusses five hundred plants and their healing qualities. Another early and most valuable medical book to emerge from the religious sector during the Middle Ages was Hildegard's Medicine, written by Hildegard of Bingen (1098–1179), Abbess of the Rupertsburg Convent in Germany. She was a nun from the age of fifteen and claimed that visions of God commanded her to treat the sick and compile her herbal formulas. Her book combined

Catholicism and folk medicine. She was the only medieval woman who left a written account of the practices of 'wise women'. Another pharmaceutical and medical book from the Middle Ages is the Compendium of Medicine (circa 1250) by Gilbertus Anglicus (*Gilbert the Englishman*). Translated in the early fifteenth century from Latin to Middle English it consists of medicinal recipes with guides to diagnosis, medicinal preparation and prognosis. The text names over four hundred different ingredients. Treatments are presented roughly from head to tail, beginning with headache and ending with hemorrhoids.

Further reading
Culpepper's Complete Herbal. N. Culpeper. W. Foulsham & Co. London.
The Simmonite-Culpeper Herbal Remedies. W. J. Simmonite & N. Culpeper. W. Foulsham & Co., London. 1957.
http://www.lewespriory.org.uk

7. 1066 – Before and After

Wales, probably more than any other country, has been known as 'the land of saints'. Many saints, or early Christians, lived here and were responsible for the spread of Christianity throughout the land during the fifth and sixth century.

Wales was a committed Christian country before St Augustine arrived in England in 597. The first of our Welsh saints – Dyfrig, with other men and women following suit, established their churches all over the country. The Welsh word *llan*, meaning a religious enclosure, bears testament to their work from Llanbadrig on the north coast of Anglesey to Llantwit Major (*Llanilltud Fawr*) in south Wales with hundreds of others in between. The influence of such characters as Dyfrig, Non, Gwenffrewi, Melangell, Dwynwen, Illtud, Padrig, Dewi, Teilo, Padarn, Deiniol, Beuno and many more spread far and wide over the Celtic fringes of the Roman Empire as far as Cumbria, Cornwall, Brittany, Ireland and Scotland.

Llanilltud Fawr played a leading role in these important events. The monastery, established in the fifth century, by Illtud was a centre of learning and training for monks. Illtud, who had been greatly influenced by Germanus of Auxerre and Dyfrig, led many of his contemporary saints on their pilgrimages to establish their own churches and *llannau* (more than one *llan*) in Wales and beyond. (as mentioned above.)

By about the year 600, due to the European influence, a Catholic Christianity was being introduced in Britain, while at the same time the Celtic Christianity still existed especially so in the west. The two branches had different histories; their organisational structure was different and Celtic monasteries were far more independent. By the seventh century, the Catholic structure of the church consisted of a Bishop for each diocese who would live and rule from a 'see' or a city which was able to support a cathedral.

The structure of the Celtic church was based on a monastic network ruled by Abbots. Bishops were still needed because of their sacramental duties but unlike on the Continent, they had little authority within the Celtic church.

There were other differences – Easter was calculated in a different way so would be at a different date; the Monastic tonsure or hairstyle was different. It was possible tell who a person was by the way their hair was cut. Celtic monks had their hair cut up from the bottom, known as a 'pudding bowl' cut, leaving hair on the top of the head, while the Catholic monks had their hair cut completely from the top of the head but a band of hair left around the head.

There were also differences of practice and belief, rites and orders. Prayer, baptism and confession were different. The Celtic Christians saw nothing wrong with this but the Church of Rome could not accept them.

In time, the Catholic Church of Rome became the public face of all Christian religion, and a strong political and financial force, supporting Kings, war and oppression.

When the new Christian influences were accepted in Wales after 1066, the remoteness of the country and sites of the abbeys and priories appealed to all orders of monks and to the Cistercians especially. Thirteen Cistercian monasteries were founded in Wales by 1226, the first at Tintern Abbey, in the Wye valley. Strata Florida, Abbey Cwmhir and Strata Marcella were all daughter houses or offshoots of Whitland Abbey in south-west Carmathenshire.

One very influential Welsh saint, David, who became the patron saint of Wales, established a distinctive form of Christian patron saint of Wales, established a distinctive form of Christian life, one that was more or less independent from Canterbury and Rome. The Welsh Church operated the 'clas' (a monastic community, 'monastica classis'; a body of collegiate canons or clergy common in Wales in pre-Norman times.) system which meant that it was made up of a number of mother churches in charge of a bishop or an abbot rather than being led and tied to the edicts of an archbishop. This system, though, was abolished by the Normans which led to their way of worshiping, the parish structure and ruling the church coming into existence. Ecclesiastical control was lost in Wales and when Gerald of Wales (*Giraldus Cambrensis*) was twice nominated to be bishop of St Davids, he was twice rejected by the king, who was, of course, a Norman. By the time of the Norman invasion in 1066 a gentle relaxing of rules had occurred in many religious houses. They had also suffered a great deal from Viking attacks and a much more lackadaisical attitude was prevalent. A change was needed–a change for the better which arrived with William I. William the Conqueror, made sure that all candidates for important posts were politically as well as ecclesiastically correct. In other words, they had to be approved by him before being appointed and many who were members of his close circle of friends and supporters, such as the barons and lords of the Marchers (the Welsh/English border lands) became bishops through his patronage.

The Norman period was one when many Benedictine abbeys and priories were founded but were not overly successful in Wales although the Cistercians that followed them were far more so. The Cistercians were much patronised by the Welsh lords, especially Lord Rhys, who was patron of Strata Florida and Whitland Abbey. His support meant that they and other establishments were welcomed as were the Premonstraterians at

Talyllychau (Talley) Abbey and the convent of Llanllŷr. These became noted centres of learning and teaching and were frequented by the best of the early Welsh poets. The Cistercians monasteries were heavily influenced by their French roots and their Welsh contemporaries followed their pattern of life in many ways. The Cistercian way of life was based on a three-way system of manual labour, community service and worship. This was better suited to the Celtic inclination. These continental influences helped the Norman mind-set to take root in Wales, though only slowly, very slowly. The Norman conquest of England was achieved in twenty years but the Norman conquest of Wales took a little longer – almost two hundred and twenty years. The Benedictine, Cistercian and Norman influence replaced religious establishments and traditions in England and in Wales. Building the new Westminster Abbey had begun before the death of Edward the Confessor and the eastern end had been completed before 1065 but when William I built his thank-offering of Battle Abbey near Hastings, on the order of Pope Alexander II as a penance for killing so many during the conquest of England, the Norman influence was clearly seen in the architecture as it was in other English masterpieces that followed such as Chester, Colchester, Selby and Reading. One of the first Norman religious establishments in Wales was Chepstow Priory founded by William fitzOsbern in c.1072. It was modelled on the Normandy abbey of Cormeilles.

When William I died in 1087, the transformation of England's abbeys had started. The same process would not take long before its full effect was felt in Wales.

Further reading

Abbeys and Priories in England and Wales. B. Little. Batsford Books. 1979.

Abbeys and Priories of Wales. R. Cooper. Christopher Davies. 1992.

The Story of Wales. John Gower. BBC Books. 2012.

8. The Ancient Abbeys and Priories of Wales

AUGUSTINIANS

On 16 December 1243, Pope Innocent IV issued a Papal Bull *Incumbit nobis* calling on several religious communities in Tuscany to join together into one religious order and to follow the Rule and way of life of St Augustine. In March, 1244, under the guidance of Cardinal Richard Annibaldi the Order of St Augustine was formed.

Ordained a priest in 391, Augustine obtained the use of a garden at Hippo to build a monastery. He later wrote a Rule for his brothers, inspired by the Christian community in Jerusalem:

'Before all else, live together in harmony, being of one soul and one heart seeking God.'

When Augustine became bishop of Hippo he lived in the Bishop's Palace but continued to live a community life with his clergy. Later a monastery of women was founded within the city, bringing together three different forms of Augustinian religious life: masculine, lay and clerical and feminine.

Between 430 and 570 the Augustinian life-style was carried to Europe by monks and clergy escaping from persecution.

By the eleventh century the Augustinian Rule was taken as a basis for the reform of monasteries and cathedral chapters.

On 9 April 1256 Pope Alexander IV's bull *Licet Ecclesiae catholicae* joined together a number of small religious orders under the auspices of the Rule of Saint Augustine. Many of their settlements in Wales were in remote places such as the priories of Bardsey, Beddgelert and Penmon. The Augustinian friary at Newport, founded in 1377, was the last medieval religious house to be established in Wales.

Name: **THE ABBEY OF ST MARY, BARDSEY ABBEY**
                    AN ISLAND RESTING PLACE FOR TWENTY
                    THOUSAND

Order: **Augustinian**

Location: **island off the coast of Llŷn Peninsula, Gwynedd**

Ordnance Survey Map Ref.:   SH 1221

Bardsey Island, lying off the coast of Llŷn in north Wales has long been known as a place of pilgrimage and if the pilgrims of the Middle Ages were unable to reach Jerusalem or Rome, Bardsey was a suitable alternative. It was said that making the pilgrimage to Bardsey three times was equivalent to going to Rome once.

St Dyfrig retired to Bardsey and died there about 522. In May 1120 his relics were moved to Llandaf by Bishop Urban and installed in Llandaf Cathedral. Other well-known saints who are said to have been buried in the island are Lleuddad, David, Deiniol, Berme and Cawrdaf.

Bardsey has always been an important church/abbey. Cadfan, from Brittany, founded the first monastery on the island in 429 and was the first abbot. He was followed by St Lleuddad, after whom *Gerddi Lleuddad* (Lleuddad's Gardens) on Bardsey, *Ogof Lleuddad* (Lleuddad's Cave) at Aberdaron and *Ffynnon Lleuddad* (Lleuddad's Well) at Bryncroes are named.

The *Book of Llandaff* states that Bardsey was known as *Rome of Britain*, because of its *sanctity and dignity, and because there were buried therein the bodies of 20,000 holy confessors and martyrs*. Some of the survivors of the massacre of the Monks of *Bangor Iscoed* (Bangor-on-Dee) by King Aethelfrith of Bernicia in 613 fled to Bardsey.

Gruffudd ap Cynan donated many gifts and left ten shillings in his will to the abbey on his death in 1137. The first written record of Bardsey dates back to 1011 in an obituary for a monk from the island. In 1212 two canons of Bardsey appeared as witnesses for an Augustinian charter from the abbey of Haughmond, Salop and its church in Nefyn, Gwynedd. This suggests that the monks from Bardsey were of the same order. Gerald of Wales (*Giraldus Cambrensis*) wrote in 1188 that:

> Beyond Lleyn, there is a small island inhabited by very religious monks, called Caelibes, or Colidei. This island, either from the wholesomeness of its climate, owing to its vicinity to Ireland, or rather from some miracle obtained by the merits of the saints, has this wonderful peculiarity, that the oldest die first, because diseases are uncommon, and scarcely any die except from extreme old age. Its name is Enlli in the Welsh and Berdesey in the Saxon language; and very many saints are said to be buried there, and amongst them that of Daniel, bishop of Bangor.

Bardsey's reputation for longevity was said to be because St Lleuddad, when on his deathbed, was visited by an angel who arranged a healthy atmosphere for the island. Because of this and the belief that twenty thousand saints had been buried on the island, it became a very popular pilgrimage destination. The Pope declared that three pilgrimages to the island were equivalent to one to Jerusalem. The most popular pilgrim route was the one following the north road from Bangor to Clynnog Fawr. The Bangor Diocese held its own pilgrimages to Bardsey during the twentieth and twenty first century. There are a number of holy wells along the way and at Pistyll, is a farm at which every pilgrim could ask shelter and a meal of bread and cheese. In Aberdaron, is a farm called Cwrt which had been released from paying the tithe on condition that it provided free shelter for Bardsey inhabitants who had to wait for favourable weather to make the dangerous crossing over the Sound.

Giraldus in his writings says that Bardsey was a Celtic monastery unconnected with any other order. Two of the family of Owain Gwynedd: Cadwallon, c.1169, and Robert ap Meredydd were onetime abbot of the abbey. The abbey was dedicated to the Blessed Virgin Mary. The dedication to Mary probably dates after the establishment of the Augustinian or Austin Canons in the island sometime between 1200 and 1240.

The *Record of Caernarfon* contains a document concerning the Abbot and Convent of Bardsey in 1252. It is an agreement between the Abbot and the Secular Canons of Aberdaron settling disputes over tithes and fines. Another document states that the Abbot was asked to show by what title he claimed some of his privileges, for example, freedom from toll on the sale of cattle and the right to a Wreck by Sea. Another manuscript states that Sir John Salisbury, Knight of Lleweny, founded a religious House of Carmelites in Denbigh and gave it to the Abbey of Bardsey in 1284. The *Taxatio* of Pope Nicholas IV, in 1291, states that the value of the abbey's property was £16 2s. 0d. including property on the mainland amounting to 24 cows, 120 sheep, four mills and 35 shillings per annum from selling rabbits and rabbit skins. In the *Valor Ecclesiasticus*, from the time of Henry VIII, the value of the temporalities was £28 3s. 2½d and of the spiritualities, £30 3s. 0d.The latter included the tithes of Aberdaron, Bryncroes, Tydweiliog and Llangwnadl.

It was an Augustinian community by the mid-thirteenth century and remained so until 1537 but originally it may well have been a hermitage and allegedly a favourite burial spot of the saints. Many desired to be buried there, amongst them St Dyfrig, the first abbot, Bishop Ainan of Bangor and Einion ap Gwalchmai, poet. Some sources quote a figure of twenty thousand saints buried on Bardsey. Whether that is true or not, when a new road was being built close to the abbey tower in 1875, many graves and coffers were found buried facing east.

The abbey stood at the north end of the island but only a

thirteenth century tower, twenty one feet high and nineteen feet square remains in the burial ground. The walls are three feet six inches thick at ground level. Many of the stones have been removed especially the shaped quoins. The entrance to the tower is in the south wall, leading to a passage that leads into the interior. On the ground floor, the walls are bare of any windows apart from a central one in the east wall.

As well as being beneficial to the island, the sea could also cause problems. The island was open to attacks from pirates; at dawn on 6 May 1346, it was attacked by thirty armed pirates on two sailing ships led by John Bannebury. The canons were locked in their house, and food and drink stolen from the kitchen.

A list of the abbots of Bardsey contains many interesting characters:

Ralph: noted as Abbot of 'Ynes' (*ynys* – island), probably 'Bardsey' in July 1221.

Kenric: who resigned from office, though it is not known why, on 23 December 1346 when a licence was granted to elect his successor.

Gregory de Eglewyskadell: Gregory was a canon of Bardesy. After the Bishop of Bangor had confirmed the election, Gregory received the temporalities of the abbey on 27 February 1347.

Gervase ap David (1377–81): as canon of Bardsey, Gervase's election received royal assent in October 1377. Gervase resigned on 30 April 1381.

John Conwy: abbot in March 1507 and in 1523. In 1509 the abbot of Bardsey was fined 40s for failing to attend the Augustinian General Chapter at Leicester.

The last abbot of Bardsey may well have been the above John Conwy of Bodnithoedd in Meyllteyrn. His monastery, like all others, came under the scrutiny of Henry VIII's commissioners.

It was worth only £46 and was dissolved in 1537.

When the abbey was dissolved, its annual income was very little according to the *Valor Ecclestiaticus*: the pilgrims' offerings were only two pounds per annum and the abbey itself only worth £46. No-one lived there by then. The choir stalls, two screens and the bells were removed and used in the building of Llanengan church.

Ten years after Bardsey Abbey's dissolution a survey of the island was made in 1547. The details can be seen in the accounts of the 'Court of Augmentations' – a tribunal set up in 1539 to deal with Monastic properties. The property of the Abbey was held in 1538 by Thomas Jones of London, at a rent of £6 3s.0d per annum.

Another document records that Siôn Wyn ap Hugh, of Bodvel in Llŷn, was Standard-Bearer to John, Earl of Warwick – afterwards Duke of Northumberland – at the Battle of Norwich in 1549. In return for his services, he was given Bardsey by the Duke and the Abbot's demesne house of Cwrt near Aberdaron. The island had been granted by Edward VI to his uncle, Sir Thomas Seymour, and afterwards to the Earl of Warwick.

Rev. J. Evans wrote in 1812:

A singular ruined chapel, or oratory, not far distant, consists of a long vaulted room, with an insulated stone altar near the east end. Here on Sundays, one of the natives, in bad weather, reads the liturgy of the established church. Thus the island, which is said to have afforded an asylum to twenty thousand saints during life, and a secure interment after death, has its spiritual concerns committed to the care of a single rustic.

Thomas Pennant mentioned the abbot's house after his visit to the island in 1773. That house survived until 1814. Today, all that remains of the former Augustinian abbey is the thirteenth-century tower.

According to the Rev. P. B. Williams, in 1821, a Court of the

Lord of the Manor of Bardsey was still held as the need arose at Aberdaron, Bryncroes or Tudweiliog, with a Recorder, Bailiff and Constable. The Marquis of Anglesey was then the Lord of the Manor. A hundred years later it was in the hands of Colonel Vaughan Wynn of Boduan who inherited it from his uncle, the Hon. F. G. Wynn of Glynllifon, son of the 3rd Lord Newborough.

Bardsey has by now been designated Site of Special Scientific Interest. It is owned by the Bardsey Island Trust who maintains it as a nature reserve and seabird sanctuary.

Further Reading

Abbeys, Priories and Cathedrals of Wales. M. Salter. Folly Publications. 2012.

A'u Bryd ar Enlli. E. Roberts. Gwasg Y Lolfa. 1993.

Gerald of Wales. The Journey Through Wales. Trans.: L. Thorpe. Penguin. 1978.

Monastic Wales http://www.monasticwales.org

The Beauties of England and Wales. J. Evans. 1812.

Y Ffordd i Enlli. G. T. Jones. Canolfan Genedlaethol Addysg Grefyddol. 1996.

Name:	**BEDDGELERT PRIORY**
	'THE MOST SOCIABLE'
Order:	**Augustinian**
Location:	**Stryd yr Eglwys (Church Street), Beddgelert, Gwynedd**
OS Map Ref.:	**SH 591480**

The church at Beddgelert is supposed to have been erected on the site of an ancient priory of Augustinian monks. These holy fathers, it further appears, belonged to that class of monks – assuredly the most sociable, and consisted of both sexes, who resided under the same roof, divided, however, by a wall. There is a piece of ground, not far from the spot, which still goes by the name of Nun's Meadow.

Wanderings and Excursuons in North and South Wales.
T. Roscoe. 1835

The mountains of Snowdonia have long been a shelter and a place of refuge for the people of north Wales and Beddgelert, being situated in the heartland of Snowdonia and far from most of the turbulence of the Welsh Wars, proved to be an ideal setting for a monastic settlement. This is emphasised by Thomas Pennant who was of the opinion that Beddgelert is,

seated in a beautiful tract of meadow at the junction of three vales . Its situation was the fittest in the world to inspire religious meditation, amidst lofty mountains, woods and murmuring streams. The church is small, yet the loftiest in Snowdonia.

Bishop Anian of Bangor was well aware of this and had voiced his sentiments almost five hundred years earlier in 1286.

The house of the Blessed Mary of Snowdon is the senior religious house of all Wales except the Island of Saints, Bardsey, and of better hospitality and is of more common resort for the poor and for the English and Welsh travellers passing from England and west Wales to north Wales and for those going from Ireland and north Wales to England.

No better testimonial could have been received from anyone for a small priory located in a rugged countryside. In 1536, there were only three cannons and nine religious men resident at the priory. Its annual income was said to be £69 in 1535. This meant that it was to be dissolved in 1536 but in 1532, the writing had been seen to be on the wall for Beddgelert Priory at the death of Dafydd Conway. He had been in office for thirty years and more and on his demise there was no one to take responsibility for the post so the Priory became the Crown's property in May 1536.

The original name of the parish was Llan y Bor – a corruption of Llan y Porth. There was, probably, a Celtic church in the area. The Priory of the Blessed Virgin of Snowdonia at Beddgelert was, at one time, believed to be the oldest religous foundation but one in Gywnedd. The Priory church and monastic buildings were situated on the banks of river Colwyn. It served an area with a small population in the parish of Llanfihagnel y Pennant in the commote of Eifionydd.

All the early records were destroyed in a fire that took place in 1283. Before that, Owain Gwynedd in 1137 had given land as had Llewelyn the Great to the church. What little remains there are in the twenty first century date from that period of the early thirteenth century. Not all the church was destroyed by the 1238 fire but the wooden roof may well have been completely destroyed. Luckily, *Giraldus Cambrensis'* description of the holy men of Beddgeleret still survives. They were

> devoted to serving God, living in a holy and common bond, having nothing private, in the manner of the Apostles. They were bound to no particular order of monks or cannons, but were celibates or culdees, that is, worshipers of God, given alike to continence and to abstinence, chiefly outstanding for their works of charity and hospitality.

By the time it was closed, only the prior was left – Prior David Conwey. He was well known as an educated man who was easily approached for a favour, as did Lewis Daron, who wrote him a *cywydd* (a poem in strict meter) on behalf of Siôn Wyn ap Maredudd ab Ifan of Gwydir asking for a horse.

> The priory seal was seen by Thomas Pennnat, who described it in his book *A Tour of Wales*.
> In my possession is a drawing of the seal of the priory dated 1531;

on it is the figure of the virgin and child; but no part of the legend except *BETHKELE.*

An actual seal was found attached to a lease made by the Abbot of Chertsey in favour of John Goch of Eifionydd. The lease and seal, were presented to the National Library of Wales in the early 1970's. The seal is in the shape of a *vesica piscis* (fish bladder) with the inscription set in a border around the edge. In the centre is a figure of the Blessed Virgin, crowned and holding the Child Jesus. She is seated on a cusped and decorated niche flanked by pinnacles. In a rectangular space below is a male figure, robed and possibly with a tonsure which may well represent St Augustine or the Prior. The worn inscription can be read as:

SIGILLUM V PRIORIS (ET) CONVENTU(S DE) BETH…

By the early 1990's the priory was in a sorry state with a leaking roof and other problems such as plaster damage but enough was raised by the 'Friends' to pay fo repairs.

Further Reading

'*A lease from the last prior of Bethkylhert*'. Colin A. Gresham. Cylchgrawn Llyfrgell Genedlaethol Cymru Rhifyn 17. 1972.

Monastic Wales http://www.monasticwales.org

The Priory and Parish Church of St Mary Beddgelert. A. Bott & M. Dunn. Coastline Publications.

T*he Old Churches of Snowdonia*. H. Hughes & H. North. Snowdonia National Park Authority. 1984.

Tours in Wales (1773–76). Thomas Pennant. 1883.

Name: HAVERFORDWEST PRIORY
IN A LITTLE ENGLAND BEYOND WALES
Order: Augustinian
Location: Union Hill, off Freemens Way, Haverfordwest,
Pembrokeshire
OS Map Ref.: SM 957152

Haverfordwest town is the only one in Wales to have three parishes and three parish churches within its boundaries:

i. St Martin of Tours – the earliest of the town's parish churches.

ii. St Thomas a Becket church from the end of the 12th century (sometime after 1173).

iii. St Mary the Virgin from the beginning of the 12th century. The thickness of the south wall and traces of round headed windows in the interior of the building suggests that it is a Norman church. On the north wall of the chancel are corbel tables which could have been the outer wall of a church with no aisle. The church was dedicated to The Blessed Virgin Mary, a familiar Norman dedication.

In 1188 Baldwin, the Archbishop of Canterbury, spent time travelling through Wales with *Giraldus Cambrensis*, recruiting for the Third Crusade. Gerald recorded that *a great crowd of people had assembled, some of them soldiers, others civilians* had attended. He preached in Latin and French but *those who could not understand a word of the language were just as moved to tears as the others, rushing forward in equal numbers to receive the sign of the Cross*.

The Priory was a house of Augustinian Canons Regular on the banks of the western Cleddau at Haverfordwest, Pembrokeshire. It was founded around 1207 on land given by Robert Fitztancard, the lord of Haverfordwest, dedicated to St Mary & St Thomas the Martyr.

Robert of Haverfordwest gave the three town churches to the Priory which had a rich income from the tithes of the churches. The Priory would have been responsible for appointing a vicar or chaplain or one of their canons to serve in the three churches.

Records from 1405 and 1409 of ordinations of brethren from the Priory held at St Mary's show the close link between the two establishments. In 1534 the Lordship of Pembroke was held by Anne Boleyn and under her patronage a new Prior, William Barlow, was appointed. He strongly opposed papal authority, and he and his five Canons subscribed to an oath under the Act Of Supremacy.

Wealthy merchants presented the church with gifts. John Miles gave two seats in the north aisle in 1488 and in 1509 William Dier gave two candlesticks, to be placed in the chancel in front of the High Altar.

Early in the sixteenth century, extensive alterations were made to the church. The north aisle was widened, the north wall with perpendicular windows was added, clerestories were added in the nave and chancel. The oak roofs, the parapets on the exterior walls, and a large room with a groined roof in the tower all date from this period.

The priory flourished until the sixteenth century despite being built on a site prone to flooding, as it had been built on a platform. In 1535 the priory was valued at £133. It was dissolved in 1537. The ownership of St Mary's Church eventually passed to Queen Elizabeth I. In 1560 she ordered that timber from the forest of Coedrath (in south Pembrokechire) be used for repairs to the chancel.

The Town Corporation paid for the running of the church. Regular attendance at church was obligatory but difficult to enforce. In 1630 an order was made:

If any person above 21 years shall absent himself from his parish church during divine service or sermon or be found loitering or playing any game... and after divine service ended in his own parish church shall not resort to the public lecture at such other of the churches of the town where it shall be appointed to be, he shall forfeit 12d. at the least at the discretion of the mayor and common council.

Wealthy patrons left money to the church. In 1715 John Laugharne of St Brides left £20 annually for the Vicar of St Mary's to read prayers daily and instruct children in the church catechism. In 1723 Owen Phillips gave £40, the interest on which to be given to a poor burgess, or widow of a burgess, of good character.

Several items of church plate were donated to the church. In 1731 Edward Henry Edwards presented a tankard-shaped flagon of silver gilt to the church, and John Williams, vintner, gave a credence paten. John Phillips, Mayor in 1733, presented St Mary's with a service of silver gilt chalice, paten cover and credence paten in 1765. In 1737 a new organ was installed, the cost of over £600 was raised by public subscription. On one of the oak beams used to repair the nave roof can be seen the names of the Mayor, Minister and Churchwardens in 1739 – William Edwards, George Phillips, John Phillips and Stephen Morris. In 1751 an anonymous donor sent the vicar £100 for the interest to be spent to support poor, insolvent debtors confined in the town jail. In 1749 Martha Bowen left the vicar £50 for the relief of the poor. Restoration continued under the control of Philip Hoare and George Bowen, churchwardens in 1745.

In 1773 the Bishop instructed the churchwardens to stop anyone buying and selling goods in the churchyard. In 1785 the Vestry Meeting ordered *that the door in the old tower be shut off and an opening made from Tower Hill – into Bridewell – and that all entrances into the churchyard be shut up except for four, viz., the passages from Shut Street, Shoemaker Street, High Street and also that facing the White Hart – it is likewise ordered that the churchwardens purchase the iron gate now at Castle Hall, provided it does not exceed two pence per pound.*

In February 1797, following the failed invasion near Fishguard, seven hundred French troops were imprisoned in the church.

The life of the priory church seems to have been one long period of continuous restoration. In 1802 the spire was removed from the tower. A truss in nave roof marked 'I.A. + 1832, T. Edwards 1832' was part of an extensive restoration of the roof at this time. This costly work led to a shortage of money to pay for the repairs and one of the churchwardens was declared bankrupt. In 1844 the oak stalls were replaced by high gothic pews. The architect, Thomas Rowlands, also designed a new gallery for the organ. The church received a grant of £150 from the Church Building Society.

The 1851 Religious Census recorded the population of the parish as 1,590, with 294 free seats and 506 reserved and paid for. On Census Sunday a congregation of 333 attended in the morning and 495 in the evening. The Sunday school had 81 present on that day. By 1862 there were over 400 children in Sunday school with singing classes and a large and successful choir.

More extensive restorations in the chancel, nave and roofs were carried out based on a structural report made in 1882 by Ewan Christian, consulting architect to the Ecclesiastical Commissioners. The organ was moved to the chancel and expanded with a new console, the 1844 Gothic style pews in the nave were replaced by carved oak pews and a new heating system was installed.

Between 1901 and 1903 the nave roof was restored, the arcade was cleaned and repaired, the nave floor renewed, and some of the clerestory windows repaired. In 1948 the asphalt roof of the nave was replaced by a copper roof and the three westernmost clerestory windows repaired. In 1954 similar work was carried out to the chancel roof. Death watch beetles attacked the chancel roof which meant that further roof repairs were needed in 1964. In 1979 work began to repair chancel windows and the south wall. The organ was refurbished and the bells and their fittings repaired.

From 1983 to 1996, the site has been excavated and the outlines of the buildings are visible. Much architectural material of a high standard was discovered and can be seen in Haverfordwest museum. The church was a large cruciform shape, 165 feet in length from west to east, with transepts measuring about ninety feet. The central tower was supported by four pointed arches. Also unearthed was a unique medieval garden with raised beds, the only surviving ecclesiastical medieval gardens in Britain and the beds have now been replanted with simple plants appropriate to the period.

In 2005 a major restoration of the roof was carried out when the whole of the copper sheet covering the nave roof was removed and replaced by lead. The cost of the work was over £700,000.

Haverfordwest was near to the routes to St Davids Cathedral taken by medieval pilgrims and a pilgrim's effigy can be seen near the back of the church.

The priory was founded and endowed by Robert Fitz-Tancred, first Lord of Haveforwest, for Black Canons of St Augustine, and dedicated to the st. Mary and St Thomas the Martyr.

Beauties of Cambria. H. Hughes. 1823

Further Reading

A Tour of the Abbeys, Priories and Cathedrals of Wales. D. S. Yerburgh. Yerburgh. 1999.

Monastic Wales http://www.monasticwales.org

The History Of St Mary's Church, Haverfordwest. Pat Barker. 2009.

Name:	**LLANTHONY PRIORY**
	BLACK MOUNTAIN MAGIC
Order:	**Augustinian**
Location:	**Llanthony Priory (on unmarked road),**
	Llanthony, 12 miles north of Abergavenny,
	Monmouthshire NP7
OS Map Ref.:	**SO 289279**

North of Abergavenny, Llanthony, once known in Welsh as *Llan Ddewi Nant Honddu*, is situated in a narrow valley, no more than three arrow-shots in width. According to an old, local tradition, St David himself accidentally came across the valley and took such a liking to its remoteness that he built a small chapel in which he spent much of his time in prayer.

In 1100, after the Norman Conquest, William – one of Walter de Lacy, Earl of Hereford's most stalwart supporters retreated to Llanthony to live the life of a hermit. He was joined in 1103 by Ernisius, chaplain to the Empress Maud (also known as Matilda), who was the daughter of Henry I. They built themselves a small church dedicated to John the Baptist. With support from de Lacy, Henry I and Maud, Bishop Sarum and Roger the Builder, the church became a monastery. When the building work was completed, Ernisius was consecrated the abbey's first abbot. When de Lacy died, he was buried in the new abbey's Chapterhouse.

The second abbot was Robert de Béthune, who worked to enhance the abbey's good name. In 1129 he was appointed Bishop of Hereford and was succeeded in the post of abbot by Robert de Braci. During his period of office the abbey was presented with a gift of many acres of land by Milo, then Earl of Hereford but due to Milo's and the monk's anti-Welsh attitude it was attacked and severely damaged. The monks were forced to leave and reside in Gloucester for twelve months where they started building another church, Llanthony Secunda, for themselves outside the town walls.

The fourth abbot of Llanthony was William of Wycombe, appointed in 1137 but he remained in Gloucester which made his position very weak as he did not have the support of the monks or the community in Wales. He had a strict regime that was another bone of contention between him and the canons and the monks. He was not well supported by the then patron – Roger, Earl of Hereford and was deposed in 1147. He retired to a cell of Llanthony at Frome to concentrate on writing.

Clement of Gloucester was appointed in his place and remained in office from 1150 until 1174. He returned to Wales and much building work was completed during his tenure. The sixth abbot was Roger of Norwich (1174–1189). Edward IV permitted Llanthony to be closely associated with Llanthony Secunda as another abbot – Abbot John Adams and four of his canons led a very degenerated lifestyle.

Giraldus Cambrensis visted in 1188 and saw the lead roofed, square stone built chapel of St David. He was not best pleased with the weather:

> *It rains a lot there because of the mountains, the winds blow strong and in winter it is always capped with clouds. The climate is temperate and healthy, the air soothing and clement, if somewhat heavy, and illness is rare.*

He obviously had a good local knowledge and it is thought *Giraldus* might well have stayed in the abbey as a boy. He also knew of the abbey's history:

> *This was formerly a happy and delightful spot, most suited to a life of contemplation, a place from its first founding fruitful and to itself sufficient. Once it was free but it has since been reduced to servitude through the boundless extravagance of the English.*

In my opinion it is fact worthy of remark that all the priors who did harm to the establishment about which I am telling you about were punished by God when their moment came to die.

Around 1200, the Priory's Church was built and at that time was considered to be one of the greatest buildings in Wales. The church which measured 212 feet long and 96 feet wide was in the shape of a cross with a large central tower and two others, smaller in size on the western side stood in a seven acre, walled site.

After the rebuilding the Priory suffered a steady decline of its fortunes and the Canons and monks gradually left for Gloucester. The decline was accelerated during the rebellion of Owain Glyndŵr and his followers during the beginning of the 15th century. Records show that by 1504 the Priory had only four Canons living there. When Henry VIII closed the priory as part of the dissolution, the Priory and its lands were sold for the sum of £160 and left to rot. Much damage was done to the buildings in 1801, 1803 and in 1837 during violent storms.

The west and south side of the crossing tower still survive though originally they had one more level on top. Recent evidence suggests the Church tower housed a 'clock' in the fourteenth century. It would have been primitive in design and without any face but rather having a bell that was struck upon the hour.

Llanthony Prima was the mother church of Llanthony Secunda in Gloucester, founded in 1136.

Further Reading
Cymru Cyf. II. O. Jones. Blackie & Sons. 1875.
Monastic Wales http://www.monasticwales.org

Name: **PENMON PRIORY**
                 ANGLESEY'S 'LAND'S END'
Order: **Augustinian**
Location: **Saint Seiriol's Church, Penmon, Ynys Môn LL58**
OS Map Ref.: **SH 603808**

Pilgrims who walk The Way of St James to Santiago de Compostella, Spain are invited to go even further to complete their journey. Not until they have reached *Cabo Fisterra* (Cape Finisterre) can they claim to have walked all the way. As the name suggests, that is where they will meet the end of the earth just as they will in *Penn an Wlas* in Cornwall for that also translates from Cornish into the English Land's End. Visit Anglesey and Penmon on the eastern side of the island is about as remote as one can go.

Gerald Morgan, writing a review of a book about *Eglwysi Cymru* (Churches of Wales) in 1985 was incensed because the authors had left out such Anglesey churches as Aberffraw, Trefdraeth, Llanddyfnan and Llanwenllwyfo with all their varied treasures but he was willing to forgive them but not for the unforgivable sin of omitting Penmon where T. Gwynn Jones went on his famous 'pilgrimage'.

Seiriol had royal blood in his veins and was a member of one of the ancient royal families of Britain, born c.494. He was the son of King Owain Danwyn (*White-toothed*) of Rhos and the younger brother of Kings Cynlas of Rhos and Einion of Llŷn. He was also the cousin of Maelgwn Gwynedd – both descendants of Cunedda Wledig. Maelgwn, who was also Cybi's patron, gave land to Seiriol to build his church on. After studying with St Illtud at Llanilltud Fawr-Seiriol returned to north Wales and abandoned all his worldly possessions. He entered a religious life and chose Penmon as a site for his hermitage. Seiriol's brothers were not best pleased with his choice of living. It wasn't that they wanted to persuade to persuade him to give up his calling but they thought that a prince should be living in much more regal surroundings rather than a small cell close to a well. They founded a monastery and Seiriol became the first abbot of Penmon.

On retirement, Seiriol left the monastery to live on the nearby island called *Ynys Lannog*, today known as *Ynys Seiriol* or Puffin Island. Other hermits and monks followed Seiriol onto the island, creating a small community of solitary monks. *Giraldus Cambrensis* visited Penmon, with Archbishop Baldwin of Canterbury in 1188. According to Gerald:

> *There is a small island (Ynys Seiriol), almost adjoining to Anglesey, which is inhabited by hermits, living by manual labour, and serving God. It is remarkable that when, by the influence of human passions, any discord arises among them, all their provisions are devoured and infected by a species of small mice, with which the island abounds; but when the discord ceases, they are no longer molested. This island is called in Welsh, Ynys Lenach, or the Ecclesiastical Island, because many bodies of saints are deposited there, and no woman is suffered to enter it.*

(A modern day plague of rats has also affected the island. Ynys Seiriol also known as Puffin Island had large numbers of puffins and other seabirds such as guillemots but their population was greatly reduced by brown rats which found their way to the island in 1890s. In 1998 the Countryside Council for Wales began an attempt to rid the island of the rats and, hopefully, encouraging the birds to return.)

Ynys Seiriol (Seiriol's Island)

A lonely island out of the world's view –
Where hermits lived:
There, ancient relics still
Speak to us of the past.
            (a translation of Richard Rowlands. Myfyr Môn's work.)

St Seiriol died in the middle of the 6th century. The year of his death is given as 550 AD. Most historians believe that he is buried on Ynys Seiriol. His feast day is February 1st. Seiriol was a friend of St Cybi who lived at *Caergybi* (Holyhead) on *Ynys Cybi*, or Holy Island, on the far western side of Anglesey. The two would walk to meet up for prayers at Clorach Well in Llandyfrydog in the centre of the island. With his back to the sun to and from Clorach, Seiriol's skin was pale. He was called *Seiriol Wyn* (Seiriol the White). Cybi faced the sun on both journeys so was called *Cybi Felyn* (Cybi the Tanned). *Rhyd-y-Saint*, or Ford of the Saints, near Pentraeth, was so called as Seiriol and Cybi are said to have met there as well.

The oldest building on the Pemnon site is probably St Seiriol's Well. Many Celtic churches were associated with a holy well as they were thought to be healing wells and were the subject of pilgrimages. St Seiriol's Well had a fish pond built by the monks. The well is found inside a small building dating from the eighteenth century; the flooring and lower parts of the wall are probably older. Nearby are the remains (foundations) of what may be the remains of Seiriol's cell.

The monastery in its early years was probably a wooden church building but it was destroyed during Viking raids in 971. When it was rebuilt in the twelfth century local stone from nearby quarries was probably used. When the monastery was dissolved in 1537 the land passed into the hands of the Bulkeley family, of Baron Hill, Beaumaris and was used as a deer park. They still collect a toll from those who venture past the church on their way to *Trwyn Du*. The church remained in use and much of it was rebuilt in 1855.

It is of a cruciform arrangement with the nave being the oldest part, completed about 1140. The transepts and the pyramid-crowned tower were built in 1160–70 and the chancel was added in 1220–1240 during the rule of *Llywelyn ap Iorwerth* (Llywelyn the Great). This was when the king convinced the monasteries in north Wales to reorganize under the Augustine Order. The entrance to the church is up steps to the small garden of the Priory House, a sixteenth century addition and which, at one time was the cloister, and through the south door. Inside, which was restored in the nineteenth century, is a Norman Arch leading into a crossing with Norman pillars into the transepts and a nave where the font is situated. In the south transept, the walls have twelfth century arcading and there are fragments of medieval glass in the windows.

Two high crosses from the entrance of the medieval monastery are now positioned in the church. The larger cross stood in its original position in the deer park until 1977 but was removed to the nave. It is badly worn, but just barely visible is a decorative pattern and a pictorial scene showing the temptation of St Anthony, and a hunting scene. A smaller cross located in the south transept is in better condition as it was used as a lintel for one of the refectory windows. To ensure a close fit, one of the arms of the cross was cut off. It is decorated with knot work and two animal heads on the sides. A baptismal font in the church has similar patterns and it is thought that it could have been the original base.

Other carvings can be seen in the nave of the church and on

the outside of the south western end of the church, above a door, is a carving of a self-consuming beast.

A refectory, a large dining hall, cellars and a dormitory was also built, which is still standing but without a roof.

According to Anthony Carr, an expert medieval historian, the priory at Penmon lasted for nearly a thousand years but little is known about it. The size of the buildings, the extent of its endowment and how much it was worth is known but the nature and strength of its spiritual life is an unknown quantity.

It must be suspected that Penmon was not exactly a centre of fervent spirituality and other evidence indicates that by the late fifteenth century the prior and canons were leading a moderately comfortable bachelor existence.

Whatever happened at Penmon, it remains as one of the treasures of the ecclesiastical buildings of Wales.

Closely associated with Penmon Priory is the religious settlement on Ynys Seiriol (*Puffin Island*). It was only a small settlement for the Augustinian monks who lived there. The only remains are the central tower of the church, which has a pyramid roof similar to that of the church at Penmon.

Further Reading

An Anglesey Anthology. D. Roberts. Gwasg Carreg Gwalch. 1999.

Cathedrals, Abbeys and Priories of England and Wales. H. Thorold. Collins. 1986.

Cristion. A Review. G. Morgan. November 1985.

Crwydro Môn. Bobi Jones. Llyfrau'r Dryw. 1957.

Dictionary of the Place Names of Wales. H. W. Owen & R. Morgan. Gomer Press. 2007.

Gerald of Wales. The Journey Through Wales. The Description of Wales. Trans.: L. Thorpe. Penguin. 1978.

Monastic Wales http://www.monasticwales.org

The Old Churches of Snowdonia. H. Hughes & H. North. Snowdonia
    National Park Authority. 1984.
The Priory of Penmon. A. D. Carr. Journal of Welsh Ecclesiastical history.
    1986.

BENEDICTINES OR BLACK MONKS

Founded about c.515; the Benedictines were known as 'black monks' because of the colour of the habits they wore. St Benedict did not lay down a rule regarding clothes to be worn but merely said that they should suit the area where the monastery was sited. The habit was modelled on what Shadrach, Meshach and Abed'nego wore,

> *These men were bound in their coats, their hose, their hats and other garments.*

> Daniel Ch. 3, v. 20–21

They were able to trace their beginnings back to St Benedict who gave all monks The Rule but all Benedictine abbeys and monasteries were self-contained and not dependant on a mother house. The rule laid down by St Benedict for monks and nuns were:

- to relieve the poor
- to clothe the naked
- to visit the sick
- to bury the dead
- to help the afflicted
- to console the sorrowing
- to avoid worldly contact
- to prefer nothing to the love of Christ
- to reverence the old
- to love the young

- to pray for one's enemies in the love of Christ
- to make peace with one's adversary before sundown
- and never to despair of God's Mercy.

The Benedictine order was a fast growing organisation and by the end of the fourteenth century had 3,700 monasteries to its name which produced 24 popes, 200 cardinals, 7,000 archbishops, 15,000 bishops and 1,500 canonized saints.

The English Benedictine houses such as Glastonbury and St Albans were some of the wealthiest and most powerful of the medieval period. Some Benedictine abbeys were also cathedrals.

Benedictine monks became very lackadaisical in their attitude to their calling and their work which gave an opportunity for other orders to develop. Many Benedictine priories were founded in south Wales by Norman lords after the 1066 Norman Conquest, near to the castles in places such as Abergavenny, Brecon, Cardiff, Cardigan, Chepstow, Kidwelly, Monmouth, and Pembroke. These priories were also burial places, guest houses and medical centres.

Name:	**ABERGAVENNY PRIORY**
	FRENCH CONNECTIONS
Order:	**Benedictine**
Location:	**off Monk Street, on south east side of**
	Abergavenny, Monmouthshire
OS Map Ref.:	**SO 301141**

The choir remains in its antique state, with stalls for a prior and his monks, formed of oak, and rudely carved; and the aisles on either side are furnished with the monuments of several illustrious personages.

A Tour throughout South Wales. J. T. Barber. 1803

The Benedictine Priory of Abergavenny was established c.1090 under Hamelin de Balun, the first Norman holder of the title Lord Abergavenny. It was a cell of the Abbey of Saint Vincent at Le Mans, France but not a very important one. It became an independent priory and was of importance as a burial place for several families of note. During recent archaeological digs, pieces of Roman Samian pottery have been discovered which point to the possibility that the priory and its church may have been built on a Romano-British or a Celtic site.

Henry de Abergavenny was the Prior and later held the same post at Llandaf. In the late 12th century he was chosen to assist at the Coronation of King John of England in 1199.

Many holders of the title of Lord of Abergavenny have been benefactors of the abbey including the pious and ruthless William de Braose, 4th Lord of Bramber. In 1320 John Hastings, 2nd Baron Hastings was so incensed that he called on the Pope to set up an investigation into the Priory, as the monks were accused of failing to maintain the Benedictine Rule and the Prior Fulk Gaston, absconded.

By the Dissolution of the Monasteries the Priory had only the Prior and four monks but due to the close connections between the Lords of Abergavenny and the Tudor king the priory was spared and became the parish church.

The church is cruciform in shape with a chancel and nave 172 feet long. There are ten bells in a vaulted space in the central tower. The style of the church building is of the Decorated and Perpendicular Period but when it was refurbished during Queen Victoria's reign, in the nineteenth century, many original Norman features were removed. The Norman font was rediscovered in the churchyard in the 19th century; having been removed from the church in the seventeenth century by a Baptist minister, John Abbot, who proclaimed that he did not believe in infant baptism.

The oak choir stalls with carved misericords and carved lattice work backs are fifteenth century originals. Carved on them is the name of the Prior Wynchestre whose stall remains, slightly raised and surmounted by a mitre.

The church contains many effigies made of wood, alabaster and marble ranging from the thirteenth century to the seventeenth century. There are more effigies in Abergavenny Priory than in any other Welsh church. One is of John de Hastings, Lord of Abergavenny (died 1324) showing him as a knight, wearing a surcoat over a hauberk and a chainmail hood.

The Lewis Chapel, named after Dr David Lewis, first Principal of Jesus College, Oxford, also contains his tomb. There are also two female effigies in the chapel, one holding a heart in her palm, showing a possible 'heart only' burial and dating from the end of the thirteenth century. Her identity is not known but she must have been someone of a high status as she has a shield with a coat of arms, which is rare for a female effigy. The second female effigy, dating from the fourteenth century, may well be that of Eva de Braose who died while trying to catch her pet Red squirrel when its escaped and ran along the castle walls at Abergavenny Castle, causing Eva to fall to her death. The effigy has a light chain around her waist which, at one time, was attached to a small carving of a squirrel. It has since been knocked off or was defaced during the Commonwealth of England (1649–1660).

The Herbert Chapel contains monuments and effigies in alabaster and marble of the ap Thomas and Herbert families. Sir Richard Herbert was brought up with Henry Tudor, later Henry VII, at Raglan Castle. In 1485 Herbert supported Henry's claim to the throne, fighting with him at the Battle of Bosworth. This support saved St Mary's at the time of the Dissolution of the Monasteries.

At the time of the dissolution the priory's income was £129 per annum and there were only five monks in residence.

The Jesse carving is an elaborate, large fifteenth century wooden carving which would have been part of a larger carving of a Jesse Tree showing the lineage of Jesus Christ. It is unique in Britain and described by Tate Britain Gallery as one of the finest medieval sculptures in the world. Only the carving of Jesse survives; the trunk and branches having been sawn off. On a board in the south transept are Royal Arms dating from 1709.

The nave was used by townsfolk, who later took over the whole building. For some time the chancel was used as a school but is now part of the church again. The priory suffered much damage due to many attacks on the town by the Welsh in 1172, 1176 and 1262 in particular. As it was outside the town walls, it was probably one of the first buildings of the town to be attacked. In 1291 the priory was valued at £51 and owned 241 acres of land. In 1294, when war with France broke out Abergavenny Priory was put under the control of the English Crown. It never grew to its full size and in 1319 there were only five monks in residence when it was intended for twelve. The Five Monks of Abergavenny were well-known for their lack of discipline – the rule of silence was ignored and when they should have been attending divine services, they preferred to play dice. They had also been tempted by the weakness of the flesh and were seen with 'loose women'. Unfortunately, they were not shown a proper example by their Prior-Fulk Gastard, for he was also known for his immorality and before the priory was visited by the mother abbey's officials, he vanished with much of the priory's valuables. The nave and the transepts are fourteenth century work, altered after being damaged by Owain Glyndŵr in 1402 when the priory was set on fire and many books, ornaments and buildings were destroyed. They have been repaired and restored several times. The nave and north aisle were entirely rebuilt 1882–96.

Gwladys ferch (daughter of) *Dafydd Gam* (*Dafydd ap Llywelyn ap Hywel*), was a well-known local lady known as *the star of Abergavenny* or as *Gwladys the happy and the faultless* by the poet Lewys Glyn Cothi. He was much taken by her beauty and generosity and described her being *like the sun – the pavilion of light*. Both she and her husband, William ap Thomas were patrons of Abergavenny Priory and both were buried in the church of St Mary's, where their alabaster tomb and effigies can still be seen. Gwladys was so popular that, according to legend, 3,000 knights, nobles and weeping peasants followed her body from Coldbrook House (her son Richard's manor) to the Herbert Chapel of St Mary's Priory Church where she was buried.

St Mary's has been called 'the Westminster Abbey of Wales' (not the only one) because of its size and the number of tombs and the medieval effigies it has. The church was listed a Grade I listed building on 1 July 1952.

Further Reading

Abbeys and Priories in England and Wales. B. Little. Batsford Books. 1979.

Abbeys and Priories of Wales. R. Cooper. Christopher Davies. 1992.

A Tour of the Abbeys, Priories and Cathedrals of Wales. D. S. Yerburgh. Yerburgh. 1999.

Monastic Wales http://www.monasticwales.org

The Old Parish Churches of Gwent, Glamorgan & Gower. Mike Salter. Folly Publications. 1991.

Name: **BASSALEG PRIORY**
             HOME OF ST. BASIL AND GWLADYS
Order: **Benedictine**
Location: **Bassaleg, west of Newport, Monmouthshire**
OS Map Ref.: **ST 277872**

Bassaleg's earliest known inhabitant was Saint Gwladys, a hermit and wife of St Gwynllyw or Woolos, who founded her own hermitage at Pencarnu. There she bathed in the Ebbw river and the Lady's Well at Tredegar may have been dedicated to her. The site of St Basil's church in Bassaleg was originally dedicated to her. In the 14th century (fl. c.1320–1360/1380), a Welsh lord, *Ifor Hael* (Ivor the Generous) Ifor ap Llywelyn lived in Gwernyclepa manor near Bassaleg. He was a well known promoter of poetry and a friend to Dafydd ap Gwilym. Evan Evans (*Ieuan Fardd*) wrote an extended poem about the condition of his manor:

> *The hall of Ifor the Generous, how poor it looks*
> *A cairn, it lies amongst alders,*
> *Thorns and the thistle own it,*
> *Briars, where once there was greatness.*
> *(a translation of Evan Evans' work)*

Bassaleg Priory was founded c.1100 but the foundation charter has not survived. Fortunately, it was copied by Adam of Domerham, a monk of Glastonbury, and a thirteenth-century copy is preserved in Trinity College, Cambridge.

The charter tells that Robert de Hay and his wife, Gundreda, granted the church at Bassaleg to the monks of Glastonbury. Robert recorded that he had acquired the permission of his lord, Robert fitz Hamon, and his wife, Gubdreda, to do so.

Robert of Hay, lord of Gwynllŵg had accompanied Robert fitz Haimon (founder of Tewkesbury Abbey, Cardiff Priory and

Llantwit-Major Priory) into SE Wales, c.1093, and for his loyal support was rewarded with the overlordship of Gwynllŵg. He made his base on Stow Hill, by St Woolos' Cathedral, Newport.

Robert's endowment included the tithes, alms, and burial of the dead in the parish of Bassaleg – the churches of Lower Machen, Bedwas, Mynyddislwyn and Manmoel, and the chapels of Coedkerniew and Pulcrud. To prevent later disputes over boundaries the charter set out clearly and in English the precise limits of the parish *'so that the native people shall clearly understand them.'*

Robert gave Glastonbury monks the right to take whatever timber they needed to build the church at Bassaleg from his woods; they were also allowed to pasture their pigs there. He granted the monks fishing rights and their own court. Support for the monks' clothing was provided and Hay promised to give them 20/- per annum in alms. The charter also permitted any of Hay's men to grant or sell the monks their lands or even to take the habit at Bassaleg should they wish.

The first monks arrived from Glastonbury in 1116 to occupy the cell. Bassaleg was a small priory and was occupied by just one or two monks of Glastonbury. In 1146 the monks were involved in a dispute with the chaplain of St Gundleus over the boundaries of their parishes.

In c.1175 Hywel ab Iorwerth gave the monks lands in Rumney Moor in 1175.

Monastic life at Bassaleg had ceased by 1252.

Further Reading

A Tour of the Abbeys, Priories and Cathedrals of Wales. D. S. Yerburgh. Yerburgh. 1999.

Monastic Wales http://www.monasticwales.org

Name:	**BRECON ABBEY, ABERHONDDU**
Order:	**Benedictine**
Location:	**Priory Hill, Brecon, Powys**
OS Map Ref.:	**SO 044290**

Brecon Cathedral was the parish church of St John the Evangelist until the Diocese of Swansea and Brecon was established in 1923. Previously it was the Benedictine Priory of St John the Evangelist, founded by the Normans in 1093 which became the Parish Church in the sixteenth century at the time of the Dissolution of the Monasteries. It is thought that the Priory might have been built on the site of an older, possibly Celtic, church.

After the Norman conquest of Britain in 1066, an uneasy peace was kept between the Welsh chieftains and the Norman invaders but as the Norman lords broke free and gained more independence from the Crown, they began to occupy lands on the Welsh border with England. One such Norman was Bernard of Neufmarche who, after a battle near Brecon in 1093, built a castle at Brecon to control the area. He donated the church of St John the Evangelist *sine muris* (without the walls) to a monk of Battle Abbey in Sussex, called Roger, who with other Benedictine monks established a Priory on the site.

Brecon Priory was then a daughter house of Battle Abbey and, with the support and patronage of the Lords of Brecon, became an important religious establishment which survived for over 400 years from about 1125 until the Dissolution of the Monasteries in 1537.

Almost the whole of Brecon Cathedral and the buildings surrounding are from this period. Some parts of the Cathedral are from the Norman period but it was expanded in the thirteenth century in the Early English style, altered and added to in the fourteenth century in the Decorated style. In the late Middle Ages it became a place of pilgrimage following the construction of a Golden Rood on the screen at the east end of the Nave.

The family of Bernard of Neufmarche were loyal to the Duke of Normandy for years but his father fell out with him. As a result, he lost all of his possessions and Bernard was forced to serve William Rufus, son of William the Conqueror. In 1087, Bernard, through marriage to the heiress of Osbern FitzRichard, acquired lands in Herefordshire. By 1088, Bernard and his followers had gone past Clifford Castle, which was held by the Tosny family, and invaded parts of south Wales. He built a rudimentary castle for himself and his army at Gasbury and refused to move from there. Over the next five years, Bernard and his men fought many skirmishes in *Brycheiniog* (modern day Breconshire). Rhys ap Tewdwr, prince of Deheubarth (*South Lands*) was called in to defend the lands and in 1093 he and the Normans were involved in a battle on the banks of the river Honddu where it flows into the river Usk. In the battle Rhys ap Tewdwr was killed and the way into south Wales was opened for the Normans. Bernard was a fine soldier and a noble warrior. It is said that his enemies would turn and run at the sight of him and that some dropped dead from terror when they saw him. His authority was absolute and he ordered castles to be built to strengthen his hold on the conquered lands. His main castle was castle at Aberhonddu, named Brecon by the Normans and there he founded a priory church and a small borough. He gave it protection by building an outer line of defence and his knights established their own castles in the surrounding area. Bronllys and Hay guarded the approach from Herefordshire; Tretower and Crickhowell controlled the route which would lead to Abergavenny and Gwent; Aberyscir and Trecastell were the defences on the western side of Brecon towards Cantref Bychan.

Bernard was patron of Battle Abbey in Sussex and it was there that William the Conqueror wanted to establish a monastery as a memorial to his victory of 1066. His son William Rufus made sure that Battle was completed and dedicated. Bernard was one of Rufus' new men and was expected to support his lord but his loyalty lay with the monks at Battle Abbey and at Brecon Priory. The priory at Brecon came under the governance of the abbot of Battle. Priors of Brecon were appointed and removed on his orders and both establishments became closely linked.

Bernard de Neufmarche, to establish himself as ruler and ingratiate himself with the Welsh married Nest, the daughter of Nest daughter of Gruffudd ap Llywelyn. She took the name Nest from her mother but it was changed to Agnes by the English. One of their children became a knight called Mahel. He lost his inheritance by an injustice after his mother broke her marriage vow and fell in love with a knight with whom she committed adultery. Mahel assaulted her lover one night when he was returning from his mother and gave him a beating, mutilating him, and sent him out of the country in disgrace.

Mahel's mother needed to revenge her lover's treatment. She went to Henry, King of the English, and swore to him that Mahel was not Bernard's child, but the illigitemate son of another man with whom she had had an affair. Henry, in 1121, gave Nest and Bernard's daughter Sybil in marriage to a knight of his own family, Miles FitzWalter, constable of Gloucester, adding the lands of Brecknock as part of the marriage deal. In 1125 Bernard died and Miles became Lord of Brecknock in his wife's name.

The choir and the transepts were rebuilt in during the thirteenth century and a tower was added. Further rebuilding work was undertaken in the fourteenth century when the nave, north and south aisles were rebuilt. The chancel was restored by Sir Gilbert Scott in 1862–65 and in 1923, the church became a cathedral. The priory domestic buildings became the cathedral offices after restoration in 1927.

After the Dissolution of the Monasteries, the church was used as a chapel by Christ College, which occupied the site and other buildings of the friary. In 1855 it became a public secondary school. The chapel was partially restored in the 19th century, but the choir is from the thirteenth century with shafted lancets. A fourteenth century arcade still stands and two halls have fifteenth century timber roofs.

> *The history of the original foundation at this place is not known. It is ascertained to have been a monastery of Black Friars, with an appurtinant church dedicated to St Nicholas.*
>
> *The Beauties of England and Wales, South Wales.* T. Rees. 1815

Further Reading
Abbeys, Priories and Cathedrals of Wales. M. Salter. Folly Publications. 2012.
A Tour of the Abbeys, Priories and Cathedrals of Wales. D. S. Yerburgh. Yerburgh. 1999.
Monastic Wales http://www.monasticwales.org

Name:	**CHEPSTOW PRIORY**
	STRIGUIL
Order:	**Benedictine**
Location:	**Upper Church Street, Chepstow,**
	Monmouthshire/Gwent NP16 5HAM
OS Map Ref:	**ST 536930**

Anciently called Striguil, the priory at Chepstow, a Benedictine priory, was founded c.1072 by William fitzOsbern and his son Roger de Breteuil, 2nd Earl of Hereford. FitzOsbern had been granted the Lordship of Striguil by his second cousin King William for his support during the Norman conquest of England, and was responsible for starting the building of a new castle overlooking the river Wye. At the same time he established a nearby monastic cell, so as to collect rent from the lands in Gwent which he had granted to his home Priory of Cormeilles in Normandy.

By the early twelfth century, the monastic establishment, about 300 metres from the castle, had the status of an alien priory in its own right. It held no more than about 12 monks. It superseded an earlier Augustinian priory, dedicated to Saint Cynfarch, a disciple of St Dyfrig.

Chepstow grew into a market town and port around the castle and priory in medieval times and the nave was used by the locals as their parish church. Accommodation was built on the south side of the church, in the 13th century and the king appointed the first vicar John de Hemmyngburg, in 1348. The priory was surrounded by extensive grounds, including most of the land south of the church enclosed by Chepstow's town wall or Port Wall. During the Hundred Years' War between England and France in the forteenth century, the priory became attached to both Llantarnam Abbey near Caerleon and, from 1414, to Bermondsey Abbey in Southwark, London. The priory was closed during the Dissolution of the Monasteries in 1536, when there were only three monks living there and the revenue was £32.

Roger Shrewsbury was made prior in May 1533 and was still there when it was surveyed and dissolved in September 1536. He had been granted a pension in June 1536.

Most of the priory buildings, including the choir part of the church, the cloister, chapter house, lodgings and kitchens, were demolished and the foundations are buried beneath a car park beside the current church. Remains of a large barn and well were also found during excavations in the 1970s.

Part of the Norman church remains, but it has been altered over the centuries. The original Priory Church was built in local yellow Triassic sandstone, with a long vaulted nave, huge piers and an ornamented west entrance doorway with zig zag and lozenge patterns which can still be seen today. Later alterations and additions used other types of stone in different architectural style. The church is now described as being *an extraordinarily disjointed building.*

The nave of the church – five out of six bays, with aisles was described by William of Worcester (c.1480) as having dimensions of 50 yards long and 33 broad. The lower part of the west porch remains, with a fine Norman door flanked by blind arches, and a Norman triplet above. The nave arcade is also Norman, and the piers are not columnar but rectangular.

The triforium consists of a pair of round-headed openings to each bay, and the clerestory of single round-headed lights. The aisle windows were a later addition. The choir and crossing were taken down after the Suppression. The present east end shows the Norman Piers outside.

The main central tower of the original church fell down in 1701, destroying the transepts. A new wall was then built at the eastern end of the nave, and its western end built up to form a new tower. This was completed in 1706 when Thomas Chest was vicar from 1701 to 1740. The Norman doorway of five concentric arches was moved from a demolished north porch to provide the main west entrance, with windows from the fallen central tower placed above it.

The entrance of the west front is by a large and finely proportioned arch of Norman architecture, which is profusely decorated with the receding pillars, and various mouldings, peculiar to that people, and which remain in singular preservation.

A Tour through Monmouthshire and Wales.
H. P. Wyndham. 1781

In 1841, through the influence of Edward Copleston, Bishop of Llandaff, who lived locally, the aisles were removed, and the eastern end, crossing and transepts were rebuilt. Further work to restore the Norman character of the nave was begun in 1890, but was abandoned unfinished in 1913.

The church contains two fonts, one of Norman origin and the other from the fifteenth century. There are several notable tombs and memorials, including that of Henry Somerset, 2nd Earl of Worcester who died in 1549, and the Jacobean tomb of Margaret Cleyton with her two husbands and twelve children. It also contains the tomb of Henry Marten, one of the signatories of Charles I's death warrant. His memorial includes an acrostic epitaph.

The organ, one of the few in the country with pipework dating from the early 17th century, was originally made for Gloucester Cathedral before being moved to Bristol Cathedral in 1663 and then to Chepstow, possibly at about 1685. It was rebuilt and expanded in 1906 and has undergone much maintenance and repair work since. Eight of the ten bells in the tower date from 1735 and were made in Chepstow by William Evans; the two lightest bells were added in 1959 and were cast by John Taylor & Co. The original clock mechanism was also made locally in the eighteenth century, and kept time until replaced by an electric clock in 1965.

Further Reading

A Tour of the Abbeys, Priories and Cathedrals of Wales. D. S. Yerburgh. Yerburgh. 1999.

Monastic Wales http://www.monasticwales.org

Name: **EWENNY PRIORY**
              BUILT BY INVADERS
Order: **Benedictine**
Location: **Ewenny, Vale of Glamorgan CF 35**
OS Map Ref.: **SS 912779**

Ewenny Priory is situated on the left bank of the Ewenny river about one-and-a-half miles south-east of Bridgend. The Priory was founded in 1140 for Benedictine monks by William de Londres, lord of Ogmore. In the following year it was made as a gift to St Peter's Abbey of Gloucester, by his son Maurice de Londres. The structure has been described as one with military peculiarities being defended by a strong line of fortifications, with an embattled tower on the north side – proof that when it was originally built it stood in hostile ground, and that it had to be as much a castle as a church.

It is one of the earliest of the *great buildings of Wales*, being a fine, if not the best, example in Wales of Norman architecture. It is also an excellent example of a fortified ecclesiastical building, with both a castle and monastery in the same building. The priory is a religious building built by 'invaders' at a time when Wales was neither in completely Norman nor Welsh hands. The monks who performed their solemn rites must have done so in fear and trembling, constantly waiting to hear the sounds of battle.

The church is in two parts. The nave, now the parish church, used to be separated by a Rood Screen from the thirteenth or fourteenth century but now the Pulpitum Screen, divides the two parts of the church, and is the work of Alexander Beleschenko, installed in July 2006. The eastern or monastic end contains the tombs of the de Londres family, a medieval altar and a reproduction of the watercolour of the Priory painted by J. M. W. Turner in 1795.

J. M. W. Turner's painting of the interior of the Priory Church gives the impression that it was then being used as a farm shed. By 1803 the north trancept, north aisle and west end of the church had collapsed; repairs were made with much of the Priory Church restored between 1869 and 1886.

The north aisle and porch were reconstructed in 1895. The most recent restoration took place between 1998 and 2004 which included the insertion of a vestry, kitchen and toilet in the ruined west end, ramped access to the monastic end and a glass screen above the wall separating the nave and presbytery.

The Priory also contains several very ancient tombs. The tomb of the donor of the church to the Abbey of Gloucester is a fine specimen of medieval workmanship. It occupies a position in the transept, and has on it a carved ornamental cross, not dissimilar to a crosier, with an elaborate border of foliage, vine leaves, and grapes. The inscription in old Norman reads:

ICI GIST MORICE DE LUNDRES LE FUNDUR
(Here lies Maurice de Londres the Founder.
DIEU LE RENDE SUN LABUR AM
God reward him for his work. Amen.)

At the time of the dissolution of the lesser monasteries in 1536, the annual income was £78 8s. 0d. The Priory and its demesnes were granted then to Sir Edward Came on payment of the sum of £727 6s. 4d. but it returned to the Turberville family by marriage in the early years of the eighteenth century. Thomas Picton Turberville succeeded to the estates in 1867 and restored much of the structure.

Much of the Priory's outer defensive walls and towers remain. Not only did they protect the Priory, but played a part in the Norman conquest of south Wales.

It exists very nearly as it was originally built, and it consequently shows us what a religious edifice raised by the invaders in the midst of a half conquered country was required to be.

Sketches in Wales. G. J. Freeman. 1826

Ewenny Priory Church has been described as the most atmospheric Romanesque space in Wales and as the most complete and impressive Norman church in south Wales and one of the finest examples of a fortified church building in Europe. Who could not fail to be impressed?

Further Reading

A Tour of the Abbeys, Priories and Cathedrals of Wales. D. S. Yerburgh. Yerburgh. 1999.

Monastic Wales http://www.monasticwales.org

Wales's Best One Hundred Churches. T. J. Hughes. Seren. 2007.

Name:	**GOLDCLIFF PRIORY**
	ON THE SHORES OF THE SEVERN
Order:	**Benedictine**
Location:	**Goldcliff, Newport, Monmouthshire NP18**
OS Map Ref.:	**ST 372820**

High above the water and not far from Caerleon there stands a rocky eminence which dominates the River Severn. In the English language it is called Goldcliff, the Golden Rock. When the sun's rays strike it the stone shines very bright and takes on a golden sheen.

Goldcliff Priory was a Benedictine establishment dedicated to St Mary Magdalene, founded by Robert de Chandos in 1113. He was persuaded by Henry I to present the priory as a cell to his home abbey of Bec, Normandy. A prior and twelve monks were the first inhabitants. The monks of Bec had the special privilege of wearing white habits, unlike the traditional black habits worn by Benedictine monks. By 1295, there were twenty five monks in residence at a time when the priory has extensive estates in Devon and Somerset – on the opposite side of the Bristol Channel. Robert de Chandos was followed by his son Robert, who died in 1120 and was buried on the south side of the choir in Goldcliff parish church.

By 1291, Goldcliff Priory was the wealthiest Benedictine house in Wales, valued at £171 and had 1,300 acres of land to its name. The reason for its wealth was a hole in the sea wall leading to the priory, suggesting that the monks benefited from shipwrecks. Wine, tobacco and brandy were the favourite contraband.

The monks built a fresh water pill (*pwll* in Welsh), Monksditch, to drain the surrounding land, which is below sea level. It runs from Langstone to the Severn at Goldcliff. The monks also built Goldcliff salmon fisheries, which is why many say the priory was built 'on the hill' for the monks' Friday fish feasts. But all was not well as the priory had a bad relationship with its patron – Gilbert de Clare, earl of Gloucester. Edward I, in a rare move, tried to soothe matters between the two warring sides but by 1297 only fifteen monks remained at the priory, which had also lost much of its holdings and suffered from a loss of income. During the fourteenth century, the priory found itself in Crown hands no less than four different times.

A new patron did not ease the priory's problems. Philip de Columbers was, like his predecessor, in dispute with the prior Ralph de Runceville and due to the patron's intransigence, the priory lost much of its Devon estates. In 1318, Ralph was ousted but on leaving took many of the priory's valuables with him, leaving the place in debt. Because of this, his follower – William de Albino had a very difficult time in his post. He was imprisoned in

Usk Castle and only freed on payment of 100 marks (1 mark= 13 shillings and 4 pence or ⅔ of a Pound Sterling). The priory lost all its possessions at this time. It was also beginning to lose a battle against the sea. Due to its location on the Gwent Levels, it suffered from the effects of flooding and coastal erosion and was badly damaged by floods in 1424.

In 1322 a Tintern Abbey monk forged a Papal Bull to put himself in the position of prior of Goldcliff Priory. His patron was Sir John Inge, of Somerset and he took advantage of his position and took hold of every one of the priory's holdings in Devon and Somerset for himself.

In 1410, more monks from Bec were sent to maintain the priory but their main enemy was the sea and no one could win that particular battle. The then prior – Lawrence de Bonneville was recalled to Bec in 1439 and a monk from Gloucester quickly stepped into his office. de Bonneville refused to return to Bec but was imprisoned in Abergavenny and Usk castles. In 1441 the connection with its mother abbey in Bec was broken and in 1442 it became a cell of Tewksbury Abbey but this did not guarantee its future. At about 1445, the priory was broken into; eight monks were expelled and by 1467 the last monk had left and all monastic activity ceased. Goldcliff priory became the property of Eton College in 1462, and on one day every year the salmon fisheries had to send enough salmon to supply the whole college.

In 1606 Goldcliff suffered a disastrous flood – the Great Flood. It reached between two and three feet high in places. It was estimated there were 'twentie hundred' deaths. In Goldcliff church there is a brass plaque showing the height the flood reached on the walls. The inscription is in rhyme, presumably to make it more memorable:

On the 20 day of January even as it came to pass,
It pleased God the flood did flow

to the edge of this same brass
and in this parish there was lost
5000 and od pound
Besides xxii people was in this parish drowned.

Today, there are no remains to be seen of what was an important priory situated at an even more important port near the mouth of the river Usk. Much of the port's trade was with towns and villages on the other side of the Bristol Channel, in England.

Further Reading

Abbeys, Priories and Cathedrals of Wales. M. Salter. Folly Publications. 2012.

Abbeys and Priories of Wales. R. Cooper. Christopher Davies. 1992.

Gerald of Wales. The Journey Through Wales. The Description of Wales. Trans.: L. Thorpe. Penguin. 1978.

Monastic Wales http://www.monasticwales.org

Name:	**KIDWELLY PRIORY**
	HOME OF THE DEAR OLD LADY OF KIDWELLY*
Order:	**Benedictine**
Location:	**in centre of village, Kidwelly, Carmarthenshire**
OS Map Ref.:	**SN 409068**

In the new towne is onely a church of our Ladi, and by is the celle of blake monks of Shirburne; there the prior is parson of our ladi church.

Leland's Itinerary. 1540

The church of St Mary, Kidwelly, formerly the priory church, is a cruciform building of stone, in the Gothic style, consisting of chancel, nave, transepts, south porch and a tower with spire at the north-west angle, containing four bells: there is a monument to Prior Gilfrida Coker, died 1301, and one to Hugh Fisher, Esq. The tower was struck by lightning in 1884, and the top of the spire fell through the roof into the nave, causing great damage: since then it has been partially restored at a great cost; there are sittings for 550 persons.

Kidwelly Priory, one of the smallest Benedictine cells founded by the Normans in medieval Wales, was a daughter house of the abbey of Sherborne in Dorset. Roger, bishop of Salisbury, who was the Norman conqueror of the commote of Cydweli, founded the priory. Two Celtic saints had previously lived in the area were Cadog and Teilo and had a church of their own before the priory was built. (St Cadog's church was rededicated to St Mary the Virgin when the priory was built.)

In the twelfth century, Maurice de Londres, lord of Kidwelly, gave St Mary of Kidwelly to God, and to the monks of Sherborne he gave twelve acres of land surrounding the church of St Cadog which adjoined the lands of St Mary.

As Kidwelly was an alien priory, with French connections, the local Welsh people were very wary of those inside and gave them very little support.

On many occasions war broke out between the two factions of the community. Kidwelly castle, borough and priory suffered from attacks. The castle was demolished by Cadwgan ap Bleddyn, recaptured and strengthened in 1190 by the Lord Rhys. In 1215 another Rhys burnt it again. By 1223 Gruffudd, son of Llywelyn ap Iorwerth (*Llywelyn Fawr* – 'the Great') burnt the town, church, and religious house. Since most of the buildings were of timber construction, they were quickly rebuilt. In 1257 Llywelyn ap Gruffudd (*Llywelyn ein Llyw Olaf* – 'the Last') brought his army to south Wales and wrought havoc amongst the English settlements at Kidwelly and elsewhere. A strong Welsh power in Gwynedd was a threat to English rule in south-west Wales but despite the troubled times, from Edward I's reign there are two surviving sources of information about Kidwelly Priory.

Archbishop John Pecham of Canterbury visited many Welsh churches in 1284 after the conquest of Wales. Pecham was a Franciscan friar with strict views about maintaining high standards and keeping monastic vows. In Kidwelly Priory, he was most displeased to find a highly unsatisfactory state of affairs:

1. The prior – Ralph de Bemenster, who, because of his many faults, was sent back to Sherborne in disgrace but in a month's time was back in Kidwelly. Pecham was not pleased that his authority had been challenged and orderd that Prior Ralph be disciplined severely and that a new prior be appointed in his place. Geoffrey of Coker was named as his replacement.

2. *The Taxatio* of Pope Nicholas IV, compiled in 1291. This document states that Kidwelly Priory's main source of income was from the tithes of the parish of Kidwelly, estimated to be worth 20 marks. It also possessed one carucate of land with rents valued at £2. l0s. 0d. and five cows worth five shillings. By the late thirteenth and early fourteenth century the priors were leasing out lands to tenants. Hugh, abbot of Sherborne (1286–1310), certainly leased to one Llywelyn Drimwas and his wife, Gwenllian for life in return for an annual render of 12d, payable at Michaelmas, on condition that they were not allowed to sell or mortgage.

The priory church itself was rebuilt early in the fourteenth century in the Decorated style of architecture. Kidwelly suffered badly during the years c.1340 and c.1440 due to poor weather, a declining population and unfavourable economic conditions for all landowners. The Hundred Years War between England and France, from 1357 to 1453 (following the wars with France, heavy taxes had to be paid even though there was only one monk in residence in 1377); the outbreak of the Black Death, 1349–51 and further outbreaks of pestilence in 1361 and 1369 reduced the population and income of the priory. The Glyndŵr Rebellion also had a lasting effect; the town was attacked in October 1403, and the castle suffered a three week siege.

Kidwelly priory had many attractions to the town faithful and any passing pilgrim.The lifesized alabaster statue of the Holy Virgin and the child Jesus, in a niche on the south wall of the chancel at the entrance to the south transept, was from either the fourteenth or the fifteenth century. There was also Mary's Well (*Ffynnon Fair*) nearby; a rood screen or possibly two rood screens were set up in the church in the fifteenth century to enhance its attractiveness.

The episcopal registers of the diocese of St Davids for parts of the fifteenth and the early sixteenth century records the names of some of the monks and clergy associated with Kidwelly. The names of two fifteenth century priors can be gleaned from this source: John Sherborne in 1482, and John Henstrige, presented to succeed him in 1487 by the abbot of Sherborne. It was he who presented Bernard Tyler in 1407, John David in 1482, John Cheyney in 1491, and John Griffith in 1502. The last named had, in 1496, been ordained a priest of Kidwelly Priory, and was still vicar there in 1534. In October 1490, however, it was Hugh Pavy, bishop of St Davids, who gave the post to Master John Gunva (Gwynfe), though he was dead by May of the following year. The fifteenth century vicars had a mixture of Welsh and English names but the priors, however, continued to be Sherborne monks.

For the last two decades of the fifteenth century and the first quarter of the sixteenth century the priory was again in a poor state. Trade in the port was on a downward slope as gradual silting up of the estuary was taking place. On 29 October 1481 the priory was struck by lightning and the western end of the nave was badly damaged. In 1513 Kidwelly Priory was one of a number of smaller monastic houses in the diocese that was spared the payment of tithes because of their poverty. It was again excused in 1517. On 20 April 1524 it was described as being in *great and manifest decay* and it was decided to abandon the damaged western part of the nave and make only a small repair by closing up the nave and inserting a Perpendicular window. Reducing the nave by nearly half severely impaired the balance and symmetry of the church.

In 1534 the two monks at Kidwelly, John Godmyston, the prior, and his companion, Augustine Green, duly took the oath, as did the vicar of Kidwelly, John Griffith. In the following year, commissioners for the diocese of St Davids, acting on behalf of the King, drew up the *Valor Ecclesiasticus*. The priory possessed lands worth £6. 13s. 4d. annualy. Its spiritualities, i.e., the income derived from churches at Kidwelly and the neighbourhood, were worth £31. 6s. 8d. A number of deductions had to be made, leaving an annual net income of £29. l0s. 0d.

At the dissolution, only the prior, John Painter, was left and he was granted an annual pension of £8. In 1544, George Aysshe and Robert Myryk, king's yeomen and purveyors of wines, were granted a lease for twenty one years of Kidwelly priory.

When Sir Gilbert Scott, architect, surveyed the church in 1854, he described it as one of the most remarkable churches in south Wales. He admired the ample open space of its aisleless, thirty-three feet wide nave together with a sturdy and handsome tower. He was of the opinion that the original fourteenth century nave had been nearly twice as long as the present one, so that the tower and the porch had then been mid-way between the transepts and the western end of the church. Despite there being differences between the flowering tracery in the chancel and the plain, severe and narrow windows of the tower, Scott was of the opinion that the church was all part of a single build undertaken about the third decade of the fourteenth century. E. A. Freeman disagreed believing that the tower had been built in the thirteenth century and that the nave was a fourteenth century addition. Scott declared that the roof of the chancel, which he dated to the reign of James 1, was then the part of the church in best condition but it was also known that in 1672, and again in 1684, churchwardens reported the church as being out of repair and fallen down since 20 June 1658, when it had again been struck by lightning. Not until 1715 do the records show the church as being rebuilt and in good repair, though its spire was still suffering from lightning damage. The church was yet again the victim of a lightning strike in 1884, and had to be rebuilt.

The alabaster figure of the Madonna and Child was left *exposed to the elements* and to rough handling by the Puritans, leading to the disappearance of the head of the child Jesus, the left arm of the Virgin, and one of the birds. Until well into the nineteenth century, women curtsied to it on entering and leaving the church, dipping their fingers in a holy water stoup. The Reverend Griffith Evans (1840–80) ordered the removal of the statue and buried it in the graveyard sometime between 1865 and 1870. It had to be dug up again by popular demand and was in place in 1875 only to be stored later in a room under the tower, where it was again subjected to rough handling by *thoughtless Philistines*. About 1900, it was kept in the vestry of the church until in the 1920s it was repaired and replaced, first on the south wall of the nave above the Memorial to the fallen of the First World War, and later, in 1971, in a niche specially made for it on the south side of the east window of the church.

The Dear Old Lady of Kidwelly *(Hen Fenyw Fach Cydweli*)*

The dear old lady of Kidwelly.
A seller of sweets is she,
Counts out ten for a halfpenny.
But always eleven for me.
That was very good news for me, for me
Counts out ten for a halfpenny.
But always eleven for me.

(* – an old Welsh Nursery rhyme)

Yr Hen Fenyw Fach may have been the bountiful Lady Hawise de Londres who, as a child, lived in Kidwelly Castle in the thirteenth century.

Further Reading

A Tour of the Abbeys, Priories and Cathedrals of Wales. D. S. Yerburgh. Yerburgh. 1999.
Kelly's Directory. 1891.
Kidwelly Priory. Glanmor Williams. SIR-GÂR – Studies in Carmarthenshire History. The Carmarthenshire Antiquarian Society. 1991.
Monastic Wales http://www.monasticwales.org

Name:	**LLANGENNITH PRIORY**
	AN IRISH AND VIKING TARGET
Order:	**Benedictine**
Location:	**Llangennith, Swansea, West Glamorgan SA3**
OS Map Ref.:	**SS 429914**

Roger de Bellomont, Earl of Warwick, is said to have conquered Gowerland in Wales, and to have thereupon founded a priory here in the reign of King Stephen and to have annexed it to the Abbey of St Taurinus at Evreux in Normandy. It was dedicated to St Kenned.

Historical Notes of the Parishes of Llangennydd and Rhosili Part III. J. D. Davies. 1885

Despite what is said in the above quotation, another source names another Earl of Warwick as the founder of Llangennith priory. He will be named shortly because the saint which the priory and church were dedicated to had a much more exciting start to life. According to legend and to Sir Glanmor Williams, a Welsh academic and historian and a specialist in the early modern period of Welsh history, Cenydd was an illegitimate child and was punished for his parents' behaviour by being born with the calf of one leg attached to the thigh. He was also thrown out of King Arthur's Court and held prisoner at Loughor. Further punishments to the innocent boy included being placed in a basket a *la* Moses on the river Lliw and being carried out to sea by the flow of the river Llwchwr. As in most stories, there is a 'but'. But he was protected by seagulls and survived on food from a breast-shaped shell. During his long voyage an angel protected him and educated him until he was old enough to join St David. His feast day or '*gŵyl mabsant*' is celebrated on July 5th and was kept well into the nineteenth century.

The sixth century church of Llangennith (*Llangenydd*) was a colleigiate church and as such was fairly wealthy. This, though, made it a regular target for Irish and Viking raiders, tales of which survive in the Chronicles of the Princes (*Brut y Tywysogion*). In 986, the church was attacked and destroyed. Folk memory places the landing of Viking ships in the bay; suggesting that the people of Rhossili burnt these ships in reprisal but the actual building was left in ruins for at least a century until Caradog, saint of Llancarfan settled there.

Rebuilding took place at the end of the eleventh and the

settled there.

Rebuilding took place at the end of the eleventh and the beginning of the twelfth century after which the church had to be reconsecrated in 1102. By that time, Norman rule had spread as far west as the Gower. Henry de Newburgh, Earl of Warwick, issued a charter to the abbey of St Taurin, Everux, in Normandy which granted the abbey the soul of the king and Queen Matilda, Henry's own soul together with the church of St Kenetus (Cenydd) and land for two ploughs near the church and the tithes of parish, a site for a mill, all the wood they needed and the tithes from all his hunting and fishing rights as well as three other churches. In return, the French monastery sent out monks to establish and take possession of a daughter house in Wales. Recently rediscovered in a medieval niche in the chancel arch is a carved slab of from the ninth century, with an intricate pattern of Celtic knots. This is legendarily the grave stone of St Cenydd and, until the nineteenth century remodelling, was set flat in the chancel floor. On the village green oppostite the church gates is the mouth of a natural spring, St Cenydd's Well, on the upper capstone of which are faint traces of a cross cut into the stone.

The Welsh families of Gower did not extend much brotherly love to their Norman neighbours and the priory suffered as a result of constant quarrelling and bickering. A register compiled by the Bishop of St David's, in 1379, describes Llangenydd Priory as being *destroyed, dilapidated and wasted with divine worship at an end*.

By 1414 all alien priories, as was Llangennith, had been relieved of their wealth and properties. Two monks were left at Llangennith. On 16 March 1441 Archbishop Chichele and his colleagues surrendered the house to Henry VI. It remained in royal hands until 1442 when it was transferred to the name of All Souls College, Oxford. Hugh John, a knight, and Richard Baddelsey were intent on causing trouble for the Warden and Fellows of the Oxford college and took over the priory. After the Wars of the Roses were over the college regained the priory and parishes of Llangennith and Pennard and as they were patrons of the church, it was their right to elect a vicar until well into the nineteenth century.

Further Reading

Abbeys, Priories and Cathedrals of Wales. M. Salter. Folly Publications. 2012.

Monastic Wales http://www.monasticwales.org

The Priory at Llangenydd. Glanmor Williams. Gower (Journal of the Gower Society). 1950.

Name:	**MONMOUTH PRIORY**
	A MEDIEVAL PRIORY WITH A MODERN TREASURE
Order:	**Benedictine**
Location:	**Monmouth Priory Office, Priory St., Monmouth, Gwent NP25 3NX**
OS Map Ref:	**SO 509130)**

Today, Monmouth Priory is advertised as an ideal location for conferences, exhibitions and weddings. What would the celibate monks who used to live and worship there say to such goings on? Monmouth Priory incorporates the remains of the monastic buildings attached to St Mary's Priory Church. The priory was a Benedictine house dating from 1075. Some parts of the medieval buildings are still standing. In the nineteenth century the buildings were used for a school – St Mary's National School. Now they are part of a community centre. The buildings were listed as a Grade II listed building on 27 June 1952. The priory was founded church on the same site and it could be that the priory was built on the foundations of that church. The priory was a daughter house of the Abbey of St Florent at Saumur, and was consecrated in 1101. The priory church was extended and became the parish church later in the twelfth century. The priory was dissolved in 1536.

Despite being a House of God, life was never easy for the monks at Monmouth. The priory suffered damage during the war between Henry II and Richard Marshall. It was compensated in 1234 but the work on restoring the church of St Thomas which had been burnt was hard and difficult for the monks; the prior had to have thirteen oaks from the Royal Forest of Dean to complete the work.

In 1264, Geoffrey Moreteau, a monk from St Florent, was sent to Monmouth take over as prior in the hope that he could reverse the priory's financial problems. Geoffrey had shown himself an able administrator at St Florent and was instructed to sort out problems caused by his predecessor at Monmouth, Prior Walter. In an attempt to raise cash Prior Geoffrey sold or mortgaged a number of the priory's holdings. This was unsuccessful and in 1279 Bishop Thomas de Cantilupe of Hereford was prompted to intervene.

According to the *Taxatio Ecclesiastica* of 1291 Monmouth had at this time 480 acres of arable land and the priory's rents totalled £14 6s 8d. The priory's income was supplemented with money it received from its borough property for Wihenoc of Monmouth and William fitz Baderon granted the community the services of seven people in the market. The prior also drew pensions from eight churches and was rector of a number of others. Three of the churches were in the diocese of Llandaff [Rockfield (£2 10s), Wonastow (£2), Llangatwg Feibon Afel (£5 18s)]; three were in the diocese of Worcester [Taddington, Stretton Asperton, Longhope]; and four were in Hereford [Monmouth, Dixton, Goodrich Castle,

Llanrothal]. At the end of the thirteenth century Monmouth's spiritualities were estimated at £62 19s 2d and its temporalities at only £22 19s 6d making a total of just under £86.

In 1309, an escaped prisoner from the castle was dragged out of the priory and murdered. Griffin Goht led a band of armed Welshmen who forced their way into the priory church and seized John Carpenter, who had escaped from the prison and taken refuge in the church. They dragged John into the cemetery and brutally murdered him and as a consequence no services were held in the church which had been polluted by blood. The priory also suffered losses during the Owain Glyndŵr rebellion of 1403. A number of the priory's tithe holdings in Hereford were destroyed. On account of the damages incurred the Crown exempted the community from paying taxes.

In November 1531 reports of the priory's ruinous state were noted and an investigation was undertaken by the Bishop of Hereford. The investigations showed that the prior of Monmouth, Richard Evesham, formerly a monk at Evesham Abbey, had pilfered the monastery's valuables, including the church treasures, to pay his own debts. Richard was thrown out of office on 16 March 1534 and a new prior was appointed in his place. The last three priors at Monmouth shared the same Christian name –

Richard Burton: 1520–24 (not related to a certain south Wales actor of the same name) a monk of Winchcombe and was admitted as prior of Monmouth on 4 April 1520. He had resigned by 4 November 1524.

Richard Evesham: 1524–34, a monk of Evesham and was admitted to office on 4 November 1524.

Richard Taylbus: 1534–6, a monk of Bermondsey and was admitted as prior of Monmouth in March 1534 and was there at the time of the dissolution.

The decision to dissolve the house had been taken by the end at the time of the dissolution.

The decision to dissolve the house had been taken by the end of June 1536. On 21 June, the president of the Council of Marchers (Roland Lee) visited the priory to consider removing the monastery's timber and stone to help with the rebuilding of Monmouth Castle though nothing came of his plans. Monmouth Priory was in a very poor condition at the time of its dissolution with only one monk and a prior in residence. The priory at that time had an income of £56. The priory's goods were sold on 28 February 1537 and the house was granted to Richard Price and Thomas Perry. The priory church was stripped of lead and left to ruin. The church continued to be used by the parishioners but a wall was built to seal off the east end which had housed the monks' choir.

The monastic buildings were located on the north side of the priory church. Traces of an infirmary were discovered in 1906. The surviving buildings were the prior's lodgings. The only recognisable surviving medieval feature is a mid-fifteenth century oriel window which is said to have a connection with Geoffrey of Monmouth but as he lived over three hundred years earlier it cannot be so. The window contains three corbels in the form of carved heads of high quality, although there is some uncertainly as to exactly what they depict. Newman describes them as representing *an angel between a civilian and what may be a bedesman*, whilst Kissack suggests that they portray *a knight, an angel and a miller*. Beneath Geoffrey's Window, three sandstone heads – the Knight, the Angel and the Miller – represent the government of the town, the parish and the business community respectively. They were sculpted by an anonymous medieval mason and today they serve as symbols of the partnership between the Priory and the Town.

The prior's lodgings were extended several times during the nineteenth century, when they were used as St Mary's National School.

In the early years of the twenty first century the building was restored with the help of the Heritage Lottery Fund. During the restoration work on the Priory in 2001, half-way up the back stairs a mediaeval fireplace was discovered. Renovation of the building was completed in 2002.

In December 2000 it was suggested that a wallhanging be produced to illustrate the life of Geoffrey of Monmouth. Research, design and preparation took six months and the first stitches were worked in July 2001, at the festivities to celebrate the Priory's 900th anniversary. The work, measuring 1.5 metres (4.9 ft) by 1.6 metres (5.2 ft), was completed in May 2003, after a combined effort by the 14 volunteers after 2,750 hours.

The background design is based on Kempe's *'The Four Rivers Window'* in St Mary's Priory Church, Monmouth. A Celtic knot pattern gradually rises from green (earth) through blue (sky) to purple (heaven). These intertwining lines were also used by the Hereford School of Romanesque sculptors who were involved with the Priory at the end of the 11th century. A beaded motif from one of the capitals is used in the lower panels of each of the background.

Of the three embroidered 'windows', the central panel depicts Geoffrey of Monmouth, modelled on Father James Coutts who instigated the refurbishment of Monmouth Priory. He wears the black habit of the Benedictines. King Arthur and Queen Guinevere are shown being crowned at Caerleon by Dubricius (modelled on the Most Reverend Dr Rowan Williams, former Archbishop of Wales and Canterbury and former Bishop of Monmouth). Here the river Usk echoes the river theme of Kempe's nineteenth century stained glass window. The Monnow and the Usk link up with the river Wye in the third panel. In this scene King Vortigern listens to the young Merlin telling him the legend of the red and white dragons. Vortigern, a lord of Gwent, was, according to legend, three circular designs in the lower panels. Beneath Geoffrey is the head of the angel that can be seen outside, sculpted underneath 'Geoffrey's Window'. Below Arthur is his shield, '*Pridwen*', with its image of the Virgin Mary, whilst 'Caledfwlch', his sword, can be seen in the initial 'A'. The red and white dragons can be found in the Vortigern panel.

Further Reading

Monastic Wales http://www.monasticwales.org
The Buildings of Wales: Gwent/Monmouthshire. J. Newman. Penguin Books. 2000.
The Lordship, Parish and Borough of Monmouth. K. Kissack.

Name:	**USK PRIORY**
	THE PRIORY OF BRYNBUGA
Order:	**Benedictine Nuns**
Location:	**Priory St., Usk, Monmouthshire NP15**
OS Map Ref.:	**SO 370008**

Some towns and villages in Wales have two names, one Welsh, the other English such as Caergybi/Holyhead or Abertawe/Swansea. The translation of the name can be worked out but there are exceptions to every rule, of which Usk is one. Usk is named after the river Usk which rises in Breconshire and flows past the town of Usk to the Severn estuary at Newport, Monmouthshire. A Roman fort beside the river at Caerleon was named Isca after which the river and town were probably named. Brynbuga, the Welsh name for Usk takes some understanding. Bryn means hill but what of Buga? It is apparently a personal name, little heard of and never seen elsewhere, which first came into use in 1450.

'far from the castle is the church (of St Mary), still a large structure,

though much contracted from its original extent. This church belonged to a Benedictine priory of five nuns, and part of the priory house is now standing, a little southwards of the church.

A Tour throughout South Wales. J. T. Barber. 1803.

Nothing beats a good ghost story, especially in a cold, winter's night with snow flurries in the air and a roaring fire to sit by. Such a story is the one told by Maria Hubert. She was looking for a property to buy when she came across the fire-damaged Usk Priory. Thinking it would be ideal and unusual as a restaurant and hotel, she went to view the property. Her companion wasn't sure about escorting her into the building and neither were some builders from a nearby site but with the estate agent's details in her hand, she ventured in – alone. Some parts of the downstairs impressed her with their potential but an upstairs staircase proved to be rather different if not difficult. For some reason she could not bring herself to climb the stairs even though she made three attempts. On looking out through one of the windows she was rather disappointed to see five nuns walking by. Thinking they might be a party of potential buyers, she left the house at about six o'clock and returned the keys to the estate agents.

As it was a cold winter's day she went into the local pub for a warming drink and there the locals were very keen to know of her plans for the old priory. She explained that if the nuns were to make an offer, she would not stand in their way but if not, she was very keen to buy. On which one who had been listening said,

I don't think the nuns will buy it as they've been here for a long time already.

For more than one reason, her plans fell through and she left the area but on returning, she remembered the old priory and researched its history. What she found was most interesting. The original convent was for five Benedictine nuns who had been researched its history. What she found was most interesting. The original convent was for five Benedictine nuns who had been pensioned off at the time of the Dissolution of the Monasteries. In winter, they would have most probably have made their way to the Vespers service at about six o'clock in the evening using a path passing the very spot where Maria Hubert had seen them. True or not? I could well believe it as I'm still not sure whether it was my wife in a hooded coat or a medieval monk that I saw at Valle Crucis on a cold February morning in 2013.

The original building was commenced by Gilbert de Clare, Earl of Pembroke, also known as Strongbow, who died in 1148. Richard de Clare (son of Gilbert) also known as Strongbow, was Earl of Chepstow and Lord of Raglan, and having property in Usk, completed the Priory and granted a charter. By his charter, granted before he started on his expedition to Ireland in 1169, *The nuns used to pray for Richard de Clare and his father Gilbert, their founders.*

Richard married Eva, daughter of Dermot MacMorough, King of Leinster and died in Dublin in 1177. He was buried in Christchurch, Dublin. He left an only daughter, Isabel, who married William Marshall, Earl of Pembroke. A room on the first floor was decorated with thirty devices, representing coats of arms, probably the armorial bearings of the founders.

At the dissolution Elen Williams was the Lady Prioress. His Grace the Duke of Beaufort disposed of the property to Mr Thomas Watkins, who had the old structure pulled down, and a new house built in 1869. The style of architecture has been partly preserved. The entrance to the Priory grounds is through an arched portal at the churchyard gate in an Anglo-Norman style of architecture.

Usk Priory had suffered in the dissolution and for four and a half centuries has been in lay hands which gave it a new history.

The position of the Priory is in direct juxta position to the church of St Mary's which stands in the Priory grounds and whose walls form the northern boundary of the grounds. The original chancel or choir of the church, and all eastward of the tower, stood on part of the Priory garden and probably a south transept of the cross extended over a part of the garden.

Dugdale in *Monasticon Anglicanum* records that as early as 1236 there was a Priory at Usk for five Benedictine nuns, which had then been some time in existence. There is also a valuation of the Priory in Pope Nicholas' taxation dated 1291. Another document from about 1535, said to be *The True reckoning of all the rents of Assize, Demesne, Lands, Tythings, Oblations, Offerings and of all other commodities, Issues and Profits, belonging or appertaining to the Monastery or Priory of Uske* has details of the receipts from rents and tythes and other items or offerings in the Parish Church of Usk. The total amount was £69 9s 8d. but there were deductions of £14 5s 3d, which included a pension to a former Prioress and payment for prayer to be offered for the dead in the church of Usk. There was also an item of £1, to be paid annually on ShroveTuesday in alms to pray for the Founders – Sir Richard de Clare, Sir Gilbert his son, Earls of the Marches and for other descendants and benefactors. This dates the completion of the Priory in the lifetime of Richard and Gilbert de Clare, i.e. mid twelfth century and begun by their father in about 1148 in the reign of Stephen.

The priory enjoyed much patronage. Very early in its life the Prioress and Convent had six livings at Raglan, Llangadock, and Usk. A watermill in Llanbaddock, called the 'Prioress Mill', was about a mile from Usk, in the village of Rhadyr. At the dissolution the last Prioress was Dame Elen Williams, but her predecessor was then living and in receipt of a pension of £7 a year *for her mete and drynke*. Ten years after the dissolution, in 1546, Roger Williams

Marsh, Williams bought everything else connected to or part of the Priory for £931 2s 11d.

At the beginning of the nineteenth century it had been remodelled as a farm house after being sold by one of the descendants of Roger Williams, of Llangibby, to Alderman Haley but he didn't live long to enjoy his new purchase. One of the most striking parts of the priory was on the first floor. It was a room, part of an apartment decorated with thirty emblematical devices or shields with emblazoned arms, probably the coats of arms of the original benefactors. These, while the Priory was possessed by the Duke of Beaufort, were moved to Cefntilla. It was then purchased and restored by Mr Watkins, of High Mead, Usk followed by his son who rented the property to Mr Lawrence, of Llangibby Castle, Sir William Heathcote and later General Barnard.

The church of St Mary, close to the Priory, was both a convent and a parish church. In the thirteenth century the nave was rebuilt; in the 15th century the aisle was replaced. The church had 344 additional seats in 1844 for which space had to made for, so a wall at the east end was demolished, which brought into view four Norman arches, which were previously unseen.

At the base of a carved screen and near the pulpit was an inscribed brass plate twenty inches long by three inches wide. In the nineteenth century, the language on the plaque caused some confusion as no-one really knew which one it was. Translated into more modern English it tells the reader to:

Mark this object of fame to the disgrace of the blade;
Were he not cover'd, Loudon would be in difficulty.
Then let us consecrate the grave of Briaut the son of Llydd,
Who in judgment was an elder;
Solomon, profound of word was he;
And the sod of Isca his bed of sleep!
Ardently he would reconcile the eloquent, and the wise,

And the sod of Isca his bed of sleep!
Ardently he would reconcile the eloquent, and the wise,
The clergy and the laity would be fully illumined.

Another story from Brynbuga, little known, is well worth repeating. David Lewis, the last Welsh martyr, was born at Abergavenny in 1616, the youngest of nine children, in a district that was predominantly Catholic. Margaret Pritchard, his mother, was a devout Catholic who brought up eight of her children in the faith, but Morgan Lewis her husband had David educated at Abergavenny Grammar School, of which he was headmaster and brought up his youngest son a Protestant. But David though was still a Catholic at heart. In 1625 the Jesuit Mission of St Francis Xavier was founded at the Cwm, near Monmouth. In the same year John Kemble (the Martyr), a relative of David Lewis, came from Douai, to begin his mission in Herefordshire. When David Lewis began to study law in London at the age of sixteen, he visited Paris and become a Catholic. In 1638 when both his parents died, David went to the Venerable English College at Rome, where he was ordained priest in 1642. The college Diary records his entry: *Charles Baker, vere David Lewis, a south-Welshman of the County of Monmouth was admitted as an alumnus Nov. 6, 1638.* Later was added: *Vir prudens et pius. (A devout and prudent man). Hanged for the Faith and the priesthood in the year 1680 in Wales.* In 1645 he entered the Society of Jesus. His uncle Fr. John Pritchard was already a member. In 1648 he was sent to the Jesuit Mission of St Francis Xavier at Cwm where he worked for thirty-one years until his martyrdom. Fr David Lewis was arrested at Llantarnam on 17 November 1678 and imprisoned in Monmouth gaol. On 13th January 1679 he was transferred to the gaol at Usk. On 28th March he was again back in Monmouth to be tried at the spring assizes which was presided over by Sir Robert Atkins. The charge against him was *David Lewis pro Sacerd Roman,* that is *David Lewis for being a Roman Priest*. Fr Lewis pointed out that it was necessary for the prosecution to prove him guilty of the charge of being ordained overseas and that he had taken Orders from the See of Rome but Atkins said that it was proof enough that he had taken services and worn the vestments of a priest. At about 10 o'clock the following morning, 29 March 1679, the trial of Fr David Lewis began. Witnesses were called who swore that they had seen him celebrate Mass but some refused to give evidence against him. He was found guilty and Judge Atkins pronounced the sentence:

> *David Lewis, thou shalt be led from this place to a place whence thou camest, and shalt be put upon a hurdle and drawn with thy heels forward to the place of execution where thou shalt be hanged by the neck and be cut down alive; thy body to be ripped open and thy bowels plucked out; thou shalt be dismembered and thy members burnt before thy face. So the Lord have mercy on thy soul.'*

On 27th August 1679, Fr David Lewis was taken from Usk Gaol and bound to a hurdle, feet up and his head to the ground. He was carried along the path by the river to the place of execution, the Island or the Coniger. The Jesuit's body was taken in procession to Usk's Priory Church of St Mary and respectfully buried in the churchyard. His grave is the one nearest the door of the west porch and just to the left of the path. The stone is relatively new, having been placed there after the canonisation of St David Lewis. It replaces an old and broken stone generally believed to be the original gravestone.

Fr David Lewis had the love and respect of many and it was a Protestant man who prevented the priest from being mutilated while still alive. On or near to where the priest was hanged an un named Protestant held his hand until he was dead, thus ensuring that Fr Lewis was not cut down while still alive to suffer the agony of disembowelling. The body was decapitated and mutilated but not quartered. Fr David Lewis was beatified in 1929 and on 25 October 1970, he was canonised by Pope Paul VI as one of the Forty Martyrs of England and Wales. His feast day is kept on 27 August.

Further Reading

A Monmouthshire Christmas. Maria Hubert. Sutton Publishing. 1995.

A Tour of the Abbeys, Priories and Cathedrals of Wales. D. S. Yerburgh. Yerburgh. 1999.

Dictionary of the Place Names of Wales. H. W. Owen & R. Morgan. Gomer Press. 2007.

lastwelshmartyr.blogspot.co.uk

Monastic Wales http://www.monasticwales.org

Usk: Past and Present. J. H. Clark. Printed at the County Observer Office.

CARMELITE FRIARS/AUGUSTINIAN FRIARS

A small orders of solitary monks who placed a strong emphasis on prayer. The order of Our Lady of Mount Carmel was founded in Palestine about 1154. Albert of Vercelli laid down a strict rule of extreme poverty, abstinence of flesh and solitude. Their habit was dark brown with a white mantle. They were known as the White Friars.

Name:	**DENBIGH FRIARY**
	A 'HOME' FOR BISHOPS
Order:	**Carmelite**
Location:	**Denbigh, Denbighshire**
OS Map Ref.:	**SJ 060666**

Denbigh Friary, also known as Henllan Friary is a ruined religious house situated at the north east end of the town of Denbigh, at house situated at the north east end of the town of Denbigh, at the foot of the hill, at the end of the lane, leading east off Rhyl Road. There appears to be confusion over the date of its founding. Some sources quote 1270s–80s. Others say it was in 1343–50. It was a Carmelite community, the only one of its kind in Wales, dedicated to St Mary and patronised by either Sir John Salusbury or John de Sunimore.

> The priory of Carmelites, or White Friars, stood at the bottom of the town. It was founded by John Salusbury, of Lleweni, who died, as appeared from a mutilated brass, found in the conventual church, on the 7th of March, 1289.

> Thomas Pennant. 1784

The Salusbury family were involved with the friary in the fifteenth and sixteenth century and a number of family members were buried there. In the sixteenth century also, Henry Standish, Bishop of St Asaph and a Carmelite friar himself, was a patron. The eastern friar's choir is still standing but the roof was badly burned in 1899.

The English Benedictine abbot Robert Parfew, a Cluniac monk, was involved in the surrender of the Carmelites of Denbigh Friary on 18 August 1538 when there were only four friars in residence. Parfew had been elected Bishop of St Asaph on 8 June 1536. He lived mostly at Denbigh. In 1537 he was present at the christening of Prince Edward and the funeral of Jane Seymour; in 1538 he was at the reception of Anne of Cleves, and his was also one of the signatures on the declaration of the nullity of her marriage. At the beginning of Queen Mary's reign he was made a member of the commission which expelled most of the bishops. He was, on 1 March 1554, translated to the diocese of Hereford in place of John Harley. He died on 22 September 1557.

During the Dissolution, some of the buildings were turned

into houses, while wool was sold in the church.

On the dissolution, this house was granted to Richard Andreas and William L'Isle. The church, now converted into a barn, is the only remaing building.

Thomas Pennant, 1784

In the early sixteenth century the friary was home to the bishops of St Asaphs who resided in the Bishop's Chamber. They were also responsible for much building work. After the Dissolution the bishops leased the property and an inventory from that period lists the choir or church, vestry, chamber, hall, kitchen, brewhouse and buttery. Another document mentions the house, stables, demesnes, terraces, gardens and orchards. The Friary, labelled The Abbey, is also shown on Speed's town plan published in 1610.

The remains consist of the ruined church, intact until it was gutted by fire in 1898, and the greatly altered dormitory and refectory block, now Abbey Cottage. The church is a late thirteenth century building with several later features, notably the great blocked Perpendicular east window. It consisted of the Friar's choir to the east and the public nave to the west, divided by a screened passage with a leaden spire above. The cloister was on the south side of the church with the chapter house and bishop's chamber in the east range and the dormitory and refectory block on the south. This block appears to be a late medieval building, possibly early sixteenth century. Few other medieval features survive.

The apex stone of a medieval cross from the Friary was in the grounds of Dolhyfryd in 1963.

Further restoration was carried out in 1954.

During building work, which was carried out at different times, bones were found in a trench. A sample found in 1985 was taken to be radiocarbon dated and found to be from 1435. Later works, in 1994, uncovered bones from at least 170 different individulas.

Further Reading

A Tour of the Abbeys, Priories and Cathedrals of Wales. D. S. Yerburgh. Yerburgh. 1999.

Denbigh Castle, Town Walls & Friar. Butler. DoE. 1976.

Monastic Wales http://www.monasticwales.org

CISTERCIANS

Founded in 1098, the Cistercians were known as 'white monks' because of the colour of their habits, an unbleached material, worn to reflect the purity of the Blessed Virgin Mary. The order began as an attempt to reform the Benedictine monasteries and followed the Rule of St Benedict very closely. They willingly accepted an offer of land to build upon but refused all other gifts. Led by Abbot, later Saint, Robert of Molesme, the monks built a wooden monastery and chose to live an extremely hard life. Robert was replaced firstly by Alberic and then, when he returned to the abbey at Molesme, by Stephen Harding.

The success of the Cistercians increased with the arrival of Bernard of Fontaines who joined the order in 1112. St Bernard of Clairvaux became the Abbot of Clairvaux in 1115. By the time of his death in 1153 there were up to 340 Cistercian abbeys in Europe. From Citeaux, the Cistercians spread across France and in 1128 moved to England to create their first abbey in Britain at Waverley in Surrey. Harding of England and Bernard of Clairvaux were canonised as saints after their deaths. Almost all Cistercian abbeys were dedicated to the Virgin Mary. The Cistercians became the most numerous order in Wales with the abbeys of Aberconwy, Basingwerk, Cwmhir, Cymer, Llantarnam, Margam, Neath, Strata Florida, Tintern, Valle Crucis and Whitland all founded in their name. Due to linguistic differences, the names of Welsh abbeys were often mixed up especially so by later researchers:

Aberconwy – was known as Conwy, or Maenan at its later site.
Whitland – was known by its Latin name of Albaland, and
sometimes Blanchland or Tŷ Gwyn.
Valle Crucis – was known as Llanegwe(y)stl (the original Welsh
name for the locality).
Llantarnam – was known as Caerleon Abbey, sometimes
Vallium or Duma.
Strata Florida – was known as Ystrad Fflur.
Strata Marcella – was known as Marchell or the abbey of Pole
(from nearby Welshpool).
Cwmhir and Cymer have often been mistaken for each other.
Many were patronised by the Welsh princes. All Cistercian
houses, whatever their size, were known as abbeys. All Cistercian
abbeys were descended from the mother church at Citeaux, but
were more independent than the Cluniacs and were administered
by their own abbots.

Name: **ABERCONWY ABBEY**
               MOVED TO MAKE WAY FOR A CASTLE
Order: **Cistercian**
Location: **Rose Hill Street, Conwy**
OS Map Ref.:   **SH 781775**

The exact site of Aberconwy Abbey is unknown as it was
demolished to make way for Edward I's castle at Conwy but St
Mary's, Conwy parish church still stands on the extensive site but
all other signs of the abbey were razed to the ground. All that is
known is that it stood as the only building on the western side of
the Conwy estuary.

A Cistercian house was founded at Rhedynog Felen near
Caernarfon in 1186 by a group of monks from Strata Florida

Caernarfon in 1186 by a group of monks from Strata Florida Abbey. Later they moved to Conwy and in 1199 were presented with grants of land by Llywelyn the Great, ruler of Gwynedd. A statue of Llywelyn ap Iorwerth (*Llywelyn Fawr* – Llywelyn the Great) was created by E. O. Griffith of Liverpool in 1895. It stands on a fountain by architects Grayson & Ould in Lancaster Square, Conwy.

Aberconwy Abbey had a rather strained relationship with the Cistercian General Chapter itself. In the General Chapter of 1202 it was said that the abbots of Aberconwy, Valle Crucis and Llantarnam rarely celebrated Mass and abstained from the altar. The three abbots were called to answer the charges but the journey from north Wales to the General Chapter was long and expensive, especially for the abbot of Aberconwy, the most distant of the Welsh houses. For him it could take a month or more to travel. The king of England wrote letters requesting that certain abbots be excused from attending. Edward I, in fairness, wrote twice for this purpose. In 1293 he requested that the abbots of Aberconwy and Valle Crucis be excused from attending because he needed them to stay in England. Again in 1298 the king requested that the abbots of Aberconwy and Valle Crucis be excused attendance as they *were staying in Wales by the king's command for the king's business and the quiet of the land* and that the abbot of Aberconwy was not in a fit state of health to travel.

When Llywelyn died in 1240 he was buried at the abbey as was his son and Dafydd ap Llywelyn who was also buried there in 1246. In 1248 Llywelyn's other son, Gruffudd ap Llywelyn, who had died after a failed escape attempt from the Tower of London in 1244, was reburied at Aberconwy after the abbots of Aberconwy and Strata Florida had arranged for his body to be brought home from London. The abbot of Aberconwy was an important figure in negotiations between Llywelyn the Last and the English crown and in 1262 was entrusted with the task of being Llywelyn's sole representative in negotiations.

The Welsh Cistercian abbots occasionally wrote in defence of their country and princes. In 1274 the abbots of Aberconwy, Whitland, Strata Florida, Cwmhir, Strata Marcella, Cymer and Valle Crucis wrote to the pope defending the reputation and integrity of Prince Llywelyn ap Gruffydd against the charges laid against him by Einion II, bishop of St Asaph. The Treaty of Aberconwy was forcibly signed by Llywelyn in the abbey in 1277. Llywelyn, in an attempt to make his link to royalty more plausible decided to marry Eleanor de Montfort, daughter of Simon de Montfort and King Edward's cousin. They were married by proxy in 1275, but when she sailed from France to meet her intended husband pirates, who had been hired by Edward, captured her and she was imprisoned at Windsor Castle.

Edward saw Llywelyn as a threat and was not keen for the marriage to take place because de Montfort had also been a threat to the English Crown. Despite being summoned more than once before Edward, Llywelyn refused all invitations as he thought that he would be in great danger.

In 1276, Edward had reached the end of his tether, declared Llywelyn an outlaw and decided to march against him. By the summer of 1277, Edward and his army were in north Wales and confiscated the harvest in Anglesey, reputedly the 'bread basket of Wales' (*Môn Mam Cymru*), forcing Llywelyn and his army to surrender.

The treaty of Aberconwy was drawn up, to guarantee peace in Gwynedd but Llywelyn had to make concessions. His authority was confined to lands west of the river Conwy, and he had to concede lands east of the river to his brother Dafydd ap Gruffudd, whom he had earlier fought. Llywelyn was allowed to keep his title of Prince of Wales but most of the other Welsh princes or rulers were not expected to recognize him as their master. In independence from England. Once the treaty was signed, Edward wasted no time in building castles at Aberystwyth, Builth, Flint and Rhuddlan.

Llywelyn had been humbled and was left with little power. He was forced to pay homage to Edward, who finally agreed to him marrying Eleanor de Montford. The ceremony took place in 1278 in Worcester Cathedral, with Edward present.

Aberconwy Abbey was damaged by the English in 1245 and again in 1283, which was the year Edward I, king of England, lord of Ireland, duke of Aquitaine stayed there from 13 March until 9 May during his survey of building sites for his castles in north Wales. He soon decided that Conwy would be the ideal site for the first in a ring of defensive castles designed to enclose north Wales. The monks had to be moved elsewhere and were paid £40 compensation for their troubles.

Henry III fought against Dafydd ap Llywelyn and sent his army to Conwy. They got no further than Deganwy Castle on the opposite bank of the estuary in sight of the abbey. An unknown, un-named English soldier wrote home to his family to describe his miserable tour of duty in north Wales:

The King with his army is encamped at Gannock (Deganwy), and is busy fortifying that place (sufficiently strong already) about which we lay in our tents, in watching, fasting, and praying, and freezing. We watch for fear of the Welsh, we fast for want of provision, we pray that we may speedily return safe, and scot-free home, and we freeze for want of winter garments.

A ship from Ireland sailed into the estuary on the Monday before Michaelmas day loaded with a supply of food and wine for the English army but due to the captain's lack of local knowledge, it struck a sandbank on the Welsh side of the river. The Welsh army waded into the water to try and relieve the ship of its cargo but hunger and thirst drove the English to do the same. The English army was the stronger for a time and sent the Welsh packing and crossed over to attack the abbey and set it on fire but the Welsh gave as good as they got and prepared to battle over the ship still high and dry on the sandbank. Victory was claimed by the Welsh army despite the burning abbey behind them but the most important prize was claimed by the English – the ship's cargo! Despite their losses, some very relieved soldiers took back to Deganwy the food and wine from the ship and celebrate their loss!

In their return back our soldiers being too covetous, and greedy of plunder, spoiled the Abbey of Aberconwy, and burnt all the books, and other choice utensils belonging to it. The Welsh being distracted by these irreligious practices got together in great number, and in a desperate manner setting upon the English, killed a great number of them, and following the rest to the water side, forced as many as could not escape into the boats.

In this skirmish several men of note were killed, including Richard, Earl of Cornwall, Sir Allan Buscell, Sir Adam de Maio, Sir Geoffry Estuany, and others, and about one hundred soldiers, so retribution came quickly upon them for their sacrilege.

John, the abbot of Aberconwy, raided Strata Florida in 1428, with a band of men and archers. Many monks were imprisoned by him in Aberystwyth Castle while he stole valuables and drove away stock worth two thousand marks. His villainy took forty days. Another abbot of Aberconwy was thrown from his horse in 1489 and died of a broken neck.

The few remains of the abbey have been incorporated into St Mary's Church, Conwy – the east and west buttresses and parts of the walls. The west door of the church is probably from the chapter house of the original abbey. The abbey church was about 43m long and part of it is preserved in the east and west walls of the present church. The western part would have been a great aisled nave. Llewelyn's Hall may have been a guest house aisled nave. Llewelyn's Hall may have been a guest house associated with the abbey. The church was largely rebuilt in the late thirteenth century. It consisted of an aisled nave, a chancel and north vestry, and a western tower built in the end bay of the abbey church. The south trancept was added soon after. There were other additions and rebuilding and the church was restored in 1872. Fittings include a fine rood screen of about 1500 separating the nave and chancel.

Of special interest are:

i. The marble bust of John Gibson sculpture, christened in Conwy church in 1790. One of the contributors to this memorial was the Prince of Wales (later Edward VIII).

ii. Effigy in south aisle of Mary (died 1585) mother of John Williams, Archbishop of York, during the reign of Charles 1 and keeper of the great Seal of England.

iii. Seventeenth century floor slab in the chancel inscribed Nicholas Hookes, forty first child of his father and himself father of 27 children!

iv. A rare reproduction of Andrea Del Santo's 'Christ' near the pulpit.

v. The Tudor Font replacing an earlier one is unique. It has a heavily moulded octagonal base and panels of the pedestal and bowl are moulded and decorated with tracery. John Williams Archbishop of York was christened here on 27 March 1582.

vi. In the graveyard is a grave with the inscription 'We are Seven' immortalized by William Wordsworth's poem *We are Seven* inspired after his visit to Conwy in 1798, when he was eighteen years old. The poem is a conversation between the poet and a young girl about her life after the death of two of her siblings.

Further Reading

An Introduction to the History of Wales. Vol. II. A. H. Williams. University of Wales Press.

A Tour of the Abbeys, Priories and Cathedrals of Wales. D. S. Yerburgh. Yerburgh. 1999.

Crwydro Arfon. A. Llywelyn-Williams. Llyfrau'r Dryw. 1959.

Dathlu Tywysogion Cymru. E. Meek. Gwasg Carreg Gwalch. 2009.

Monastic Wales http://www.monasticwales.org

RCAHMW Caernarvonshire Inventory. 1956.

The Architectural Remains of The Mendicant Orders In Wales. A. W. Clapham.

The Welsh Cistercians. D. H. Williams. Hughes & Son, Ltd., Griffin Press. 1969.

The Complete Poetical Works of William Wordsworth. Thomas Y. Crowell & Co., New York. 1888.

The Monastic Order in South Wales 1066–1349. F. G. Cowley. Cardiff. 1977.

We Are Seven. www.gradesaver.com/wordsworths-poetical-works/study-guide/section14/

Name:	**BASINGWERK ABBEY**
	A SHELTER FOR PRIESTS, PRINCES AND POETS
Order:	**Sauvignac/Cistercian**
Location:	**Greenfield Valley Heritage Park, Greenfield Road, Holywell, Flintshire**
OS Map Ref.:	**SJ 195774)**

The refectory is the most entire portion left, which has a recess with superincumbent circular arches, where formerly the well supplied sideboard used to stand. The columns, or supporters of these arches, are almost unique.

Think of the Greenfield Valley (*Maesglas*) in Flintshire and its industrial heritage immediately comes to mind but the history of this particular valley in north Wales has much more to offer than industrial remains. It was the *cradle of Christianity* in the area.

King Offa, Mercia's ruler, is probably better known for the dyke that bears his name but he was also responsible for another – Watt's Dyke, which was built as part of the defence of his realm against the Welsh. So, even in the eighth century, the locals were known but not for all the right reasons. The valley had its attractions even then and attracted many pilgrims and travellers to St Winefride and the well named in her honour. It was a well of great religious significance drawing welcome and unwelcomed visitors from far and near even in Norman times. Owain Gwynedd attacked Henry II at Basingwerk as he made his way to Rhuddlan Castle. A church built in 1093 and a castle, where Henry II stayed and sheltered became the focal point of a small, agricultural community but the founding of Basingwerk Abbey, circa 1131 led to the development of the valley and the beginning of its 'industrial age'. Originally the abbey was built on a site three miles south further along the coast at a place called Hen Blas, Basingwerk but the building and the name was moved to its present day site. The abbey church was a little over fifty metres long, making it one of the smallest Cistercian churches. The abbey was meant, amongst other things, to care for the visitors to St Winefride's Well and due to the ever increasing number of visitors corn mills, fulling mills and malt houses were built, a weekly market, and an annual fair were held. As Holywell became known as the 'Lourdes of Wales' the abbey and the valley prospered until 1536 when the abbey was closed and allowed to deteriorate following the dissolution of the lesser monasteries.

Benedictine monks from the Savigny region of France built the abbey in 1131, which by 1147 had become under the

Cistercian rule. Henry II granted the abbey its charter in 1157 and Gilbert was appointed abbot of Basingwerk in mid-summer 1159. From the Weekly Mail, dated 13 October 1900, an article about the history of Basingwerk Abbey gives details of a military raid in the twelfth century and a long forgotten poem was brought back to light.

HENRY II

In 1157 King Henry II made preparations for his first Welsh war. The domestic quarrels of the Welsh princes furnished him with an excellent pretext. Cadwaladr appealed to Henry against his relatives, and, of course, found a gracious reception. Orders were issued for an expedition into north Wales. The invasion was two-fold – by land and sea. The host assembled near Chester, on Saltney Marsh, and was joined by Madog, prince of Powys. Owen Gwynedd, with his three sons and all his forces, entrenched himself at Basingwerk. The King himself set off by the sea coast, hoping to fall upon the Welsh all unawares. Owen's sons, however, were on the watch, and in the narrow pass of Consilt the English suddenly found themselves face to face with the foe. Entangled in the woody, marshy ground, they were easily routed by the nimble, light-armed Welsh, and the cry that the king himself had fallen caused the constable, Henry of Essex, to drop the royal standard and fly in despair. Owen, however, thought it prudent to withdraw from Basingwerk, and seek a more inaccessible retreat. Henry pushed on to Rhuddlan, and there fortified the castle. Meanwhile, the fleet had sailed under the command of Madog ap Meredith. It touched at Anglesey, and there landed a few troops whose sacrilegious behaviour brought upon them such vengeance from the outraged islanders that their terrified comrades sailed back at once to Chester, where they learned that the war was ended.

This battle is referred to in a poem by Hywel, son of Owen

Gwynedd, an accomplished poet, as well as valiant warrior:

The ravens croaked, and human blood
In ruddy flood, poured o'er the land;
Then burning houses war proclaimed,
Churches inflamed and palace halls;
While sheets of fire scale the sky,
And warriors cry, "To Battle!"

They clearly heard the conflict's roar
On Menai's shore from Seiont's fort;
Three hundred ships, so heroes say,
The third of May, were set on fire.
Ten hundred times as many fled,
And not a beard staid on Menai.

Owen, in terror of being hemmed in between the royal army and the fleet, sent proposals for peace, reinstated his banished brother, performed his own homage to King Henry, and gave hostages for his loyalty in the future. As the south Welsh princes were all vassals of north Wales, Owen's submission was equivalent to a formal acknowledgment of Henry's right as lord paramount over the whole country, and the king was technically justified in boasting that he had subdued all the Welsh to his will. So says the English historian, but, as a matter of fact, Henry's expedition of 1157 against the princes of north Wales had little practical result. Henry had gained nothing by it, but had lost many brave men, and, as matters in France were calling for his attention, he was glad to leave Wales for that country.

Due to the high volume of visitors to Holywell, it became one of the richest abbeys in Wales at the time and the owner of many acres of land and mineral rights in Holway and Whitford. Other visitors were *Giraldus Cambrensis* and Archbishop Baldwin of Canterbury were *Giraldus Cambrensis* and Archbishop Baldwin of Canterbury on their journey through Wales recruiting for the Crusades.

After celebrating Mass at St Aspah, we set out again almost immediately. We passed through a district where there is a rich vein of silver and successful mining-works, and where by delving deep, they penetrate the very bowels of the earth. We spent the night in the small priory at Basingwerk.

In the early thirteenth century, Edward I stayed at Basingwerk while Flint Castle was being built. A monk from the abbey took divine services in the chapel of Flint Castle for which he was paid fifty shillings in 1285. Such generosity guaranteed their support to the English cause. Later in the same century, Basingwerk Abbey was affiliated with Buildwas Abbey in Shropshire. *Llywelyn Fawr* (Llywelyn the Great) also became patron during the thirteenth century and his only son, Dafydd ap Llywelyn, formally presented the abbey with St Winefride's Well. This increased the abbey's wealth and the monks made use of the Holywell river to treat the wool from their flocks of sheep.

The abbey was home to a number of Welsh poets including Tudur Aled (1480–1526), who wrote a poem of praise to Thomas ap Dafydd Pennant, onetime abbot of Basingwerk, saying:

Your poets and tables are praiseworthy
As are your choir, your drinking vessels and library.

Gutun Owain was another who had connections with the abbey and the fifteenth century manuscript – The Black Book of Basingwerk, contains much of his work. Although known as the Black Book of Basingwerk, it was probably copied at Valle Crucis Abbey. The manuscript was created between 1488 and 1498 and still has its wooden boards covered with calf leather. Gold was used in its decorated letters and a blue-green ink used in the text. Its contents include:

a volvella of the moon (a moveable device for working out the position of the sun and moon in the Zodiac),

tables for situating the moveable holy days of the Christian year,

a chart showing the parts of the body to be bled for different diseases,

a chart of the planets,

a calendar of saint days,

a chart showing urine colours and their meaning,

the life of Saint Martin,

genealogy and history including a list of the kings of Britain.

Gutun Owain was a very important and well known genealogist and was appointed by Henry VII to trace the family tree of his grandfather Owain Tudur. Another poet with Basingwerk connections was Guto'r Glyn (1440–1493). Guto was well known for his 'praise poetry', *cywyddau* of asking favours and of thanks. When Tomas ap Dafydd, Abbot of Basingwerk Abbey, asked the poet Tudur Aled who was the best for composing poetry praising the nobility, his answer was Guto'r Glyn. Guto died at Valle Crucis Abbey. Owain Brogyntyn (1160–1188) was not a poet but benefactor of the abbey. He was a prince of Powys, the son of Madog ap Maredudd, the last king of Powys.

Much renovation was made over the years but little of the twelfth century remains are seen today. The church dates from the thirteenth century and has seven bays in the nave and two south side chapels in each transept. A warming house was added in the fifteenth century which contained the upper floor dormitory with direct access to the choir of the church, down a night stair. No-one paid much attention to Robin Ddu, a Welsh seer, when he predicted that the roof of the refectory would suit a little church on Moel Famau but his prophecies came to mind after the dissolution of the monasteries in 1536, when parts of the abbey were dismantled and recycled in other local churches. Part of the roof was used to cover the aisle in Cilcain parish church and another given to Ruthin parish church. The choir stalls were removed and reassembled at St Mary-on-the-Hill, Chester. Lead was taken to castles at Holt and Dublin and a stained glass Jesse-window was put into the church of Llanrhaeadr-yng-Nghinmeirch.

According to a fifteenth century description of the abbey, it had lead roofs and a new guest house. So many visitors came that meal times always had two sittings. Thomas Pennant, a relative of another Thomas Pennant who was a noted Welsh naturalist and antiquary, was the abbot between the years 1481–1522 but he left the post after becoming married. He was noted for nurturing and patronising many poets especially Tudur Aled, who described him as a very good man with fine taste but more importantly as *a generous patron of the bards*. His son Nicholas was the last abbot of Basingwerk, whose handwriting may be seen in the margin of the Black Book of Basingwerk. When he was forced to give up his post after the Dissolution, he was given a pension of £17 per annum.

The site of the abbey was given by Henry VIII to Henry ap Harry of Llanasa. His daughter married into the Mostyn family of Talcare which renovated parts of the abbey as living accommodation. By the early 1800's it had fallen into disuse with stones from the building being used by John Smalley to build the first cotton mill in the valley. Other abbey out-buildings housed a tannery.

In the Liverpool Mercury (Saturday, 23 August 1890) there appeared a report of the Cambrian Archaeological Association's Rambles about Holywell written by Mr Thomas Hughes of Greenfield. Though the report is short, it gives much valuable background information about one of the least well known abbeys in Wales.

A short walk brought the members of the Association to the neglected ruins of Basingwerk Abbey, which occupy a commanding position overlooking the Dee. The abbey is supposed to have been built in 1131 by Ranulph, Earl of Chester, supposed to have been built in 1131 by Ranulph, Earl of Chester, although a society of monks are known to have existed there in 1119, and it was the first house of the Cistercian order in this part of the county. The architecture is mixed, being partly Saxon and partly Saracenic. The house was dissolved in 1535, and the present ruins consist of fragments of the abbey church, the refectory, and dormitories. King Richard I in 1119, it is stated by an old writer, attempted a pilgrimage to St Winifred's Well, and either in going or returning, he was attacked by the Welsh, and took shelter in Basingwerk. Having in this emergency applied to St Winifred for assistance, the saint raised up a quantity of sand between there and the opposite coast in the river Dee, which enabled the Constable of Chester with his armed bands to march over the estuary to the king's relief. The shoal retains to the present day the name of The Constable's Sands.

The most important remains of the abbey is its literary legacy. *The Book of Aneirin*, one of the Four Ancient Books of Wales, transcribed in the second half of the thirteenth century, has been credited to Basingwerk Abbey. Basingwerk is also thought to have contributed to *Brut y Tywysogyon* of the *Chronicle of the Princes*.

Like many ancient buildings, Basingwerk Abbey was allowed to gradually fall into disrepair, while the ones who could have done something to save it from further deterioration did very little as shown in an article in the Rhyl Journal, dated 28 June 1902.

HOLYWELL

Basingwerk Abbey. Everyone will regret that the Flintshire County Council have felt it their duty to decline to repair that venerable ruin, Basingwerk Abbey, near Holywell. Mr J. J. Fitzpatrick, president of the Liverpool Science Students' Association, writes to the Press pointing out that in France the authorities look after the preservation of their ancient monuments in the most careful manner, and he expresses the hope that the Cambrian Archaeological Association, which has amongst its members some of the most intellectual of living Welshmen, may be induced to take the matter in hand. A society of monks existed at Basingwerk previous to the year 1119, and the Abbey itself was probably founded by one of the native princes of north Wales The Cistercian rule was introduced late in the twelfth century, when the Abbey received a charter from King Henry II, and the present building which is of the early pointed style of architecture, probably dates from that period. It is a thousand pities that a structure surrounded by many historical associations should be allowed to go to ruin.

Another article in the same paper, dated 6 April 1907, shows that had something been done five years earlier, storm damage might not have had such a disastrous effect.

DISAPPEARING ABBEY

Welsh archaeologists and antiquarians will regret to hear that recent severe storms have done great damage to the ruins of Basingwerk Abbey at Holywell. One of the best preserved and interesting portions of the buildings was the chapter-house, which has unusual architectural features, but the whole of the outer wall has fallen, hundreds of tons of stone having been cast to the ground. Other portions of the walls are only kept together by dilapidated and shaky archways, and must soon fall too. The abbey belonged to the Cistercian Order, and was probably erected in the twelfth century.

Today, most of Greenfield Valley's industrial past is, like the abbey, in ruins but at least the abbey ruins are easily recognised and their purpose realised. Though it receives scant recognition for what it was, it remains the most obvious evidence of the valley's past.

Abbeys, Priories and Cathedrals of Wales. M. Salter. Folly Publications. 2012.

A Tour of the Abbeys, Priories and Cathedrals of Wales. D. S. Yerburgh. Yerburgh. 1999.

Basingwerk Abbey. D. M. Robionson. Cadw. 2006.

Crwydro Sir Fflint. T. I. Ellis. Llyfrau'r Dryw. 1959.

Gerald of Wales. The Journey Through Wales. The Description of Wales. Trans.: L. Thorpe. Penguin. 1978.

Monastic Wales http://www.monasticwales.org

The Cistercian Abbeys of Britain. D. Robinson (ed.). B. T. Batsford Ltd. 1998.

The Greenfield Valley. K. Davies & C. J. Williams. Gwasg Gee. 1986.

The Monastic Order in South Wales 1066–1349, F. G. Cowley.

Name:	**CRIDIA ABBEY, POWYS**
	DID IT EXIST?
Order:	**Cistercian**
Location:	**Unknown**

Very little information is available to decide if this abbey ever existed. Reputedly it was near Bryntalch in Llandyssil. It is mentioned by Roger of Wendover. In 1228, after Henry III relieved Montgomery from a Welsh siege, he followed them into the forest beyond and came to the abbey of Cridia which belonged to the white monks (Cistercians). Henry destroyed the abbey and ordered Hurbert de Burgh to build a castle on the site.

In 1778 Warrington claimed that the monastery was situated on the Goranddu ridge, in Llandyssil parish between Bryntalch and the river Severn. Other sites of its location could be Brynderwen, near Abermule, Cymmer Abbey and in the vale of Kerry. Samuel Lewis called it a castellated mansion. Above the vale of Kerry *is Cefn y Mynach*, (Monks Ridge), reputedly the site of Cridia Abbey. Some believe it may also have been confused with Cwmhir.

It has also been said Cridia Abbey was occupied by the 'White Friars' or Carmelites but they were not known in Britain in the early thirteenth century.

Further reading

Monastic and Religious Orders in Britain, 1000–1300. J. Burton. University of Cambridge Press. 1994.

Crida Abbey. M. C. Jones. Montgomeryshire Collections 6. 1873.

Religious Houses of England and Wales. D. Knowles & R. N. Hadcock. Longman. 1971.

Cridier Abbey. R. Williams. Montgomeryshire Collections 15. 1882.

Name:	**CWMHIR ABBEY**
	THE ABBEY OF THE LONG VALLEY
Ordrer:	**Cistercian**
Location:	**Abbeycwmhir Village (north of Llandrindod Wells), Powys**
OS Map Ref.:	**SO 055711**

The Chronicle of Chester states that Cwmhir Abbey was founded in 1143 after Maredudd ap Madog ap Iorwerth offered Cistercian monks the land at Tŷ Faenor in Maelienydd, on which to build but Hugh of Wigmore attacked and conquered Maelienydd and the monks left for Pembrokeshire, where they founded a house at Trefgarn in 1144. In 1151 they moved on to Tŷ Gwyn, Whitland. Maredudd's two brothers – Cadwallon and Einion helped the monks from Whitland Abbey to proceed with the work in 1176. A wooden church was the first structure on the site and a fish pond was dug two miles further up the valley. They worked at growing was dug two miles further up the valley. They worked at growing corn for food, flax for linen, hay for cattle and rearing sheep for wool, building mills to grind corn and to make cloth. The Cistercian way of life was one of self-sustenance. Cwmhir Abbey was meant to maintain sixty monks. Plans were in hand for a sizable abbey in a very rural part of Wales. Work began on the church in the 1190's which at 242 feet in length would have been longer than any other in Wales but only the nave was completed and about a third of the foundations laid and finished. It contained thirteen huge round pillars on the north and south side to divide the nave. Permission to baptize was given in 1232 as the nearest parish church of Llanbister was so far away. The first abbot was Meurig, who died six years after the founder in 1184. Llywelyn the Great became patron in 1220.

The abbey suffered from internal problems. In 1195 the lay-brothers of Cwmhir stole their abbot's horses because he had forbidden them to drink beer. The offending monks were sent to Clairvaux on foot and told to abide by the decision of the abbot of Clairvaux.

In 1231, during the war between Henry III and Llywelyn, the abbey was plundered and burnt by English soldiers. It was thought that a monk from the abbey had misled the English army and misdirected them. This, they believed, led to their defeat by Llywelyn. Henry would have completely destroyed the abbey had they not paid him a fine of three hundred marks. In 1282, when Llywelyn was betrayed and killed at Cefn y Bedd, Cilmeri on the banks of the river Irfon, it was the monks of Cwmhir Abbey who took his body for burial in concecrated ground.

After Llywelyn's death the abbey's fortunes declined and the monks were found guilty of fraud and stealing sheep and land. They lost their good name in the locality and a local saying which came to be used was, *to be bad neighbours like the White monks.*

An anonymous poet composed a verse:

A certain friar, to increase his store
Beneath his cloak holy Curig*'s image bore,
And to protect good folk from nightly harm
Another sells Seiriol* as a charm;
But each for luce his good prayers repeats,
And of nine fat cheeses the farmer cheats.

(* Curig and Seiriol were both Welsh saints)

Owain Glyndŵr found that he had many problems with the monks of Cwmhir Abbey and had to punish them and destroy the abbey in 1401. This proved to be the final nail in the abbey's coffin for it never fully recovered.

In 1536, there were only three resident monks at Cwmhir when the value of the abbey was calculated to be only £24 19s 4d. After the Dissolution, the property was kept by the Crown and sold as and when it needed money. The second person to buy some of the abbey's land was John Williams, a relative of Oliver Cromwell. By 1542, much of the abbey's stonework had been removed and used to build and repair other churches such as Llanbister and Llananno. The people of Llanidloes took away five of the pillars while the screen went to Newtown church. By the early 1600's gentry folk such as Richard Folwer had carried away enough material to build his own mansion but who, to his credit, defended the property for the royalist cause during the civil war of the 1640s. Despite their best efforts, the house was unfortunately stormed and wrecked in 1644.

During the Civil War (1642–1649), the abbey was held for Charles I. Sir Thomas Middleton was sent to attack it and take any prisoners. Forty local soldiers were captured but Richard Fowler escaped. Some cannonballs from the period have been found locally. It was thought that they had been dropped by Cromwell's

Fowler was made High Sheriff and another anonymous poet set to work with his tongue in cheek:

Poor Radnorshire, poor Radnorshire,
Never a park and never a Deer,
Never a Squire of £500 a year,
Save Richard Fowler of Abbeycwmhir.

Another effect of the dissolution was that the inhabitants of the local community had to live without a church for about 160 years until the beginning of the eighteenth century.

In 1935, Gildas Tibbott wrote of a photograph of a most interesting document sent from France to the National Library of Wales, in Aberystwyth. The document is a record, in Latin, of grants of land made to Cwmhir Abbey by Madog ap Maelgwn, a Welsh prince from the thirteenth century. Unfortunately, the document was not dated. All that is known is that was presented to Bibliothèque Nationale in Paris in 1886 by Ernest Theodore Hamy, director of the Ethnological Museum in the Trocadero, Paris. It is a vellum document and attached to it a seal, probably dating from the twelfth century showing a warrior on horseback with a helmet, shield and sword. An English translation reads:

To all Christian faithful, both present and future, Madauc the son of Mailgwn gives greeting and peace. Know ye all that I have granted and given as a charity for ever to the monks of Cumhyr, who serve God and the blessed Mary there, the land which is called Brinecrois in its entirety and with all its appurtenances; also the land which is called Cayrwetun equally fully and in its entirety; likewise too, the land which is called Maysecrur with all its appurtenances and its uses in wood and plain, in meadows and waters, in forests and fields, and in respect of all its uses absolutely. These said lands I granted to the above mentioned monks as a permanent gift, free and unhampered by any secular taxes or services, and in the presence of many.

The document was witnessed by the Lord Maredudd the son of Robert; Trahayarn the son of Grifut Weleu; Griffith the son of Heylin; Iorwerth the son of Meyraun and many others. The letters are dated by the hand of the Lord Rired, the abbot in the month of May.

Who was this kind benefactor Madog ap Maelgwn? Nothing is known of him apart from the fact that he was one of the foremost princes of Wales and the date of his death in 1212 when he and two others were hanged in England. The four named witnesses do not figure prominently in Welsh history apart from Maredudd ap Robert, prince of Cedewain, Montgomeryshire who changed his allegiance from King John to Llywelyn in 1212. In 1211 Maredudd was in Chester with five other Welsh princes ready to march with the king's army to attack Llywelyn. In 1212, he supported Llywelyn and three other princes in the successful attacks on the north Wales castles.

Only one other question remains unanswered – How did the original document find its way to Paris? Again no one knows so we can but guess that it was taken by one of the monks at the time of the dissolution as he fled to the Europe in the hope of refuge. What became of the other abbey treasures which were taken at the same time, for the monks must surely have tried to save them all? Again, the answer is blowing in the wind in the Long Valley.

Further Reading
Abbey Cwm Hir. D. S. Davies. Radnorshire Society Transactions. 1934.
Abbey Cwmhir. D. R. Davies. Radnorshire Society Transactions. 1946.
Abbeys, Priories and Cathedrals of Wales. M. Salter. Folly Publications. 2012.
An Abbey – Cwmhir relic abroad. Gildas Tibbott. Radnorshire Society

An Abbey – Cwmhir relic abroad. Gildas Tibbott. Radnorshire Society
Transactions Vol. 5. 1935.

Monastic Wales http://www.monasticwales.org

Name:	**CYMER ABBEY**
	AT A SITE OF BATTLE OR A MEETING OF WATERS
Order:	**Cistercian**
Location:	**off A470, Llanelltyd, Dolgellau, Gwynedd**
OS Map Ref.:	**SH 722195**

According to the University of Wales' Dictionary, the word *cymer* has two possible meanings. One is the confluence of two or more rivers; the second being a meeting-place or a clash of armies. As Cymer Abbey is situated on the east bank of the river Mawddach, near its confluence with Afon Wnion, in Llanelltyd, near Dolgellau the first meaning seems appropriate but on studying a map of the area another river by the name of Afon Gamlan and Cwm Camlan Waterfalls can be seen near Ganllwyd. According to the dictionary *camlan* means a grim battle, giving the second meaning of *cymer* some credibility.

Cymer Abbey was built in 1198/99 of local slate, dolomite and boulders. Fine grained sandstone was used for the carvings. Its mother house was Cwmhir Abbey, in Radnorshire (present day Powys) Gwenwynwyn was burnt down by Henry III in 1241 and royal officials removed all traces of Llywelyn the Last from the abbey in 1282. Owain Cyfeiliog gave lands at Llwydiarth and Cwmcelli, in Powys to the abbey. Edward I passed through Cymer in 1283/84 and gave the monks £5 towards future building work as Cymer was the poorest Cistercian house in Wales. By 1291, almost a hundred years after its founding, it had lands worth £11 14s 11d according to the *Taxatio* of Pope Nicholas IV. Despite its almost empty coffers, Cymer Abbey struggled to exist and survived by rearing sheep, mining and metallurgy. It also kept a noteable stud of horses in readiness for Llywelyn ap Iorwerth (*Llywelyn Fawr*) and by the late thirteenth century was able to grow grain in Gellisarog and Rhydygarnedd. It also had twenty five sheep to look after.

In 1360 the abbot of Cymer was appointed tithe collector for the diocese of Bangor, a tax granted to the King, by the clergy of Canterbury. By 1388 it was home for only five monks.

Although situated on an important site which was the lowest fording place of the estuary, it remained small and unimportant and was nearly always in a state of poverty. Cymer did, however, possess a very large and fine silver gilt chalice and paten, which must have been hidden on the mountainside at the time of the Dissolution. These objects were rediscovered in the nineteenth century and are now in the National Museum of Wales in Cardiff. At the time of its dissolution, probably 16 March 1537, Abbot Lewys of Cymer was granted a pension of £6 13s 4d and appointed Bishop of Shrewsbury.

What survives is only part of an uncompleted thirteenth century church, with an aisled nave. The eastern end was used as the monks' choir until the crossing, transepts and choir could be built. Unfortunately, they never were.

Only a few ruined and degraded walls and a small window, show where the powerful Cistercian Abbey of Kymmer stood. We paid a visit to the spot where it once flourished covering a large space of meadowland near the river.

The Falls, Lakes and Mountains of North Wales.
L. S. Costello. 1845

A few remains of the cloisters and other buildings can be seen but the chapter house remains is in the nearby farmhouse – Tŷ Fanner, which more than likely was also part of the guest house.

SONNET

(In Llanegryn Parish Church is a Rood Screen, carved by the

Mute in the holy stillness of this place,
Great product of an age's careful toil,
A masterpiece of art in every face,
Grave monument to workers of this soil;
The pomp and gorgeous ritual of men's vow,
Rich vestments, incense, odours rare, the gold
Once knew thee in a solemn mass – but now,
In mystic silence rest; Thy tale is told.
Yet in th' obscure and quiet teach us still,
While petty quarrels run their futile course.
That there embedded in the mighty hill,
Memorial none to power nor brutal Force
But Peace engraven in the very wood
The Peace of patient labour and of good.

J. Alban Evans

Cymer Abbey, in its present condition, has been described thus by an unknown writer on the World Wide Web:

The ruins are underwhelming, but the secluded location provides a tranquil and picturesque setting that lends an evocative atmosphere to the site. Cymer Abbey is probably not worth making any great effort to visit, but it's worthy of a short detour if you find yourself in the area.

Further Reading

A Tour of the Abbeys, Priories and Cathedrals of Wales. D. S. Yerburgh. Yerburgh. 1999.

Gwynedd. F. Lynch. HMSO London. 1995.

History of Merioneth. Vol. II. J. & Ll. Beverly Smith. Merioneth Historical & Record Society. University of Wales Press. 2001.

Welsh Outlook. March 1930.

http://www.isleofaslbion.co.uk

Name: **DORE ABBEY**
                   OVER THE BORDER
Order: Cistercian
Location: **nr. Ewyas Harold, Herefordshire HR2 0AA**
OS Map Ref.: **SO 3870 3045**

Dore Abbey, a Cistercian settlement, close to the Welsh border in Herefordshire's Golden Valley (the valley of the river Dore), was founded in 1147 by Robert, son of Harold of Ewyas and grandson of William I. It was the only Cistercian monastery to be founded directly from Morimond in France. The church was begun in 1175 and consecrated one century later. The consecration was conducted by St Thomas Cantilupe, Bishop of Hereford despite the objections of the Bishop of St Davids, who claimed jurisdiction over the area. Cantilupe had expected trouble and posted armed guards around the church!

The monks raised sheep, and their fleece or wool was exported as far as Italy. The abbey's position, being close to the Welsh border, meant that it was attacked quite often by Welsh raiders. In 1405 the abbey narrowly avoided being sacked by Owain Glyndŵr.

Most of the original buildings have long disappeared but the present church was begun in c.1180. The Abbey was closed in 1535 and the accompanying lands were granted to the Scudamore family but the site soon fell into ruins. In 1633 the building was extensively renovated by John, Viscount Scudamore and the church was re-dedicated in 1634 as a parish church. Tree ring analysis show that re-used timbers was used in the restoration; some were timbers felled in 1205–1238, others were timbers dating to a few decades before the 1633 restoration. The interior was refurbished with magnificently carved oak, a fine restoration; some were timbers felled in 1205–1238, others were timbers dating to a few decades before the 1633 restoration. The interior was refurbished with magnificently carved oak, a fine Renaissance screen inserted, and many windows replaced with seventeenth century stained glass. There are suggestions that Scudamore had a pang of conscience about inheriting church lands and felt he should give something back to the community. Whatever the reason (some say that it was his lack of a male heir that troubled him), with the help of his friend William Laud (who later became an Archbishop of Canterbury), in 1630 John Scudamore carried out a restoration. In hope of producing an heir, Viscount John restored the abbey as a parish church, and it was reconsecrated in 1634. His next child was a son, who lived to adulthood!

Around 1700 the church underwent another restoration, when a number of paintings were added onto the walls. In 1900 the church was again rebuilt. The current church is only the original presbytery dating from the twelfth century. Inside can be seen a collection of elaborately carved stone roof bosses. One shows the Abbot of Dore kneeeling before the Virgin and Child. The church also has a carved Carolean screen made by John Abel showing the arms of Charles I, Archbishop Laud, and Viscount Scudamore.

In the late nineteenth century, Roland Paul excavated and made measured drawings of all the foundations of the abbey buildings and monastic quarters on northern side of church. The north side of northern transept is roofless. The Chapter house is entered by vestibule on northern side of sacristy. North of the northern aisle is the kitchen garden. To the north of the garden, about 84 feet west of the present western face of the church and running northwards from kitchen garden wall is substantial aged wall nearly 100 feet long. At its southern end it is 2 feet 9 inches thick and at the northern end 4 feet 4 inches. It probably formed part of the west wall of the frater.

The monastic chapterhouse has almost entirely disappeared. To the north of the northern transept was the east range and first a sacristy whose tunnel vault can still be seen indicated in the transept wall. In the west wall was a book cupboard open to the cloister walk. To the north is the vestibule to the twelve sided Chapter House (one of only two in Britain) which had a central column. Above the east range was the dormitory. Slight traces of the wall of the northern range still exist. Between the cloister and the western range ran a lane. About 180 feet east of the dormitory stood another building, probably the infirmary.

A Geophysical survey and archaeological excavation were carried out in 2009 in conjunction with repairs to the nave and cloister walls. A trench within the cloister garth, showed evidence of a collapsed building with some stones that had been heated to a high temperature, supporting the theory that the kitchens may have been located here. Another trench excavation showed two sandstone walls which were not contemporary with each other. One joined the north wall of the nave, and the other was most probably built at the same time as the nave. Another trench, located within the eastern cloister walk, exposed a grave containing a buried body consisting of the entire skeleton of a mature adult, probably between 25 and 35 years of age.

Further Reading
Dore Abbey. R. Shoesmith & R. E. Richardson.

Name:	**GRACE DIEU**
	THE LAST OF ITS TYPE
Order:	Cistercian

Location: **3 miles west of Monmouth, Gwent – exact site unkown.**

No-one knows the exact site of Grace Dieu Abbey but, after excavations, archaeologists believe it was on the east bank of the river Troddi. Offa's Dyke Path passes nearby. In 1217 John, Lord of Monmouth (d. 1248) raised the possibility of founding a new community with monks from Dore abbey but it took until 1226 for a colony of monks to finally settle at Grace Dieu. The delay was thought to have been caused by local unrest and a lack of the benefactor's money. It was one of three Dore daughter abbeys; Trawscoed in Wales, Grace Dieu (1226), and Vale Royal (1274).

The abbey was finally founded in 1226 by John. Monks from the Cistercian order were sent from Dore Abbey, in Herefordshire. It was a small, poor house (*Pwros* in Welsh.) It did not make much of an impression during its lifetime, compared to other abbeys close by such as Cwmhir, Llantarnam or Tintern because of the remoteness of its site and because of poverty. The local Welsh people maintained that Grace Dieu occupied land which had been seized illegally from them. The abbey was attacked several times. In 1232 the abbot and a monk were kidnapped and held captive. The monk was wounded and another summoned to take his place. The abbot and substitute monk eventually escaped by stuffing hay into their cowls, which they posed in a praying position. Their captors only realised the figures were dummies after the abbot and monk had got clean away.

The abbey was destroyed by the Welsh during a raid by Llywelyn ap Iorwerth and Richard Marshall, Earl of Pembroke in 1233 when they rebelled against Henry III, and the monks were forced to take refuge at nearby White Castle. The abbey was re-established in 1236, on the other bank of the river, within easier reach of the English centre of Monmouth. John had managed to secure the monks a new location and the community began rebuilding the abbey. Henry III allowed them a grant of twenty trees from the Forest of Dean to rebuild their house. In 1236 they moved from their original site to the site on the river Troddi bank. More trees were given by Henry III in 1240, this time from the Grosmont Forest and another two trees from Seinfremy Wood in 1253. Still the troubles continued to such an extent that another move was proposed in 1276. In 1351, Hugh, the abbey's abbot, expressed a desire to resign as he found the arguments with the monastery's neighbours too much to endure. He was well provided for in his retirement and had his own private chambers at the abbey; he ate with the new abbot and, like him, was permitted to speak anywhere. Hugh was also allowed to have at least one servant and an annual pension of £20. In 1484 John Mitulton resigned from the abbacy on account of the persecution by his enemies.

The community had little luck at its new site and forty years later Edmund of Lancaster, also known as Edmund Crouchback, lord of Monmouth, proposed moving the abbey yet again. It is not known whether a second move took place, but it is clear that Grace Dieu remained one of the poorest Cistercian houses in Britain.

This parish was known in Welsh as *Llangatwg Feibion Afel*, anglicised as Llangattock Vibion Avel (now Llangattock-Vibon-Avel). In 1254 it was written as Lancadok Avel, as Lankadok Webonawel in 1350, and Llangotocke Vybon Ave'll in 1535. The name describes the church of Cadog and the sons of Afel.

By 1535 the abbey's annual income was just over £19, lower than at any other Cistercian abbey in Wales or England. After the Dissolution of the Monasteries in 1536 Grace Dieu fell into ruin. Archaeologists have been unable to establish precisely where the buildings stood.

Grace Dieu was the last Cistercian foundation in Wales and also

Grace Dieu was the last Cistercian foundation in Wales and also the least well known. The abbey appears to have been wrecked by the Welsh in 1233, who claimed that the abbey site was on land that rightfully belonged to them. The abbey was dissolved on 3 September 1536 with the smaller monasteries and it was afterwards left to ruin. The site was acquired by the Herberts of Wonastow. By today the site of the abbey cannot be precisely fixed but it is thought to be marked by slight earthworks in Abbey Meadow, on the east bank of the river Troddi.

Some of the known abbots of Grace Dieu included:

John: abbot in March 1236 but was no longer officiating as abbot in the November.

Walter: abbot in July 1236.

Roger: abbot in August 1246.

William: abbot of Grace Dieu in 1267.

Warin: abbot in August and September 1281.

Robert: abbot in 1350 and May 1351.

Hugh or possibly Roger of Chepstow: ?–1351, he resigned in July.

John Wysbeche: abbot of Grace Dieu before 1387. Subsequently abbot of Tintern, from 1387 until 1407.

Richard Clifford: abbot of Grace Dieu on 1 May 1447. Previously abbot of Dore in Herefordshire.

John Mitulton: ?–1484: abbot in 1473 and on 31 August 1484 is described as having resigned from office.

Richard Dorston: abbot in May 1486 and March 1488. He had left office by 1495 when he was abbot of Dore.

Stephen Green (Grene): abbot of Grace Dieu in March and December 1515 but left office by 1521 to become abbot of Buildwas.

John Ryldos (Byldos): abbot in 1530.

John Rothwell (Rowthwelle): had left office by September

1535; awarded a pension as former abbot of Grace Dieu.
William Ipsley: abbot in September 1533. Had been a monk of
Flaxley Abbey, Gloucestershire.
Thomas Perptn (Perpym): left office by December 1534 and
granted a pension as the former abbot.
John Griffith/Griffiths: final abbot of Grace Dieu, from August
1534 until the dissolution in September 1536. John may have
formerly been abbot of Margam

Further Reading
Monastic Wales http://www.monasticwales.org

Name:	**LLANLLUGAN ABBEY**
	CISTERCIAN STAINED GLASS
Order:	**Cistercian Nuns**
Location:	**Llanllugan, Powys SY21**
OS Map Ref.:	**SJ 058022**

Llanllugan Abbey in Powys was a monastery of Cistercian nuns,
one of only two women's monasteries in Wales. It was founded
around 1188 on land donated by Maredudd ap Robert, Lord of
Cedewain, and was founded as a dependency of the Cistercian
monks at the Abbey of Strata Marcella. Maredudd ap Rhobert
granted the nunnery the whole vill of Llanllugan, Talhalun, and
other lands circa 1216–17. The nunnery acquired other lands from
lords of Powys Wenwynwyn or their tenants.

In the fifteenth century the convent had a wealthy patron in
Richard, Duke of York, father of kings Edward IV and Richard III.
Richard probably donated the stained glass to the church, dated
1453 with an inscription *Orate pro bono...qui fecit fabrica*. It is
recognised as a most important example of medieaval glass. The

Crucifixion, which depicts a scatter of bones at the base of the cross, including a crude skull which dates the window to the fifteenth century. The glass also depicts a jawbone of an ass which would have stood originally in close association with the figure of the crucified Jesus; this image would have provided a subtle reference to the resurrection and triumph of life and love. The figure of Jesus is shown at the moment of death, naked but for a waistcloth, hands clenched, wearing the crown of throns. There are now no accompanying figures, but in the original arrangement the Virgin Mary and John the Evangelist would have been depicted. A figure of John does survive, now placed incorrectly in one of the small upper lights. The apostle is shown as a beardless young man, holding the palm given him by the Virgin Mary to carry before her coffin at her funeral and bearing a chalice from which a serpent or snake emerges. Two angels also exist. The final complete figure of the scheme is perhaps the best known: the kneeling nun. The Llanllugan nun is a very important figure, painted in great detail; her mantle and habit are very carefully and skilfully delineated (despite the fact that some experts have commented on her big nose!). She is shown kneeling and in an attitude of prayer, but she is not the donor of the glass. The most likely explanation is that it is a depiction of the convent superior in office at the time that the glass was put in place. A fragment of the representation of John the Baptist also exists. The community probably possessed glazed windows in the chapter room, refectory and the superior's chamber, as well as in the church.

The monastery church serves as the parish church of Llanllugan but the site of the abbey buildings remains uncertain: they might have been in a meadow 200 metres to the south of the church but very little archaeological evidence survives from the site of the abbey.

Dafydd ap Gwilym wrote a poem – *Cyrchu Lleian* (Wooing a nun) about his love life. His lover, Morfudd, may have been the nun in question and could have been sent to the abbey by her father to keep her out of harm's way. Dafydd's poem (written before the Black Death) suggests there were some sixty nuns at the abbey but there were never more than a dozen there. The abbey was small: only four nuns and an abbess were recorded in 1377, and it might have been closed before the Dissolution of the Monasteries when its annual income was only £21.

> *LLANLLIGAN, or LLANLLUGAN (LLAN-LLUGAN), a parish in the lower division of the hundred of NEWTOWN, county of MONTGOMERY, NORTH WALES, 4 miles (S. W.) from Llanvair, containing 361 inhabitants. This place is distinguished as the site of an ancient Cistercian nunnery, which, according to Bishop Tanner, was founded here prior to the year 1239, at which time the tithes of the parish of Llanvair Caereinion were given by Bishop Hugh to the "nuns of Llanllugan in Powys," to whom also the tithes of the parishes of Llanllwchaiarn and Bettws were subsequently appropriated by Anian, Bishop of St Asaph, in 1265. This establishment, of which the founder is not known, had, at the dissolution, a revenue estimated at £ 22. 13. 8.: the site was granted, in the 37th of Henry VIII., to Sir Arthur D'Arcy, Knt.: the only remains are some fragments of painted glass in the chancel window of the parish church.*

Further Reading

A Topographical Dictionary of Wales. Samuel Lewis. 1833.
Medieval Religious Houses in England and Wales. D. Knowles, R. N.

Medieval Religious Houses in England and Wales. D. Knowles, R. N. Hadcock. Longman. 1971.

Monastic Wales http://www.monasticwales.org

Name:	LLANLLŶR PRIORY
	'WHERE GLORY REIGNED'
Order:	**Cistercian Nunnery**
Location:	**on private land, Llanfihangel Ystrad, Cardiganshire.**
OS Map Ref.:	**SN 542560**

Llanllŷr Priory, a Cistercian nunnery and dedicated to The Blessed Virgin Mary, was founded in c.1180/ 90 by Lord Rhys ap Gruffudd in the Aeron valley. The site was remote and uncomfortable. There may well have been an earlier settlement in the area. Llanllyr has one of the earliest inscribed stones in Wales, recording the gift of a patch of waste land belonging to Ditoc, which Occon son of Asaitgen gave to Madomnuac. These are Irish names and Madomnuac was possibly a priest, possibly the head of a religious community.

It became a mansion house during the post-medieval period but has now disappeared completely although traces of the chapel/church, and a cemetery enclosure, were visible until the late 19th century.

Abbess Anne from the fifteenth century is described in the poetical works of Huw Cae Llwyd (fl. 1431–1504); he mentions her wish for an ape!

Nothing is now left of the abbey apart from a carved beam over the fireplace at Gwernfyda, to the south-west. The site is occupied by a large Victorian house set in landscaped gardens of formal ponds and fountains. The present owners are the direct descendants of the family (William Sackville and John Dudley) who bought the site and land at the Dissolution on 26 February 1537.

As there are few signs of the abbey left, only local people would have known about it had it not been for the work of Rhiannon Davies Jones, a Welsh historical novelist. Her novel about Sister Anna, one of the nuns, possibly an abbess of Llanllŷr won the Literary Medal at the Swansea National Eisteddfod of Wales 1964 with high and deserved praise. Although only very few facts are disclosed about the priory, we learn a great deal about life in such an establishment. We are told that there was a barn, cloister, cloister house, fish pond, garden, kitchen, mill, orchard, refectory, scriptorium, stable and a well but that it was a poor house, well out of the way and off the main roads. Very little else is said about the buildings but the life of a nun through the eyes of Sister Anna is fully described.

Further Reading
Lleian Llanllŷr. Rh. Davies Jones. Gwasg y March Gwyn. 1965.
Monastic Wales http://www.monasticwales.org

Name:	LLANTARNAM ABBEY
	AN OASIS OF TRANQUILLITY AND PRAYER
Order:	Cistercian
Location:	Llantarnam, Cwmbran, Torfaen, Gwent NP44
OS Map Ref.:	ST 311930

Llantarnam is but one of many names the village has been known by. In the twelfth century it was known as Nant Thirnon (the stream or valley of Teyrnon). Later it became Llanfihnagel Llantarnam, named after the church of St Michael near the abbey.

near the crossroads); Croes y Mwylach (black-bird cross) and Llanfihangel y Fynachlog (the church of St Michael by the abbey).

Llantarnam Abbey, in Monmouthsire was a Cistercian abbey founded in 1170 by Hywel ap Iorwerth.

He proclaimed:

Be it known to all the faithful of the Church of God that I, Hywel ap Iorweth, son of Owen, for the salvation of my soul and that of my parents and predecessors, I have settled the White Monks at Llantarnam and given the lands to the White Monks.

Some historians are of the opinion that the original abbey was situated at Caerleon or Pentre-bach and relocated to Llantarnam but Caerleon Abbey and Llantarnam Abbey were the same. A mandate addressed to *The Abbot of St Mary's Llantarnam* and other documents refer to *the monastery of the Blessed Virgin of Karelyn (Caerleon) alias Llantarnam.*

Although only six monks lived, prayed and worked at the abbey it had a yearly income of £71 3s 2d. and prospered though it came into dispute with Tintern and Margam abbeys. The names of the monks suggests that is was a predomianately Welsh abbey, as opposed to many Anglicised settlements found elsewhere in Gwent.

A dispute arose between the monks and the Earl of Gloucester, Gilbert de Clare. Around 1272, the abbey was at the mercy of de Clare and its possessions had been considerably reduced because *wild animals had devoured the land*. The *wild animals* could well be a sarcastic comment about the earl and his behaviour towards the church.

By 1291, Llantarnam was continuing to prosper and had fourteen granges or farms to its name in Gwent and Glamorgan which included one at Penrhys in the Rhondda Valley. A grange together with a small chapel was built there for a small community of monks. It is believed that the monks at Penrhys grew medicinal herbs for use in the infirmary at Llantarnam. At Penrhys too, was a well dedicated to the Virgin Mary, known locally as *Ffynnon Fair* or Mary's Well. Today, the area at Penrhys is still known as *Craig Rhiw Mynach* or Monks' Ridge Rock and a seventeen foot high Portland stone statue of the Virgin Mary and the Holy well is the focus of pilgrims to the area.

Another grange was established at Cillonydd, on the slopes of *Mynydd Maen* (rocky mountain). It was used to rear sheep. In 1291 a record from the *Taxatio Ecclesiastica* states that 588 sheep were reared on land belonging to the abbey, some of which must have been at Cillonydd. This was a relatively small number compared to 3,264 sheep on Tintern Abbey land and 5,285 on Margam Abbey land but another Gwent Cistercian abbey at Grace Dieu had only twenty two sheep. The wool from Llantarnam was not of the best quality and only a few sacks were exported to Europe. During the fourteenth century the abbey suffered badly from different agricultural problems and only twenty monks could eke out a living. Things got no better when they supported Owain Glyndŵr; his supporters had confessed to and had been absolved of their sins by the abbot. It was recorded that during the late twelfth century that Llantarnam was a community of sixty monks, although the numbers had dropped to twenty by 1317. This was probably a result of the damaging effects of the revolt of Llywelyn Bren which took place in 1316.

After the Reformation the abbey was dissolved and during the reign of Elizabeth I it was demolished with the materials used to build a mansion, later named Pentrebach, on the site for the Morgan family of Kilsant. William, son of John Morgan was the first owner. At that time only the stone cells of the abbey remained but they were converted into stables. The Gothic gateway – *Magna Porta* stood on the site together with a porch dated 1588 and on it the shield of the Morgan family. In the hall, the great dated 1588 and on it the shield of the Morgan family. In the hall, the great chimney had a memorial inscription to *Vindutius*, a Roman soldier of the Second Augustan Legion, aged 45.

William Morgan, a devout Catholic, maintained a Catholic Chapel in the house. He faithfully paid the fines for non-attendance at the Established Church and eventually paid a large sum to be exempted from having to pay further fines. Lady Frances Morgan, an aunt of The Jesuit Martyr, St David Lewis, married a descendant of William Morgan and lived at Llantarnam until her death in 1676. The property passed to her son, Sir Edward who, although a Deputy Lieutenant and a Justice of the Peace, kept to the Old Faith. He also kept a Catholic Chapel which was frequently crowded with Catholics of the surrounding area. In 1670, the priest hunter, John Arnold, informed the House of Lords, that:

At Llantarnam, an eminent papist's house in Monmouthshire, there is a room fitted up chapel wise for saying of Mass where Fr David Lewis, a popish priest, hath said Mass for many years past.

For several years Fr Lewis lived at Llantarnam Abbey with his relatives and ministered to the local Catholics. To avoid endangering his relatives, the priest moved to a cottage adjoining the blacksmith's opposite the church of St Michael, Llantarnam. However, Fr Lewis continued to say Mass in the Morgans' Chapel. David Lewis, one of the Forty Martyrs of England and Wales was captured outside the Abbey grounds and martyred at Usk on 27 August 1679. His portrait hangs in the Chapel corridor of the present day abbey.

Edward Morgan (one of William's descendants) added to the house. The Morgan family helped to establish the Jesuits, on their return to Wales, at the Cwm near Monmouth.

No other work was done to the abbey till the nineteenth century. Reginald James Blewitt, a relation by marriage to the

Morgans, restored the property in 1836. The abbey estate passed down into the hands of Edmiund Blewitt, of Saltford and Charles Fettilace, of Swinebrook, Oxfordshire. The Blewitt family were bankers, newspaper magnets and politicians but not very successful businessmen. They were not very good managers and the estate was heavily mortgaged. After Blewitt's death Clifford Cory J. P. bought the Estate and after his death the property was sold to the Government.

During the Second World War, the property was used as a storage centre for RAF uniforms. In 1946 it was bought by the Sisters of St Joseph of Annecy and is home to a large community of Sisters. *Tŷ Croeso* (Welcome House), the Retreat Centre is part of the Abbey buildings. The Sisters farm the adjoining land and their order is well known for teaching, nursing and working in prisons and parishes.

The surviving literary works from Llantarnam abbey include St Gregory's Homilies and a late copy of a set of Chester annals.

Further Reading

A post-dissolution monastic site and its landscape. David Jones. Gwent
     local history (the journal of Gwent Local Cambria Magazine).
History Council. Robert Weeks. Spring. 2002.
Dictionary of the Place Names of Wales. H. W. Owen & R. Morgan.
     Gomer Press. 2007.
Monastic Wales http://www.monasticwales.org

Name:	**MAENAN ABBEY**
	WHERE AN OLD DRAIN THREW NEW LIGHT ON AN ANCIENT ABBEY
Order:	**Cistercian**
Location:	**Maenan Abbey Hotel, Maenan, Llanrwst, Conwy**

OS Map Ref.: SH 7899655

Driving through the Conwy Valley from Conwy towards Llanrwst and Betws-y-coed, one follows the Conwy river past the Maenan Abbey Hotel and Caravan Park. Passing traffic gives little thought to its history which stretches back to at least 1277.

In 1186, a Cistercian community was founded at Rhedynog Felen near Caernarfon by a group of monks from Strata Florida Abbey. They moved to Conwy in 1190/91 and established Aberconwy Abbey. In 1283, Edward I began work on his 'ring of steel', defensive castles in north Wales on the site of the abbey in Aberconwy and where the new walled town would be situated.

Edward stayed at the monastery for a short time during the spring of 1283, whilst the building work was in progress and gave the monks £100 in compensation and a set of glass windows for damage sustained during the war. They were also given land and money for building materials on a new site at Maenan. The new abbey was dedicated to Saint Mary and All Saints. It became one of the most powerful in the land, owning 38,000 acres of land. It was also the burial place for a number of Welsh princes including Llywelyn Fawr (The Great).

Edward again moved the community to the abbey at Vale Royal in Cheshire, but the abbey at Maenan continued to exist until it was closed in March 1537 as part of Henry VIII's dissolution of the monasteries. Much of the stonework was demolished and recycled in the repairs of Caernarfon Castle and the glass, lead, slate and timber sold to the local gentry who were building their own homes in the valley. Llywelyn Fawr's stone sarcophagus was lost for many years until half of it was recovered from the Conwy river in Llanrwst. What remains of it now is in St Grwst, Llanrwst parish church.

In the 15th century the abbot, John ap Rhys, became involved in an argument with the abbot and monks of Strata Florida Abbey and led some of his own Maenan monks and some soldiers on a raid on that abbey. Maenan Abbey was valued at £162 in 1535.

In 1563, the site of the abbey was given to Elizeus Wynne, who was also granted the township of Maenan. He demolished many of the abbey's buildings, and used the materials to construct a new mansion for himself on the site. What remained of the stones and other materials were used in nearby Gwydir Castle. Very little of the original twelfth century stone work remains apart from a small arch, which was described by Samuel Lewis in his *Topographical Dictionary* as:

> remarkable for the pleasantness of its situation and the beauty of its architecture.

Sir William Dugdale (12 September 1605–10 February 1686) says of Maenan Abbey and its history in his book *Monasticon Anglicanum or The History Of the Ancient Abbies, and other Monasteries, Hospitals, Cathedral and Collegiate Churches, in England and Wales*. (1655–1673):

> In 26 Henry VIII, the revenues of Conway, otherwise Maynan Abbey, amounted in clear income to £162 15s., in gross revenue to £179 10s. 10d. The site was granted in the fifth year of Queen Elizabeth to Elizaeus Wynne, in whose family it still continues, Lord Newborough being the present owner. A large house built from the materials of the abbey still remains.

Information in the Pedigree of Wynne of Garthewin, states that:

> William Wynne of Melai married Mary, heiress of Maenan Abbey, being daughter and co-heir of Sir Richard Clough of Plas Clough, co. Denbigh. She died in 1632, and the abbey descended in the male line to John Wynne of Melai and Maenan, Sheriff of Denbighshire in 1712, who married Sydney, second daughter of

Denbighshire in 1712, who married Sydney, second daughter of Sir William Williams of Llanvorda, by whom he left two co-heirs, of whom Jane, the elder, married Sir John Wynn of Bodvean, and was so mother of Thomas Wynn, created Lord Newborough, 23 July 1776.

The grounds were excavated in 1963 and the site developed into the Maenan Abbey Hotel and, later, Caravan Park. In 2011, while workmen were working on the drains in the grounds of the hotel, three medieval walls were found. It is thought that they are early cloister walls, about 6 feet thick, and dated to 1282. The grounds are a scheduled ancient monument, because of the importance of the abbey in its day.

Further Reading

A Topographical Dictionary of Wales. Samuel Lewis. 1849
Crwydro Arfon. A. Llywelyn-Williams. Llyfrau'r Dryw. 1959.
Monastic Wales http://www.monasticwales.org
The Cistercian Abbeys of Britain. Ed.: D. Robinson. London. 1998.

Name:	**MARGAM ABBEY**
	AN ORANGERY ON THE SITE OF THE REFECTORY
Order:	**Cistercian**
Location:	**Margam Abbey, Margam, Port Talbot, Neath Port Talbot SA13 2TA**
OS Map Ref.:	**SS 791863**

Margam is famous for many things but mostly for its steel works, chimneys, blast furnaces and cooling towers. It is also close to Port Talbot and to Junction 39 of the M4 motorway should anyone feel the need to escape from such industrial sights. Much earlier than the time of the Industrial Revolution, when the need for coal dominated, Margam was a Welsh community, in the shadow of Margam Abbey. The parish church continues to operate from the nave of Margam Abbey.

The meaning of the word Margam is unknown but is thought to be the name of a saint.

The place is generally supposed to have derived its name from Mawrgan, the son of Caradoc ab Iestyn, about the year 1200, who with his brothers Cadwallon and Meriadoc, confirmed by charter their father's benefactions to the Abbey. From some old records, the earliest name of the place was Peridar, from the oak-crowned hills or headlands at the end of which the old Abbey was erected.

Robert, earl of Gloucester, founded Margam Abbey a very short time before his death and it was a few weeks later that the first colony of monks arrived from Clairvaux. Robert of Gloucester (the bastard son of King Henry I, half-brother of the Empress Matilda) was a very wealthy man and allocated to the abbey a site of 18,000 acres on the west coast of Glamorgan, '*all the land between the Kenfig and Afan rivers from the brow of the mountains to the sea*'. Over the next century the monks acquired a number of estates across the Vale and border of Glamorgan and by 1291 the abbey had an annual income of £256, making it the richest monastic house in Wales. At this time the abbey was farming nearly 7000 acres of land and reared 5,285 sheep. During its earlier years Margam Abbey was known as a house of good repute. *Giraldus Cambrensis* described Abbot Cynan *as a learned man and one discreet in his behaviour.* He added that *of all the houses belonging to the Cistercian Order in Wales this was by far the most renowned for alms and charity.*

This monastery under the direction of Cynan, a learned and prudent abbot, was at this time more celebrated for its charitable deeds than any other in Wales. On this account it is an undoubted fact that as a reward for that abundant charity, which the monastery had always, in time of need, exercised towards strangers and poor persons in a season of approaching famine, their corn and provisions were perceptibly, by divine assistance, increased like the Widow's cruise of oil by means of the prophet Elijah.

Giraldus must have enjoyed his overnight stay at Margam Abbey on Wednesday, 16 March 1188 and he left with a treasure trove of stories and fables. He was told of the young Welshman who claimed that land donated to the abbey belonged to him. Inspired by the Devil, he set light to the best barn belonging to the monks as it was piled high with corn. Soon after he lost his reason and went completely mad, howling like a dog. His relatives had to tie him up in chains but he broke free and ran to the abbey gates and howled even louder, where he died a few days later still howling.

Another story which surely appealed to *Giraldus* was that of the young man who was hit by someone in the refectory of the abbey guest house. No one owned up but the next morning the guilty monk was found dead on the very spot where the 'crime' was committed.

In the twelfth century, stories of miracles were sure to appeal to everyone and Margam Abbey had its own miracle story to tell. At a time of a serious famine, the local population were near starving and desperate for food. The monks of the abbey sent a boat over the channel to Bristol to purchase a supply of corn. Unfortunately, the boat was delayed for many days by cross winds and unable to make the return journey. On the day food finally ran out at Margam, a nearby corn field was found to be ready for reaping, a full month before time. God provided them with enough grain to last until autumn.

Such stories made good reading but were almost lost. To find out how, read the next chapter.

The other story that Gerald chronicled was one of murder and divine revenge. Caradog ap Iestyn and his wife Gwladys Rhys had four sons, Morgan, Maredudd, Owain and Cadwallon. In 1175 Cadwallon murdered his brother Owain but according to the master storyteller, *The wrath of God caught up with him*. Owain had a greyhound, a tall, handsome, multi-coloured dog. The dog tried to defend his master but was severely injured in seven places after being shot with arrows and prodded with spears. But it was a strong dog and he turned on Owain's attackers, biting them and scratching them as best he could. Owain lay dead and the dog stayed with his master. Cadwallon moved on to lead an assault on a nearby castle but one of the castle walls collapsed and killed him. The nameless but faithful dog recovered but was covered in scars. William, earl of Gloucester took him and presented it as a gift and a sign of loyalty to Henry ll.

The lay-brothers posed particular problems for Margam Abbey and in 1190 the abbot of Margam and his community were punished as they had not observed the Chapter's prohibition of beer. Other misdemeanours took place at Margam in 1190–1, and the abbot was given forty days penance and ordered to send two of his *conversi* to Clairvaux to do regular satisfaction. A serious revolt of the lay-brothers occurred in 1206. They formed a conspiracy and rose against the abbot, pulling the cellarer from his horse and chasing the abbot for twenty six miles from the abbey. They then barricaded themselves in the dormitory and refused food for the monks. Fountains Abbey stepped in and the guilty were made to walk all the way to Clairvaux as punishment. The ring leaders were sent to various other Cistercian houses. The monastery suffered badly during the rebellion of Owain Glyndŵr in the fifteenth century when the monks were reduced to wandering about like beggars.

In 1210, King John stayed at the abbey with his army en route to Ireland, and again on his return three months later. In return for the kindness shown to him by the monks the king spared

Margam from the taxes he imposed on other houses. Margam and John's foundation of Beaulieu were the only two houses to escape King John's taxes. One of the Margam abbots, John Delaware, became the thirty-ninth bishop of Llandaff, and died June 30th, 1256.

A letter sent to the Pope in 1412 stated:

that 'Margam Abbey is utterly destroyed, so that its abbot and monks are obliged to wander around like so many vagabonds.

Two reasons given for this state of affairs were:

1. The Hundred Years War with France, which led to heavy taxation and devaluation of the currency. Cistercian houses like Margam were also cut off from their mother house in Citeaux, France.
2. The Black Death. Repeated outbreaks of the plague led to the deaths of many of the monks and the local population. Farm animals died which led to a drop in the abbey's revenues. There was much less call and demand for agricultural products and this in turn made it difficult to recruit labour making a continuous circle of events which took many decades to resolve.

A document from 1384 sets out the difficulties faced by Margam Abbey:

1. The cost of the abbey's hospitality was very high.
2. The best lands near the sea had been flooded.
3. It had lost much of its livestock.
4. Heavy taxes.
5. Expensive lawsuits.
6. Debts.
7. The effects of Owain Glyndŵr's Rebellion.

   The aftermath of the rebellion was a time of acute trauma and distress. Buildings were shattered, estates devasted, and tennats dispersed. Monks were sharply reduced in numbers and morale, their discipline was sadly undermined, and their routines of *prayer and worship badly disrupted. Monastic life had touched nearer rock bottom than at any other time in the Middle Ages.*

That Margam Abbey functioned until 1538 is due to one man in particular – Thomas Franklin, abbot of Neath before being appointed Abbot of Margam 1441 to 1460. He restored both abbeys to their former glory. Thomas ap Ieuan ap Rhys, a Glamorgan poet, sang the abbey's praises and said that not only had he been born in the parish of Margam; that he was also christened there and that is where he wished to be buried.

He compared the abbey very favourably with that of Gloucester and that the Margam abbot was the best there had been since the days of Benedict himself.

Not since the days of Benedict has there been
Such a worthy wearer of the white habit.

(Translated form Welsh)

Ni bu bais wen, am dan berchen
Lanach dan gred wedi Bened.)

The good times soon came to an end and the abbot of Neath– Thomas Leyshon, was forced to dismiss the followers of Thomas Franklin. On 20 June 1536 the abbey was put in the king's name and on 23 August 1536, the abbot and monks were dismissed. The abbey seal was broken and the site taken over by Sir Rhys Mansell, a future owner who paid £2482 13s. 1d. (£422,796.00 in 2013) for the property.

At the time of the Dissolution the annual income of the abbey was £181 and only eight monks remained at the monastery. The abbey was dissolved in 1536 and the monks dispersed. Following the Dissolution the nave of the church was given over to the parish for its own use and the abbey buildings were sold. The construction of a large mansion was begun during the sixteenth century but was swept away during the eighteenth century to make way for a garden dominated by an orangery which houses a collection of orange, lemon and other citrus trees. The orangery supposedly occupies the site of the refectory of the old abbey. It was, at one time, the largest orange house in the world, being 827 feet long, 81 feet broad and about 20 feet high. Built between 1787 and 1793 at a cost of £16,000, after many alterations, it is still the longest orangery in Britain. The original trees were brought from Italy by Sir Henry Wilson, as a present for Charles I (there is another version) but the ship conveying them to England was reported to have been steered, through error, into the Bristol Channel, instead of the English Channel, and became a wreck on the coast of Glamorgan, opposite the demesnes of Margam. The lord of the manor carefully collected the trees, brought them to the mansion, intending to present them to Charles, after the Civil War but he never received them. The trees were retained until the time of Queen Anne, who made a present of them to the then owner of Margam, Sir Thomas Mansel, who was comptroller of the Queen's Household.

As a building the Orangery is long and narrow with a series of twenty seven tall windows to admit the winter light. The plain back wall contained fireplaces, from which hot air passed through flues. In its centre was the high door through which fully-grown trees could be wheeled into the garden. A collection of orange trees was maintained at Margam up to the beginning of the Second World War when the Orangery was needed for military use and was occupied by American forces. The trees had to be left outside and failed to survive the winter weather. After the end of the war, a new collection of citrus trees was formed. In 1973, when the estate was purchased by Glamorgan County Council, the Orangery was in ruins. It was restored and re-opened by the Queen in her Silver Jubilee Year. Part still remains an Orangery and is used for exhibitions. The eastern end (the Grove) still houses a small collection of orange trees.

The nave was restored at the beginning of the nineteenth century which is now used as a parish church. Other remains of the abbey include the twelve-sided chapter-house and vestibule.

Several important literary works have survived from Margam Abbey's library. The Annals *de Margam* is one of the most valuable surviving Welsh monastic chronicles. It begins with the death of Edward the Confessor and breaks off abruptly in 1232. From the year 1185 onwards the chronicle has been regarded as one of the most valuable sources for Glamorgan history. The 'Book of Taliesin', one of the 'Four Ancient Books of Wales', has also been ascribed to Margam Abbey. Margam Abbey library also possessed a copy of Domesday Book and a complete volume containing two works by William of Malmesbury the *Gesta Regum* (History of the Kings) and the *Historia Novella* (*Historical Novels*) and Geoffrey of Monmouth's *Historia Regum Britanniae* (History of the Kings of Britain).

After the time of the last abbot of Margam Abbey, Lewis Thomas, the property went into the hands of the Mansel family of Oxwich Castle, Gower. Sir Rhys Mansel (c.1487–1559), Vice-Admiral and also High Sheriff of Glamorgan, a Commissioner of Peace who served as Chamberlain of Chester to King Henry VIII of England and at the Dissolution of the Monasteries it was he who purchased Margam Abbey for the sum of £642 9s. 8d. The abbey remained the property of his descendants until 1760, when it passed to the Talbot family. The ancient gate-house before the court of the house remains unaltered, because of an old prophecy among the bards that as soon as the porch or gatehouse shall be pulled down the family shall decline and go to decay.

MARGAM, a parish, in the union of Neath, county of Glamorgan, south Wales. The present appellation is considered a corruption of Mawrgan, who was the son of Caradoc ab Iestyn, and a great of Mawrgan, who was the son of Caradoc ab Iestyn, and a great benefactor to the celebrated abbey of Margan or Margam, if not its founder. The date of the foundation was in 1147, and attributed to Robert, Earl of Gloucester, who died in this year.

There can be little doubt that it was endowed by Caradoc ab Iestyn, lord of the lordship of Avon, with extensive grants of lands, which were confirmed by a deed under the hands of Morgan, and his two brothers, Cadwallon and Meriedoc, whose descendants, for several generations, were munificent benefactors to the establishment.

At the Dissolution, its revenue was estimated at £188. 14., and the site and possessions, together with the royalty of Avon water, were purchased by Sir Rice Mansel, Knt., who, about the year 1552, built a mansion partly on the site of the abbey, which continued to be the principal seat of the family until the extinction of the male line in 1750. The chapter-house, which is a portion of the ancient conventual buildings, is in the form of a regular duodecagon within an exact circle, 49 feet in diameter. Its roof was vaulted, and supported in the centre by a single clustered column branching off into twenty-four ribs; but this beautiful roof fell in the year 1799, in consequence of the outer walls having become defective and the side walls of the chapter-house, with the spring of the arches, only, are now left standing.

A noble mansion, in the style of English architecture which prevailed in the reign of Henry VIII has been erected. Its chief external features are two grand façades, broken by bays, and a tower: the interior is superbly furnished. In the midst of the pleasure-grounds is a splendid orangery, an unusual appendage to a private residence, but there is no document in existence that shows the period of its establishment. According to tradition, this celebrated collection of exotics was intended as a present from a Dutch merchant to Queen Mary, consort of William III.; but the *vessel conveying it having been stranded on the coast here, the choice cargo was claimed as the property of the lord, and a house, 150 feet in length, was built for the reception of the plants. The late Mr Talbot, in the year 1787, built a new green-house, 327 feet in length, with a handsome Palladian front and a room at each end; and, in 1800, a conservatory, 150 feet long, with flues in the ground. There are about 110 trees in the greenhouse, all standards planted in square boxes, and many of them eighteen feet high; those in the conservatory, forty in number, are trained against a trellis framing. The collection includes pomegranate, lemon, citron, and shaddock trees, as well as orange-trees. The evergreens cultivated in the grounds surrounding the orangery are healthy and luxuriant: among these a bay-tree, supposed to be the largest in Britain, sprouting from the ground in several branches, is the most remarkable, being upwards of sixty feet in height, and forty-five in diameter; the arbutus, Portugal laurel, and holly flourish in an extraordinary manner, and present a rich appearance.*

A Topographical Dictionary of Wales. Samuel Lewis. 1849. Members of the Swansea Scientific Society enjoyed a visit to the abbey on Saturday, 24 July 1886 when they were conducted through the grounds by the *estimable* head gardener – Mr Muir, *who gave them the benefit of his botanical and local knowledge*. They were shown the orange trees, which were thought to be between three to four hundred years old and as famous for their flowers as for their fruits.

Further Reading

A Topographical Dictionary of Wales. Samuel Lewis. 1849.
Cistercian Abbeys: History and Architecture. Paris. 1998.
Dictionary of the Place Names of Wales. H. W. Owen & R. Morgan. Gomer Press. 2007.
Gerald of Wales. The Journey Through Wales. The Description of Wales.

Trans.: L. Thorpe. Penguin. 1978.

Glamorgan – an outline of its geography, history, and antiquities. A. Morris. J. E. Southall, Newport. 1907.

Medieval Religious Houses: England and Wales. Eds.: D. Knowles & R. Neville. Hadcock. London. 1953.

'*Margam Abbey*'. Glanmor Williams. Morgannwg – Transactions of the Glamorgan Local History Society. Vol. 42.1998.

Monastic Wales http://www.monasticwales.org

The Cistercian Abbeys of Britain. Ed.: D. Robinson. London. 1998.

The Monastic Order in England. D. Knowles. Cambridge University Press. 1940.

The Monastic Order in South Wales 1066–1349. Cowley.

Name:	**NEATH ABBEY**
	SERVING RELIGIOUS, RESIDENTIAL AND INDUSTRIAL NEEDS
Order:	**Cistercian**
Location:	**Neath, Neath Port Talbot SA10**
OS Map Ref.:	**SS 738973**

Like Margam, Neath was at one time much better known for its industrial history and connections with the iron and coal industry rather than with an ecclestiastical history but its early history should not be forgotten. Neath is the anglicised form of *Nedd* – the river which flows through the area. The word *Nedd* could mean shining.

In going to Neath Abbey on Thursday, 17 March 1188, *Girladus Cambrensis* nearly lost his horse and more important, he nearly lost his baggage and books. Had he lost his books, which most probably contained his early notes and writings about *The Journey Through Wales* and *The Description of Wales*, historians and scholars of many centuries would have lost a valuable resource.

It didn't happen but it was a close run thing. Luckily, as they approached the river Neath Gerald had appointed Morgan, eldest and only surviving son of Caradog as a guide and leader. They had watched *Giraldus'* horse almost being swallowed up by a quicksand and it was only with great difficulty that it had been pulled out and not without damage to his baggage and books. It was a case of *'terror giving them wings'* when it came to crossing the quicksand on foot but to hurry across was not the best way to deal with such a dangerous obstacle. It would have been much better to go slowly – which was what the guide advised. Slowly but surely they crossed the quicksands and caught the ferry rather than risk crossing over the ford as the crossings changed with every tide making it one of the most dangerous crossings to have to face on their journey.

The caretaker of Neath Abbey, Glamorgan received a mysterious parcel in late September 1936. It contained four ancient stones. They were sent by an un-named London woman motorist who believed that they had brought a curse on her.

While on a visit to the abbey she thought that they would be ideal for her rockery and placed them in the boot of her car to take back to London. Then, there started a chapter of accidents ending in a car collision in Harrow after which she had to spend a month in hospital. Firmly convinced that the stones had brought her bad luck, she returned them to the caretaker with a note of apology for having taken them and disturbed the site!

In 1129 Richard de Granville granted land on the west bank of the river Neath, to the Norman abbey of Holy Trinity at Sauvigny for the foundation of a new monastery. A year later Abbot Richard (d. 1145) and his twelve monks arrived from Sauvigny and a new community at Neath was formed: it was the second daughter – house of Sauvigny in England and Wales. The monks soon found and during the 1190s a plan was put forward for the monastery to move to the site of its property at Exford in Somerset. The plan was thwarted when, in 1198, the abbey of Cleeve was established barely ten miles from the site at Exford. So instead of moving, the community decided to stay and concentrate their efforts on land nearer to home. This paid off and by the end of the thirteenth century Neath Abbey was one of the wealthiest houses in Wales. The number of resident monks increased and after the house was burnt down in 1224 by Morgan ap Owen it had to be rebuilt for twenty-four monks and forty to fifty lay-brothers. Between 1280 and 1320 the twelfth-century Romanesque church was replaced by a new Gothic construction. The scheme attracted the attention of King Edward I and, on a visit to Neath in 1284, he presented the abbey with a beautiful canopy, intended for the High Altar.

After the death of Gilbert de Clare in 1314 rebellion broke out in Glamorgan. The monks of Neath were *plundered of their goods by reason of rebellion of certain Welshmen and their house devastated and ruined*. Neath experienced further financial difficulties during the fifteenth century but it seems that by around 1500 the house had largely recovered from these set backs. During the beginning of the sixteenth century, the southern end of the dormitory and the refectory ranges were adapted to provide the abbot with substantial private accommodation. From about 1509 until the Dissolution these new apartments were occupied by Abbot Leyshon Thomas, the most influential Cistercian abbot of late mediaeval Wales. Despite having a fine reputation, Neath Abbey had an annual net income of just £132 at the time of the Dissolution and should have fallen under the first Act of Suppression in 1536. In order to avoid closure, Abbot Leyshon paid a fine of £150. However, the house evaded suppression for only three years, and was finally dissolved with the larger monasteries in 1539. A few years later Cromwell purchased the site and converted parts of the monastic buildings into an impressive Tudor mansion. These buildings were abandoned in the early years of the eighteenth century and left to ruin. Today the remains include much of the east and west ranges of the monastic buildings, the gothic church and the mansion. The site is now under the care of Welsh Historic Monuments.

It has recently been suggested that the '*Red Book of Hergest*', one of the '*Four Ancient Books of Wales*', normally ascribed to Strata Florida, was in fact copied in a Glamorgan monastery – probably Neath.

It was reported in the press on Tuesday, 18 June 1907 that the congregation at Neath Abbey Church had had the shock of their lives when the church bell fell on the roof and bounded into the churchyard.

In the early 1920s a huge clearance operation began, before the site was excavated to reveal the extensive remains. Some 4,000 tons of debris were removed from the abbey with the help of Glen Arthur Taylor, leader of the Neath Abbey Research Party, and it is due to his efforts that the monastery was not lost among industrial waste, and the modern docks complex of Swansea.

Further Reading
Dictionary of the Place Names of Wales. H. W. Owen & R. Morgan. Gomer Press. 2007.
Hull Daily Mail – Tuesday, 18 June 1907
Monastic Wales http://www.monasticwales.org
Wild Wales. George Borrow. Collins. 1862.

Name: **STRATA FLORIDA ABBEY**
              THE 'WESTMINSTER ABBEY' OF WEST WALES
Order: **Cistercian**

Order: Cistercian
Location: Abbey Road, Ystrad Fflur, Ceredigion SY25 6ES
OS Map Ref.: SN 164458

Strata Florida Abbey, known as *The Westminster Abbey of Wales*, was possibly the most important abbey in Wales. It lies in a small, sheltered valley in western Ceredigion. Through the valley, with its broad, glaciated floor, flows the river Teifi, a mile from its source in Teifi Pools. During the many years of building work, the monks had to control the river waters to prevent flooding and from stopping their land becoming wet and marshy. They showed their skill and ingenuity by diverting Afon Glasffrwd into a small, hand-dug canal.

The new abbey became known as a centre of learning where some of the most important Welsh manuscripts were created including the history of early Wales – *Brut y Tywysogion* (The Chronicle of the Princes, started in Llanbadarn Fawr) which begins with the death of *Cadwaladr Fendigaid* (Blessed Cadwaladr) in 682 and finishes with the death of Llywelyn ap Gruffudd in 1282. Another manuscript is considered one of the most important collections of poetry from the Middle Ages – *Llawysgrif Hendregadredd* (The Hendregadredd Manuscript) containing a selection of the poetry of the Poets of the Princes (*Beirdd y Tywysogion*) and one in Dafydd ap Gwilym's own hand. Dafydd is closely connected with Strata Florida and it is believed he is buried there though the exact spot is unknown. Gruffudd Grug, in one poem, says he was buried inside the abbey but in another mentions that his grave is outside in the graveyard, under the shadow of a spreading yew tree.

> *Yr ywen i oreuwas*
> *Ger mur Ystrad Fflur a'i phlas;*
> *Da Duw wrthyd, gwynfyd gwŷdd,*
> *Dy dyfu yn dŷ Dafydd.*

(This yew-tree for the best of men,
Near the walls of Strata Florida and its hall;
God's blessing on you, happy tree,
For growing at a house for Dafydd.)

(a translation of the work of Gruffudd Grug)

The Hendregadredd Manuscript was written between 1282 and 1350 and almost forty different monks are known to have worked on this manuscript. The abbey also supported literary works and the arts in general. It flourished in the late twelfth and thirteenth century, before the conquest of Wales by Edward I. During this time it established a reputation in many fields such as education; it was also well known as a centre of healing.

The original monastery buildings were built two miles south-west of the present site on the banks of the river Fflur and are known simply as *Yr Hen Fynachlog* (The Old Monastery).

The situation of this abbey, in the wildest part of Cardiganshire, is comparatively beautiful, when contrasted with the surrounding country. Seated in a valley by the course of the Teivy, formally abounding with wood, and shut in by lofty mountains on every side, except the west, it appears well calculated for the seclusion of so severe an order as that of the Cistercians.

The Principal Rivers of Wales. J. G. Wood. 1813

A community of monks from the Cistercian Abbey of Whitland found a new monastery in the summer of 1164 by the Anglo-Norman knight Robert fitz Stephen and were given endowments of land by the Lord Rhys of Deheubarth. His generosity enabled the monks to move to the new site but he died in 1196 of a fever and was buried in the grounds. Other members of his family – a brother, son and daughter, had been buried before him in the abbey confirming the family connections. Five princes of Dinefwr in 1176. Cadell, Lord of Dinefwr was a fine hunter and would travel as far as Tenby to hunt. His English enemies, when they learnt of this, set a trap to capture him. In this they failed but he was severly injured. When he recovered from his wounds he went to the Holy Land on a pilgrimage and on his return became a monk at Strata Florida. The other four princes were Owain ap Rhys who died in 1190; Rhys ap Gruffudd who died in 1196; Gruffudd Rhys who died in 1202 and Hywel who died in 1204. Hywel was murdered and his eyes extracted from his head. During the next forty years another ten members of the family were also buried there including Maud de Breos, Gruffudd ap Rhys' widow, in 1209; Isabel, daughter of Richard, Earl of Clare and wife of William, Lord of Gower, in 1210; Rhys ap Gruffudd ap Rhys in 1221; Maelgwn, son of Rhys, in 1230 and Owain, son of Gruffudd ap Rhys, in 1235.

In 1184, the Lord Rhys gave the monks of Strata Florida a new charter for their new monastery, which was modelled on the abbeys of Citeaux and Clairvaux of the 1130's and 1140's. David, the first abbot died in 1185 and afterwards matters got so out of hand that the abbot of Whitland was ordered to hold an inquiry into allegations that the monks of Strata Florida were drunk and fighting amongst themselves.

Giraldus Cambrensis visited the abbey with Archbishop Bladwin and stayed for three nights – 3, 4, 5 April 1188. Gerald tells a tale about two famous poets of the day who had fallen out over a beautiful, young woman and a trick played on both by the abbey monks. One of the poets was the celebrated and known womaniser – Dafydd ap Gwilym. The other was from Anglesey – Gruffudd Grug of Penmynydd. The monks sent a message to both saying that the other had died and was to be buried on a certain date at Strata Florida. Together with the message was an invitation to the funeral. On their way to the abbey both composed an eulogy for the other but when they arrived to be date at Strata Florida. Together with the message was an invitation to the funeral. On their way to the abbey both composed an eulogy for the other but when they arrived to be greeted by each other, the argument was soon forgotten and both became firm, lifelong friends.

Dafydd ap Gwilym was once told by a Benedictine monk:

Cease composing poetry
And concentrate on praying.

To which Dafydd replied:

'Few know my poems
But everyone knows his prayers.'

Later Dafydd retorted:

'I hate a brother preaching.'

Later still he said that he didn't like someone in barefeet and hair like a crow's nest!

The reputaion of some monkls must have been an unenviable one as a very old Welsh saying condemns a Grey friar by naming him as one of the three necessaries of Hell! The other two being a bailiff and an Englishman. It could well have been a line first said by Dafydd ap Gwilym.

Building work was slow and laboured and it was not until 1201 that the community of monks was able to use their new church. They celebrated their first Mass on Whit Sunday 1201. One of the reasons that the work took so long was that the monks had been fined £800 by King John for their support of Llywelyn ap Iorwerth (*The Great*). He had ordered the monastery to *be destroyed or as far as possible wasted*. But his orders were not successfully carried out but such a fine was just as prohibitive as it took the monks until 1248 to pay the last instalment. When Gruffudd ap Llywelyn died at the Tower of London in 1249, the abbots of Strata Florida and Aberconwy asked for his body to be returned for burial in Aberconwy and in 1276 when the Bishop of St Asaph complained to the Pope about Llywelyn II, the abbot of Strata Florida was one who wrote to Rome to say that the accusations were without truth.

Strata Florida monks had connections with Llanddewi Aberarth, on the Cardiganshire coast.

According to local tradition, along a road named Lôn Lacs was carried many of the stones for the building work. It has been mentioned that the stone for carving and decorative work was carried by ship from Somerset and by hand from Aberarth to the abbey! The masons were paid four-pence a day for their work and the labourers only a penny a day. There was also a twenty mile long monks' road named Monks Trod from Strata Florida to Cwmhir Abbey which kept lines of communications open in troubled times. The abbey also held land at Morfa Bychan and Morfa Mawr and had rights to coastal wrecks and fishing weirs. Whether they needed to exercise those rights over the fishing weirs is in question as a local tradition has it that the monks swore so much in Welsh when they fished, that trout in Carraclwddyn Pools had been bewitched by them and were much easier to catch. In 1217, the abbot of Strata Florida was deposed for political reasons. When the new, large bell was put in its place in 1255, it was a sign that the building work was finally completed.

Soon, problems had to be faced during the war against Edward I in 1276–77 and again in 1282–83. The monastery was hit by lightning on 13 December 1284 and fire caused grave damage to the church. According to the Chronicle of St Werburgh:

> A great misfortune happened at the Abbey of Strata Florida in Wales. The fire and lightning struck the belfry, and burned the whole of it, with the bells, without the flames being seen: and then devoured the whole church, which was completely covered with lead, as far as the body of our Lord was kept there on the great altar under lock.

The monks suffered during the Welsh rebellion of 1294–95

and the abbey was severely damaged by royal troops but they were permitted to rebuild their abbey and the Crown paid for the necessary repairs.

Decline set in from the late thirteenth century onwards but new building provided some hope for the future. Plain glass rather than stained glass was fitted into the windows, walls were painted white and tiles were laid on the floors. But all was to very little avail, as much damage was done to the abbey during the reign of Henry IV, during Owain Glyndŵr's rebellion. English soldiers were allowed to garrison in the abbey buildings and their respect for anything Welsh was very short. Strata Florida was attacked by thieves and the abbot of Aberconwy and his followers in 1423. They imprisoned the monks and robbed the monastery. With a great deal of further work and support from the abbots, Strata Florida Abbey managed to survive. Llywelyn Goch ap Meurig Hen wrote a poem of thanks to God for saving the life of Llywelyn Fychan ap Llywelyn, abbot from 1344 to 1380. Guto'r Glyn, dedicated five poems to Rhys, his patron, who was abbot in February 1433. Another method of sustaining themselves and the abbey used by the monks was the holding of fairs on St James' Day and on the Feast of Assumption and Holy Rood. The fairs were held at Mevenydd and continued to be held as cattle and horse fairs until the twentieth century when they were known as Ffair Rhos.

The more important the abbey, the more problems the abbot had to face and this was certainly true of Strata Florida:

Meredith (Maredudd) Bool: abbot of Strata Florida in October 1336 but was excommunicated on 1 October 1338.

Llewelyn Vaughan: 1344–?: A monk of Strata Florida, his election to the abbacy involved him in a dispute with another claimant, Clement ap Richart, who, it was alleged, had taken away the goods of the house. The case was brought to the attention of the papacy and the bishop of Hereford duly appointed delegates to hear the case in June 1345 and April 1346. The case was decided in Llewelyn's favour. He was abbot of Strata Florida in 1377 and 1380. Llywelyn Goch ap Meurig Hen (1330–70) wrote a congratulatory poem to him following his recovery from a serious illness:

Clement ap Richard: disputed the election of Llywelyn Vaughan and took possession of the house but was ejected by Vaughan. Following several investigations the case was decided in Vaughan's favour.

Richard: abbot in May 1435. In Henry VI's reign, Richard was imprisoned in Carmarthen Castle by royal officials on account of his debts and he died in prison.

William: abbot of Strata Florida in November 1441. In 1443, he was defamed by John ap Rees, abbot of Cymer. Willam and a few of his monks were held at Aberystwyth Castle. John ap Rees took the abbacy after which William was forced to resign. The king appointed the abbots of Whitland and Margam to take control of the abbey and refused permission for the other two to enter the abbey or its grounds.

Morgan: a monk of Strata Florida who in 1446 received papal dispensation on account of his illegitimacy was abbot in February 1458 and November 1486.

William Marlow: abbot of Strata Florida in June 1487 and was imprisoned by the Abbot of Stratford on account of the dispute between Cîteaux and Clairvaux.

Richard Talley: abbot in December 1530 until February 1539. In October 1534 there was a dispute over the abbacy.

Others left for higher office:

Cadwgan of Llandyfai: c.1202 – was elevated to the abbacy at Whitland, c.1202.

Anian or Einion Sais: abbot in 1280 until August 1294. He left to become Archdeacon of Anglesey and later Bishop of Bangor (1309–28).

After the Dissolution of the Monasteries in 1539, stone work was demolished and materials taken by locals for their own building projects; its lands were taken over by Sir Richard Devereux and then by local gentry families. The Stedman's first leased and then purchased the Abbey itself and some of its lands.

It was the Stedman family who built the plas or mansion of Mynachlog Fawr where the refectory stood. In the mid-eighteenth century it became the property of the Powells of Nanteos and later to the Vaughans of Trawscoed, and finally to the Arch family, the present owners.

The abbey site has been excavated many times by the Cambrian Archaeological Association but in the late 1880s, a railway engineer Stephen Williams set about uncovering the site of the church and part of the cloister. Today the whole complex of Strata Florida is in the hands of CADW.

An inscribed slate was found at Strata Florida in 1946. It looked so nondescript that the ones who found it were about to throw it away. Luckily, it was kept and is now part of the collection of the National Library of Wales, Aberystwyth. The inscription on the slate can be dated to the 1470's, a few years before the Tudor dynasty reigned. The information gleaned from on the slate include details about the farm of Hafodwen which is spread in four different parishes between the river Aeron and the Teifi. It was a form of rent book used by the monks of Strata Florida to keep tabs on local farm tennants and how much they paid for their land. One farmer/ tennant is named as *Ieuan ap Dafydd Ddu a Dafydd ap y Mab Moel* (Ieuan the son of Black David the son of David the son of the Bald son.) On the back is a drawing of a king's head with his tongue sticking out.

Further Reading

A Tour of the Abbeys, Priories and Cathedrals of Wales. D. S. Yerburgh. Yerburgh. 1999.

Cestyll a Abatai Deheubarth. R. Turvey. Cadw. 2002.

Golud yr Oes. H. Humphreys. Caernarfon. 1864.

'Hen Fynachlogydd Cymru' Y Traethodydd Rhifyn Cyf. LVI. Hugh Williams. 1901.

Monastic Wales http://www.monasticwales.org

Musings from Gelli Fach. Hilaire Wood. Aberystwyth. 2001.

Strata Florida Abbey. T. Jones Pierce Ceredigion: Journal of the Cardiganshire Antiquarian Society Vol. 1. 1950.

Wales Vol, V no. 7. Summer 1945.

Wild Wales. George Borrow. Collins. 1862.

Name:	**STRATA MARCELLA**
	ONE OF A BAKER'S DOZEN
Order:	**Cistercian**
Location:	**2½ miles NE of Welshpool, Powys SY21**
OS Map Ref.:	**SJ 251104**

Strata Marcella Abbey was the largest of thirteen Cistercian abbeys in Wales. In 1170 Owain Cyfeiliog, prince of south Wales, invited monks from Whitland to settle at a new foundation on the west bank of the river Severn.He was also buried in the abbey in 1197. The building of the monastery took place from 1190 to the early 14th century. The church of the monastery was 273 feet long with an aisled nave, a transept and a chancel.

After only two years, the monks moved from the first site to the present one. Both abbeys were called *Ystrad Marchell* (Strata Marcella). Owain retired to the monastery and took the habit of the Cistercian monks. On his death, in 1197, he was buried in the grounds of the abbey. His son Gwenwynwyn (d.1216) took over patronage of the abbey and added to Strata Marcella's endowments. It also known that Gruffyd ap Gwenwynwyn, lord of Powys, entered a monastery, which could have been Strata Marcella Abbey, when he was close to death (c.1260) but recovered during his stay. The monks of Strata Marcella founded another Cistercian abbey, at Valle Crucis near Llangollen, in 1200, and they also had the oversight of a Cistercian nunnery at Llanllugan near Llanfair Caereinion. Gerald of Wales, tells of the abbot, Enoc (c.1190), who was guilty of misconduct with a nun and abandoned the habit.

Strata Marcella was one of several abbeys to suffer damage during the wars of Edward I and by the fourteenth century was in a state of poverty. In the late 1320s, Lord John de Cherleton of Powys (d.1353) introduced English monks into Strata Marcella as he opposed the Welsh community, complaining that there were only eight monks at the house when at one time there had been sixty. In 1330 Edward III responded by dispersing the Welsh community at Strata Marcella and sending the monks to English houses. They were replaced with English monks, and the house was made subject to the abbey of Buildwas in Shropshire.

The Strata Marcella monks were much involved in the struggle between the Welsh princes and the Marcher Lords and between Llywelyn and Edward I. In the 14th century the King demanded the monastery to be controlled by Buildwas Abbey due to Welsh leanings. Between 1400 and 1405 the buildings were subject to destruction during the Owain Glyndŵr rising and the monastery never recovered completely.

At the time of the Dissolution the abbey had an annual income of £64 and a community of only four monks. It was closed in 1536. When the last abbot John ap Rhys was appointed to his post the monastery buildings were said to be more or less in ruin. After the closure of the abbey local people helped themselves to building

After the closure of the abbey local people helped themselves to building stone, while the Crown tenant, Nicholas Purcell sold the organ to St Mary's, Shrewsbury, and three bells to Chirk parish church. Henry VIII sent his officials to Strata Maercella but upon their arrival they discovered that Lord Powis had bought the buildings from the monks the year before and all valuable items had disappeared. The site was dismantled completely and many pieces of stonework were sold in the area to Buttington church, Llanfair Caereinion church and Trewern Hall.

The cloister of the abbey formed Abbey Farm as late as 1780.Very little of the abbey remains today, apart from a few small areas of masonry and some earthworks which denote the positions of the church and cloister.

The riverside site of the abbey was typically Cistercian, and valuable both for fishing and transport. The site was excavated in 1890 by a noted antiquary, Stephen W. Williams, and was the subject of a geophysical survey one hundred years later which brought to light pillar bases and pier capitals, as well as decorative tiles. It is thought that the window of All Saints Church Buttington, Welshpool may be the remains of a much bigger window salvaged from Strata Marcella Abbey at Pool Quay, Welshpool. When the Chester Society of Natural Science, Literature and Art visited Welshpool church on an outing in June 1900 they were pleasantly surprised to see a large, flat topped stone in the churchyard which they were reliably informed was from Strata Marcella Abbey. On the dissolution of the monastery the stone found a resting place in the church but its presence there offended a very zealous Puritan, an ancestor of Major Baden Powell, who insisted it be moved outside and placed in the churchyard!

Further Reading
Cheshire Observer – Saturday, 16 June 1900
Monastic Wales

Name:	**TINTERN ABBEY**
	INSPIRATION FOR ARTISTS, POETS AND PRIESTS
Order:	**Cistercian**
Location:	**Tintern, Gwent NP16 6SQ**
OS Map Ref.:	**SO 533001**

For about two hundred years after the Dissolution of the Monasteries, few visited Tintern Abbey – unless it was to carry stone from the site. The brothers Samuel (1696–1779) and Nathaniel Buck (c.1759–1774), Yorkshire born engravers and printmakers, were among the first to visit the site in 1732 for the purpose of drawing what they could see. Between 1739 and 1742 they travelled all over Wales producing prints known as *Buck's Antiquities*.

Another landscape artist who made drawings of the abbey was Paul Sandby (1731–1809), who was very highly thought of by Thomas Gainsborough. He first visited Wales in 1770 and returned with Sir Jospeh Banks in 1773. His drawings of *XII Views in south Wales* were published in 1775 and another twelve were published in 1776 as part of a 48 plate album of engravings for Banks. Another artist visitor was J. M. W. Turner who visited south Wales in 1795 to make engravings. He travelled twenty five miles per day on foot making drawings of abbeys, bridges, cathedrals and towns and because of such work, many more visitors were

Movement of artists and poets were drawn to wild scenery and ruins. Tintern had plenty to offer.

Tintern was founded in 1131 by Walter fitz Richard, lord of Chepstow and a member of the Clare family. Walter of Clare was related by marriage to Bishop William of Winchester, who had introduced the first colony of White Monks to Waverley in 1128. Tintern was the first Cistercian house to be founded in Wales and the second in the British Isles after Waverley.

Tintern abbey, in the Wye valley, was colonised by monks from L'Aumone (Loir-et-Cher) in France. L'Aumone was a daughter house of Cîteaux, and Tintern was therefore linked to the Burgundian mother house. The community grew quickly and by 1139, had sufficient numbers to send out a colony to Kingswood in Gloucestershire. Abbot Henry, the second Tintern abbot from 1148–1157, had spent his youth as a robber but repented of his sins and took the Cistercian habit. He became a very religious man and is known to have visited both the Pope and St Bernard. In 1189 William Marshal, earl of Pembroke, became Lord of Chepstow and patron of Tintern. Earl William was also Lord of Leinster in south-east Ireland and, during a storm at sea, he promised God that he would establish a new monastery if he was saved from shipwreck. Tintern sent out her second colony to establish the abbey of *Tintern Parva* (Little Tintern) on William's lands in Ireland (1201–1203).

The abbey buildings were intended for a large community: some twenty monks and perhaps fifty lay-brothers. It was endowed with lands and possessions on both sides of the river Wye. By the late thirteenth century the monks at Tintern were farming over 3000 acres of arable land on the Welsh side of the Wye and kept 3,264 sheep on their pasture lands. In 1245 the lordship of Chepstow passed to the Bigod family. Roger Bigod III, Earl of Norfolk (1270–1306), took a keen interest in the abbey. In

1301–2 he granted the abbey his Norfolk manor of Acle. This proved to be a valuable asset and by the sixteenth century accounted for a quarter of the abbey's income. Roger Bigod was remembered primarily as the builder of the abbey church. The project, which had began in 1269, was completed under the patronage of Roger c.1301. At the time of the Dissolution the monks were still distributing alms to the poor five times a year for the repose of Roger's soul.

The abbey was at its most prosperous at the turn of the fourteenth century but was still poor compared to others in England:

> Also the Abbote of Westmystere,
>> the hiest of this land,
> The Abbot of Tynterne the poorest
>> y indeirstand,
> They ar bothe abbots of name,
>> and not like of fame to fande,
> Yet Tynyerne with Westmystere
>> shalle nowher sitte ne stande.

John Russell

Afterwards no significant additions were made to its property. Tintern was one of the few Welsh abbeys that managed to escape the suffering inflicted by the wars of Edward II. This was due to the fact that Tintern occupied a site that was more remote than its Welsh counterparts and outside the area in which most of the fighting took place. Edward II was known to have stayed at the abbey for two nights in 1326 when he was fleeing from the invading army of Roger Mortimer.

By the early fifteenth century the abbey was in financial difficulties as a result of the damaging effects of the uprising of Owain Glyndŵr. The community found relief from the offerings of pilgrims who travelled to the abbey. The abbey chapel of pilgrims who travelled to the abbey. The abbey chapel contained a statue of St Mary the Virgin which was thought to have possessed miraculous powers. It was said a great number of people journeyed to visit this sight.

In 1535 the net annual income of the abbey was valued at £192, which made Tintern the wealthiest abbey in Wales but still the abbey came under the first Act of Suppression (1536) which dissolved all houses with an annual income of under £200. The house was surrendered in September 1536 and the site was granted to Henry Somerset, Earl of Worcester (d. 1549), who was its patron. The earl stripped the buildings of their roofs for lead and during the following century a number of the monastic buildings may have been converted into dwelling houses.

During the second half of the eighteenth century the wooded slopes of the Wye became a popular site for 'Romantic' tourists, with the ruins at Tintern acknowledged as 'the jewel and highlight of the tour'. At this time the site was owned by the Duke of Beaufort who set about preserving the abbey as the perfect Gothic ruin. Reverend William Gilpin's guidebook 'Observations on the River Wye' (1782) became a bestseller and travellers flocked to the area to see and enjoy Tintern, which was supposed to be the most beautiful scene on the tour.

In 1901 the site was recognised as a monument of national importance and the property was sold to the Crown. A restoration programme was set in motion which was completed c.1928.
Today the site remains one of the most picturesque and romantic of all the tourist sites in Wales. The Gothic church stands almost complete, apart from the roof and the north aisle in the nave. The excavated foundations of the communal guest hall and other inner court structures can be seen to the west of the abbey church. The north-east side of the abbey complex does not survive to any great height but shows the layout of the infirmary

hall and the abbot's lodgings.

On a visit to Tintern Abbey there are many outstanding features to see, to study and to enjoy:

i. Outer porch – where laymen could meet and talk to the monks but could go no further.

ii. Remains of the stairs – by which the monks come down from their dormitory to the church for the night time services.

iii. The church – set diagonally in the north-west corner. The most conspicuous parts that are missing are the roof and the glass and tracery from the windows.

iv. The cloister – now consisting of four gravel paths but originally four covered passageways covered by lean-to roofs.

v. Round headed recess – used as a cupboard for books to be used in the cloister.

vi. Book-room or library and vestry.

vii. Chapter house – used for the daily meeings.

viii. Parlour – where any necessary conversation was held but kept to a minimum.

ix. Day stairs – ledaing to dormitory.

x. Lodging for novices.

xi. *Redorter* or latrine. Water to flush the drain was from a little stream that ran downhill to the north west of the abbey.

xii. Arches.

xiii. Warming house – which had a central fire place.

xiv. Monks' dining hall – 84 ft long and 29 ft wide, built in thirteenth century to replace an earlier one.

xv. Kitchen – for the monkls and lay-brother's use.

xvi. Infirmary – 107 ft long and 54 ft wide. In the fifteenth century the infirmary was divided into cubicles or separate rooms, each with its own fireplace.

xviii. Infirmary kitchen.

xix. Abbot's *camera* or living room – a separate establishment so he would not upset the routine of the monastery.

xx. Abbot's hall.

xxi. Accommodation for the lay brothers, including a dormitory and dining hall, and a storeroom.

xxii. The cellar – main storeroom of the abbey.

Tintern Abbey is said to be haunted by the spirits of knights in shining armour and a few of the monks who once lived there. One local belief is that the Devil himself used to preach from a nearby rock, trying to tempt the monks away from their religious duties. He did not succeed as the ghost of one monk is said to be seen praying near one of the arches.

Another local legend tells of a group of young men visiting the abbey to search for remains. Local men were employed to dig in the grounds and found two skeletons. So pleased were they with themselves that they celebrated their discovery, with a drink. Almost immediately, the weather changed with heavy rain clouds, flashes of lightning and thunder claps heard and seen and a heavy, dreary mist fell over the ruins but suddenly a knight in shining armour appeared before them. Monks and abbots appeared and stood in a circle around them. The terrified men fled.

Further Reading
Monastic Wales http://www.monasticwales.org
Tintern Abbey. H. Brakspear & M. Evans. 1910.
Tintern Abbey. O. E. Craster. HMSO. 1964.

Name: **VALLE CRUCIS ABBEY**
    IN THE VALLEY OF THE CROSS

Order: Cistercian
Location: Abbey Road, Llangollen, Denbighshire
OS Map Ref.: SJ 205442

When is the best time to visit Valle Crucis Abbey? Is there a best time, you may ask, to visit such a place? My last visit took place one cold, misty February morning and that, I would suggest, is the best time to arrive, when the temperature is just above freezing, when the bushes and hedges are covered in frost and the mist hangs heavily on the Berwyn Hills so as to hear not the sound of monks chanting but of a proud blackbird and a cheeky robin chirping away to their hearts content. Were I of Guto'r Glyn's ilk, I would compose a verse of praise to the feathered songster but I am not so I can only say a silent prayer of thanks for such a welcome on my early morning visit. Early February mornings are not, thankfully, the time for educational visits and few visitors occupy the caravans from across the field. Then is the time for contemplation. Then is the time to drift in thought.

Misty February mornings are just the time for peace and quiet in Valle Crucis. In 2013, it can be had a' plenty just as it was to be had eight hundred years ago when the first monks set foot in the valley. Because of the beauty of its site and surroundings, the abbey has been an inspiration to many writers including one who penned a pocket description in the Wrexham Advertiser on Saturday, 20 January 1866:

> The abbey was built by Cistercian monks, so called from Cisteux (Latin Cistertium), in Burgundy, about the year 1200. These said Cistercians were at the time very busy in colonising other habitations, and so this valley in Wales was selected for one of their finest abbeys. These same Cistercians built Fountains, and Tintern, and Jervaux, and lived at Byland and Roche, and Buildwas. They soon became a powerful order, though only

Buildwas. They soon became a powerful order, though only established in 1098, and introduced into England thirty years later, for they had the powerful patronage of St Bernard. But their glory is all departed now. Three hundred years ago Thomas Cromwell 'mauled' them horribly, as he did all other orders of monks, and now; like most other abbeys of England, Valle Crucis is only a roofless ruin. The rubbish is carried out. Where was the old church floor, is smooth green-sward, and the effigy of the armed knight is broken, and we are told this, that, and the other by a female cicerone*. We listened, but asked few questions, as we preferred to muse on the ruin present – the glory past. We were thankful to the lady that she took us out to the east, where lies a sheet of water. There was nothing remarkable about it, but when we passed it the lady said, 'Turn round and look in the water.' We turned and looked. Below the grassy margin, deep down in the clear pool, was an image of the form above, the fine unglazed oriel of the abbey. We have seen many views of the abbey published, but this we have never seen; still the memory of it is fresh with us – a golden memory of the passed away.

(a guide who understands and explains antiquities)

Sadly, on my visit CADW, the abbey's present day keepers, had decided to close all doors and keep any information sheets under lock and key. Just a few copies of the above would have added to my appreciation of what can only be described as one of CADW and Wales' 'jewels in the crown'.

Valle Crucis Abbey has many names including: Abbey of the Valley of the Cross; Abaty Glyn-y-Groes; Glyn Egwestl; Llanegwestl. The cross, mentioned in English and Welsh names, refers to the Cross of Eliseg also known as Elise's Pillar or Croes Elisedd in Welsh, which was erected by Cyngen ap Cadell (d. 855), king of Powys in honour of his great-grandfather Elisedd ap Gwylog. The spelling of Eliseg as it is on the pillar is thought to be a mistake by the carver of the inscription. The Latin inscription is one of the longest found in Wales and mentions a number of important individuals:

Concenn son of Cattell, Cattell son of Brochmail, Brochmail son of Eliseg, Eliseg son of Guoillauc and that Concenn, great-grandson of Eliseg, erected this stone for his great-grandfather Eliseg.

The same Eliseg, who joined together the inheritance of Powys...throughout nine (years?) out of the power of the Angles with his sword and with fire.

Whosoever shall read this hand-inscribed stone, let him give a blessing on the soul of Eliseg.

This is that Concenn who captured with his hand eleven hundred acres which used to belong to his kingdom of Powys... and which...the mountain

[the column is broken here. One line, if not more, lost]

...the monarchy...Maximus...of Britain...Concenn, Pascent, Maun, Annan.

Britu son of Vortigern, whom Germanus blessed, and whom Sevira bore to him, daughter of Maximus the king, who killed the king of the Romans.

Conmarch painted this writing at the request of king Concenn.

The blessing of the Lord be upon Concenn and upon his entire household, and upon the entire region of Powys until the Day of Judgement.

The Pillar was taken down by the Roundheads during the English Civil War. A grave was found underneath and opened. Edward Lhuyd examined the Pillar and copied the inscription in 1696. The pillar was broken, the lower half disappeared but the upper half was returned to its place in 1779. By now, the writing has been almost completely eroded away.

Valle Crucis Abbey is a Cistercian abbey, by the pool of Llyn Egwystl, in the parish of Llantysilio in Denbighshire and no more than two miles from Llangollen on the river Dee. The Abbey Church of the Blessed Virgin Mary was founded in 1201 by Madog ap Gruffudd Maelor, on the site of a temporary wooden church and was the last Cistercian monastery to be built in Wales. The Cistercian records show that the abbey was founded on 21 January 1201 and the presbytery, transepts all date from the first quarter of the thirteenth century. Madog had extensive lands from the Tanat valley to the outskirts of Chester. Overton castle was in his name and he ruled the route from England into north Wales. Valle Crucis was the spiritual centre of the region, while Dinas Bran castle, on an overlooking hill, was the political stronghold. Madog remained loyal to Llywelyn the Great all his life. The founder was buried in the abbey on his death in 1236. Shortly after his death, a serious fire badly damaged the abbey, signs of which can still be seen on the lower church stonework.

Originally Valle Crucis was a colony of only twelve monks from Strata Marcella Abbey, on the western bank of the river Severn near Welshpool. The original wooden structure was replaced with stone structures of roughly faced rubble. Thirteen monks and an abbot arrived from Strata Marcella near Welshpool, and the building work began almost immediately. The monks were granted access to nearby grazing lands for their flocks and herds at Mwstwr and Buddugre. They also held arable fields, water meadows and woodland areas, all of which gave the abbey a comfortable income. The completed abbey is believed to have housed about sixty brethren, twenty choir monks and forty lay-members who would have carried out the day-to-day duties including agricultural work. The numbers within the church fluctuated as the monks and the abbey suffered because of political and religious events. The abbey is believed to been involved in the Welsh Wars of Edward I of England during the thirteenth century but not extensively damaged as in a list of payments made to Welsh churches in 1284 it received only four pounds compared to £100 paid to the abbot of Aberconwy. It was again damaged during Owain Glyndŵr's Rebellion. The Black Death also accounted for some of the monks.

The General Chapter of the Cistercian Order reprimanded the abbot of Valle Crucis, along with those of Aberconwy and Caerleon, because they rarely celebrated Mass or even received the Holy Eucharist. It seems that the community lived a lifestyle bordering on luxury. During the late fifteenth century the monks' dormitory was completely taken over to be used as a grand set of apartments, in which the abbots must have lived in semi-secular comfort.

In the fifteenth century the abbey became a place of hospitality. Several important Welsh poets spent time at the abbey including Gutun Owain, Tudur Aled and Guto'r Glyn. Gutun Owain praised the hospitality of the abbots by saying that the table was usually spread with four meat courses served on silver dishes and accompanied by *sparkling claret*. Guto'r Glyn may well have been adopted as a child and brought up at the abbey. In some of his poems he described himself as being big, strong, courageous and sporting. He wore a beard and had black hair but was bald as a young man. He compared himself to a tonsured monk. Dafydd ap Edmund, another poet, wrote that Guto was not good-looking and had a nose like a billhook, whilst he was described by another as being bear-like in appearance. Guto'r Glyn spent the last years of his life at the abbey, and was buried there in 1493. This was also the century in which Abbot David had built for himself a new abbot's house which had comforts such as a fireplace and an external staircase from the cloister and even a private room!

Scandals soured the monastery's last few years. In 1534 abbot Robert Salusbury, was accused of many crimes. The following year, he was arrested for his part in a highway robbery. At the time of the Dissolution the abbey had a net annual income valued at £188 and the monastery was finally surrendered in January 1537 when under the patronage of Henry Fitzroy, duke of Richmond and Somerset. The building was given to Sir William Pickering on a twenty one year lease by Henry VIII, which was renewed by Edward VI in 1551. When Sir William died in 1574, the abbey passed to his daughter, Hester. In 1575 Hester married Edward Wotton, 1st Baron Wotton and the lease was extended to him in 1583 by Elizabeth I. The church soon fell to ruin, but the east range was converted into a dwelling house. The house was later used as a farmhouse.

In the late sixteenth century the eastern range was converted into a manor house. Valle Crucis remained in the Wotton family's possession, and was inherited by the 2nd Baron Wotton but on his death passed to Hester Wotton, his third daughter. Hester married Baptist Noel, 3rd Viscount Campden and the abbey entered the family's ownership, before being sold when the estate was taken over by Parliament in 1651. By the late 18th century the site was used as a farm before excavations were undertaken in the second half of the nineteenth century under the auspices of the Cambrian Archaeological Association. Sir Gilbert Scott, Gothic architect, worked on the repairs of the west front.

A number of original features remain, including the west front complete with an elaborate, richly carved doorway, a beautiful rose window and a fourteenth century inscription *Abbot Adams carried out this work; may he rest in peace. Amen.* In the dormitory can be seen a collection of twenty grave slabs which have been removed from the church. Though difficult to decipher, one is thought to be the gravestone of the abbey's founder – Madog ap Gruffudd Maelor and another is of his great-grandson – Madog ap Gruffydd who died in 1306. Another, much rarer gravestone (because it is dated), commemorates Gweirca ferch (the daughter of) Owain dating from 1290:

HIC IACET GWEIRCA FILIA OWENI CUIUS ANIMA PROPICIETUR DEUS ANNO DOMINE MCCLXXXX.
(Here lies Gweirca, daughter of Owain, on whose soul God have mercy; she died in the year 1290.)

There is also an effigy of Ieuaf ab Adda, Lord of Trefor who was alive in 1313 but the date of his date of his death is unknown.

In September 1888, the tomb of Madog ap Gruffudd Maelor was found at the abbey. The warden at the time, Reverend H. T. Owen was excavating and searching for pieces of stained glass when he came across a large stone slab with the name of 'Madog' and an undecipherable inscription on it. Down the centre of the stone was an inscription of a sheathed sword. Four other stones were found after further examinations, each about five feet by eighteen inches. The stones formed part of the vaulting of the slype or corridor leading to the monk's burial ground.

Another important discovery was made in 1890 during further excavations at the abbey. Another tomb of a Knight Templar, which was in a very good condition considering its age, was discovered and on it an inscription of a sword. Among the debris beneath the tomb were found decayed bones.

Other well preserved features include the east end of the Abbey, the Chapter House which has a rib-vaulted roof and the monks' original fishpond, (though restored, it is the only one of its kind in Wales and England). In December 1907 the fish pond was the scene of a tragedy when the daughter of a local priest, when out walking with her parents, leapt into the pool. Despite all

From a list of abbots at Valle Crucis, some characters of note included:

Tenhaer: mentioned as abbot more than once in 1227 and other occasions until 1234.

Madog: former abbot of Valle Crucis in 1254.

Anian ap Meredith: abbot in 1251, 1254 and possibly 1265.

Madog: abbot in September 1275 until November 1284.

Adam (Adda): abbot in 1330 until August 1343 (possibly January 1344). The abbey suffered a great deal during Edward I's campaigns in Wales in 1276–77 and 1282–83 but Abbot Adam supervised repairs and restoration especially to the western gable end.

Gutun Owain, poet, praised the standard of work on the abbey buildings especially the choir which is said to be more magnificent than the one at Salisbury Cathedral. Other abbots included:

Robert Lancaster: bishop of St Asaph in October 1409 as well as being abbot of Valle Crucis Abbey. He died in March 1433 and was still in both positions.

Dafydd ap Ieuan ap Iorwerth: 1480–1503.He was Bishop of St Asaph in 1500 and continued as abbot at Valle Crucis Abbey until his death in 1503.

Robert Salisbury: abbot of Valle Crucis in April 1528 until 1535. He was deposed in 1535 after being convicted of a robbery and held in the White Tower, the Tower of London.

John Herne or Heron alias Deram (Duram/Durham): a monk of St Mary Graces, London, abbot of Valle Crucis from June 1535 until August 1536. He was granted a pension in March 1537 at the time of the dissolution of the monasteries.

It is said that Felix Mendelssohn, on a vist to north Wales in 1829, was so moved by the abbey that he composed some music and had what he called '*a good day*.' John Gibson was an artist who was so impressed with the abbey that he wrote to the Saturday, 20 August 1853 edition of the Newcastle Journal to say how much he had enjoyed his visit:

I name Valle Crucis Abbey, 'far removed from noise and smoke,' date 1200 – of which I saw about three months ago, and from the details of which I made several drawings; and except where violence has been used by the hand of man, time has left the various mouldings, ornaments, &c. as fresh and sharp in the articulatrion, as on the day they were first chiselled.

In 1950 the property passed into the care of the government and today is managed by Welsh Historic Monuments. Extensive remains include the church, the east range of the claustral buildings and the foundations of the south and west ranges. The site is accessible to the public and can be visited at all reasonable hours.

The monks certainly have shown great taste in their choice of situations for retirement, and that of the site of this beautiful ruin is one of the mosty striking.

Welsh Scenery. Captain Barry. 1823

Further Reading

Abbeys, Priories and Cathedrals of Wales. M. Salter. Folly Publications. 2012.

A Tour of the Abbeys, Priories and Cathedrals of Wales. D. S. Yerburgh. Yerburgh. 1999.

Monastic Wales http://www.monasticwales.org

Valle Crucis Abbey. C. A. Ralegh Radford. HMSO. 1953.

Wild Wales. George Borrow. Collins. 1862.

Wrexham Advertiser – Saturday, 20 January 1866.

Name: **WHITLAND ABBEY**

Name: **WHITLAND ABBEY**
OLD WHITE HOUSE ON THE TAF
(Hen Dŷ Gwyn ar Daf)
Order: **Cistercian**
Location: **1¼ml. NNE of Whitland, Carmarthenshire**
OS Map Ref.: **SN 209181**

Whitland (probably better known in Wales as *Hen Dŷ Gwyn ar Daf*) is more famous for its connections with Hywel Dda, king of Wales 915–948 and the Laws of Hywel Dda drafted in 928 and which remained in force for almost four hundred years than for its abbey.

Today, the remains of the abbey have almost disappeared but in its day it was a most important establishment. After the monastery of Bangor-Iscoed in north Wales was destroyed by Northumbrian Saxons some of the dispersed monks under Paulinus, son of Urien Reged, found a religious society at Albalanda or Whitland which was the forerunner of the abbey. Whitland was founded on 16 September 1140 by monks from the mother house of Clairvaux, Burgundy. In 1144 it was located at Little Trefgarn near Haverfordwest and moved to Whitland on the banks of the river Gronw in 1155, to a site given to them by John of Torrington. The abbey was the first Cistercian house in Wales and founded other daughter houses including Abbeycwmhir in 1143, Cymer in 1198, Strata Florida in 1169, Llantarnam in 1179, Aberconwy in 1186, Strata Marcella Abbey in 1170 and Valle Crucis in 1201.Two Irish abbeys were also daughter houses of Whitland.

Giraldus Cambrensis visited the abbey with Archbishop Baldwin in on Monday and Tuesday, 21 and 22 March 1188. On the way to Whitland they signed twelve archers from St Clears with the sign of the Cross because they had murdered a Welshman who was on his way to meet *Giraldus* and the

Archbishop. In his journal, *Giraldus* also tells of Cynan, the abbot of Whitland from 1165 until his death in 1176 and how he had lusted after a woman just as Meilyr had done. Cynan cried bitterly and asked to be punished by being whipped by three of his monks.

Whitland Abbey came under the control and patronage of Rhys ap Gruffudd, prince of Deheubarth. Under his patronage the community prospered and by the thirteenth century the abbey had extensive landholdings organised around seventeen grange centres. In the following decades Whitland sent out a further two colonies to establish daughter-houses at Comber in 1199 and Tracton in 1224.

In the Welsh annals it is recorded that Cadwaladr, brother of Owain Gwynedd, prince of north Wales, had long running disputes between him and his nephews, the sons of Owain, gave the custody of Cynvael Castle to the abbot of *Tŷ Gwyn ar Daf*, who defended it against the assaults of the princes. The whole of the garrison was either killed or wounded, but the abbot managed to escape and retired to his monastery. Rhys's son, Maredudd, ended his days as a monk at Whitland after he had been blinded by an order of Henry II. The monastery, dedicated to St Mary, was an establishment of only eight monks but continued to flourish till the dissolution, when its revenue was estimated to be £153 17s 2d. The site was given to Henry Audley and John Cordel.

Whitland paid heavily for the support they gave to the Welsh princes. In 1257 Stephen Bauzan, Nicholas – Lord of Cemais, Patrick de Chaworth – Lord of Kilwelly and Lord of Carew, accompanied by a band of knights, invaded Whitland Abbey and killed all the monks, lay-brethren and servants in the abbey cemetery. When they left they stole all of Whitland's horses and valuables, except those in the church. The abbey also suffered great damage during the Welsh wars of Edward I. In 1277 or 1282 he was asked to pay a claim for £260 compensation for damages incurred when the English troops were garrisoned at the abbey

Whitland declined in wealth, the number of monks dwindled to eight and as low as five on some occasions. At the time of the dissolution the net annual income of the abbey was valued at £135.

In 1536 Abbot William ap Thomas avoided the closure of his abbey by offering a sum of £400 to the government but the abbey survived for only three more years and was finally dissolved with the larger monasteries in February 1539.

John Vaughan, who was the owner in the 1580's, built a manor house on the site with twenty two rooms and windows with ten lights each. In the mid seventeenth century, there was an iron works on the site but it was closed down in 1810. By the 1840's what remained of the abbey and the site was in the possession of the Morgan family who had a walled garden laid out where the old cloister used to be. The heiress of the family and her husband built a new house in the south eastern corner.

Very little of the abbey remains today apart from fragments of the abbey church. One important possession to have survived from Whitland Abbey is the *Cronica Wallia*, one of the most valuable of all the Welsh monastic chronicles. Its one time keeper – the abbot of Whitland, was a counsellor of Owain Glyndŵr.

After excavations were carried out in the 1920's and 1990's, the Community of Cistercian Nuns at Holy Cross Abbey, Whitland arrived in west Wales in 1991. This was a community founded at Stapehill in Dorset in October 1802 when Reverend Mother Augustin de Chabannes came to England to seek asylum from the French Revolution. It was she who led the group which established itself at Stapehill. The property in Dorset became too big to manage and it was sold in 1989 and a smaller property was purchased in Whitland.

Since the Cistercian Order was founded in 1098 houses of monks and nuns have been sited across Europe. From the beginning Cistercian women, or 'White Ladies' as they were known because of their cowls of unbleached and undyed wool, formed an important part of the Order.

The community at Whitland earns its living by making altar breads, used at the celebration of the Eucharist. Each member of the Community has some involvement in this industry. There is a small guest house, for people who want to retreat or those in need of a 'quiet day'.

> *It was situated in a sequested valley and sheltered by majestic groves of woods. The present remains are inconsiderable, but are sufficient to mark the site.*
>
> *The Beauties of England and South Wales.* T. Rees. 1815

Further Reading

Abbeys, Priories and Cathedrals of Wales. M. Salter. Folly Publications. 2012.

A Tour of the Abbeys, Priories and Cathedrals of Wales. D. S. Yerburgh. Yerburgh. 1999.

Gerald of Wales. The Journey Through Wales. The Description of Wales. Trans.: L. Thorpe. Penguin. 1978.

Hanes Cymru. John Davies. Penguin Books. 1992.

Later medieval and Early Post Medieval Threat Related Assessment Work 2012 – Monateries. F. Murphy & M. Page. Report No. 2012/12. Dyfed Archaeological Trust. 2012.

CLUNIAC ORDER

The Cluniac order of monks whoich was founded in 910, derived their names from the Cluny Abbey in Burgundy, France. The founder of Cluny Abbey was a Benedictine monk named Odo, who believed that The Rule of St Benedict was not being followed closely enough. The order was noted for its emphasis on church ceremonials and in the tenth and eleventh century became dedicated to formal prayer and liturgy (order of worship). They dedicated to formal prayer and liturgy (order of worship). They spent so much of their time at worship (almost constantly) that they did very little work or study and had to employ workers to work in their fields and gardens.

All Clunic houses were considered daughter houses of the mother church and were dependant on Cluny Abbey for their funds. Any donations, gifts or profits made by the daughter house were sent back to Cluny.

During the Hundred Years War between England and France, Clunic priories and houses were seen as a security risk as they could have supported the French cause. To avoid any help being given by them to a French invasion, a restriction was put on the inhabitants of the priories preventing them living within thirteen miles of the coast. In 1414 the alien or Clunic priories were confiscated by Henry V and many were taken over by other religious orders.

Name:	**ST. CLEARS PRIORY**
	'UNDISTINGUISHED AND DISREPUTABLE'
Order:	**Cluniac**
Location:	**Llanfihangel Abercywyn Church, St Clears,**
	Carmarthenshire.
OS Map Ref.:	**SN 281157**

In 1188 when Archbishop Baldwin of Canterbury and *Giraldus Cambrensis* were on their way from Carmarthen to Whitland they were stopped by messengers who told them of how a young Welshman, on his way to meet the archbishop, had been murdered by his enemies. The archbishop ordered the corpse to be covered with the cloak of his almoner, and commended the soul of the murdered youth to heaven. The next day twelve archers from the castle of St Clare who had assassinated the young man were signed with the cross at Whitland, as a punishment for their crime.

Modern day St Clears can be divided into three parts:

i. Lower St Clears;
ii. the shopping and market area, on the main London to Fishguard road;
iii. Station Road.

The second and third parts are the result of modern developments, and were during the Middle Ages undeveloped land in the parish of Llanfihangel Abercywyn. Medieval St Clears was centered on Lower St Clears, where the church and castle mound are amongst the most important signs of the Middle Ages in the area. The name St Clears was first recorded in 1189 as Seint Cler after a ninth century saint, who is also associated with Cornwall but who originated from St Clair, Normandy.

The Cluniac Priory was the most distinctive feature of St Clears during the Middle Ages. The Cluniac Order was a group of devout monks who in 910 established their own monastery at Cluny in Normandy to develop their own order and Rule distinct from the Benedictines. The Cluniac Order was very strict and each daughter-house was ruled directly from the parent-house; the Priory at St Clears was the daughter-house of the famous abbey near Paris, St Martin-des-Champs. The only other Cluniac foundation in Wales was at Malpas near Newport.

In modern day St Clears, place and field names point to the site of the priory. A field named *Parc y Prior* and a road called *Lon Prior* are near the site of the old Priory. Edward Lluyd confirms this after a visit in 1698, when he talked to men who could remember a wall in Parc y Prior which, it was claimed, represented the remains of the old Priory building. There can be no doubt that the Cluniac Priory of St Clears stood in the field adjoining the church.

than two or three monks.

There appears to be some confusion regarding the date of the founding of the priory. Rose Graham wrote:

The Priory of St Clears in Carmarthenshire was not founded until the middle of the 12th century, and the founder is unknown. It was included in the possessions of St Martin-des-Champs, which were conferred by 'Pope Eugenius III in 1184; it was not in the Bull of Pope Lucius II 1147 in which Barnstaple and St James by Exeter were noted.'

The Priory served the needs of the castle, but in doing so had only *'an undistinguished and sometimes disreputable career.'* It had very little influence on the area because:

i. It was too small to be effective. Usually it housed only two monks (the Prior and one other), and the small number often led to a relaxation of discipline. This was a charge laid by the visiting inspectors of St Martin-des-Champs in 1297: *The Prior and his companion were living evil lives and the property was in a bad state.* It seems that they had kept church funds to their own use. Another, John Soyer, is said to have led a dissolute life.

ii. the Priory was ruled directly from France. The Prior was nominated by the Prior of St Martin-des-Champs. Each year the Prior of St Clears was summoned to attended the general chapter at St Martin on July 4th (the feast of St Martin) but sometimes they stayed too long and spent too much money.

iii. frequent warfare between England and France disrupted the life of the alien priories. When war broke out the King would seize the revenues of all alien priories. In 1337 when the Hundred Years War began the Cluniac priories found themselves in financial difficulties. In 1393 *'Thomas de Tetford is charged £7 for the rent of St Clears Priory payable to the crown during the war with France.'* Previously this money would have been sent to St Martin-des-Champs. The sum of £7 also included a rent increase. Life must have been difficult for the few members of the priory. They were suspected of spying and their letters to and from France were thought to contain secret messages.

The Priory's history came to an end in 1444 when Henry VI dissolved it. Its possessions were granted to the warden of All Souls College, Oxford.

When the Priory's usefulness came to an end the church, dedicated to Mary Magdalene, continued to serve the parish. It contains many features of a Norman Cluniac church. The chancel arch is of Norman architecture. The capitals are examples of Romanesque designs. During its earlier period the church would have terminated at the west end with a flat wall and gable, but in the thirteenth century a large unbuttressed miltary type tower was added. The north and south walls of the church slope outwards at a noticable angle. This is thought to have been caused by either the weight of the roof causing subsidence or a style of building during the Middle Ages.

Further Reading

Later medieval and Early Post Medieval Threat Related Assessment Work 2012 – Monateries. F. Murphy & M. Page. Report No. 2012/12. Dyfed Archaeological Trust. 2012.

Monastic Wales http://www.monasticwales.org

R.A.C.M.: Inventory for Carmarthenshire. 1911.

St Clears in the Middle Ages 1100 – 1500. The Carmarthenshire Historian. D. A. Thomas. Carmarthenshire Community Council. 2006.

'The Cluniac Priory of St Martin-des-Champs, Paris and its dependent Priories in England and Wales.' Rose Graham. Journal of the British

Priories in England and Wales.' Rose Graham. Journal of the British Archaeological Association. 1948.

FRANCISCAN FRIARS

The friars dedicated to following the example of St Francis of Assisi were formed in 1209 and lived a life of poverty. They moved from place to place and lived by preaching and begging. Many became teachers and helped set up universities. The Franciscans came to England in 1224 and were known as the 'grey friars'. In Wales they were *Y Brodyr Llwydion* because of the coarse garment with a pointed hood of the same material, and a short cloak which they wore. Around their waist was a knotted cord – the *cordeliére* – and they went barefoot. Llanfaes, Anglesey became the most well-known Franciscan friary in Wales but they also settled in Cardiff and Cardigan.

Name:	**CARMARTHEN FRIARY**
	***'CWRTT BRODYR KAER VERDINN'* (Court of the brothers of Carmarthen**
Order:	**Franciscan**
Location:	**Church St., Carmarthen SA31 1GW**
OS Map Ref.:	**SN 419204)**

On the 11 September 1224 nine penniless men, members of the Grey Friars or Franciscan order, landed at Dover. Their passage from France had been paid for by the monks of Fécamp but once on English soil they had to fend for themselves with only their faith and their belief that God would provide for them. The order of which they were members was established in England but only three houses of Grey Friars were established in Wales. The first of which they were members was established in England but only three houses of Grey Friars were established in Wales. The first was founded at Llanfaes in Anglesey in 1237 by Llywelyn the Great, in memory of his wife, *Siwan* (Joan), who was buried there. The second was founded in Cardiff in 1280; the third at Carmarthen about two or three years later. The precise date of the foundation at Carmarthen is not known, but the earliest reference to it was in 1284. In 1538 when the houses were dissolved there were four friars at Llanfaes, nine at Cardiff, and fourteen at Carmarthen.

The Grey Friars built their house and church on the western side of Carmarthen, outside the walled town on a five acre site, bounded on the northern side by Lammas or Gell Street; on the west by a small stream that ran by Heol y Morfa and on the east by another stream running through what is now Blue Street, both streams feeding the river Towy on the south side. The main entrance was from Lammas Street. By now, the buildings have vanished but fifteenth and sixteenth century documents show that there was a church 70 to 80 feet long and 30 feet broad on the site. The friary and the church were of equal importance. Other buildings included a parlour, King's chamber, three other chambers, lavery, hall, refectory, kitchen, buttery, and brew house.

Few relics of the friary have survived. In 1917 a writer stated that a tenant, who came to live at the Friary in 1894, had come across '*a beautiful square of tessellated pavement*.' from the floor of the church or the chapter house. Unfortunately it was covered over and has not been seen since. A section of an Early English mullion of a window and a section of a fourteenth century moulding of the jamb of a doorway were found early in the twentieth century but were removed to the County Museum.

The earliest reference to the Grey Friars is in 1284 when Edward I, on a visit to Carmarthen, gave the friars certain rights over a watercourse that supplied a royal mill and formed part of the outer defences of the castle. A decade later, the King granted them a small holding in Carmarthen and the right to bring a water-course across it. Royal favour was again shown in 1329–30 when the Warden and the Friars Minor were to have a grant of land in Carmarthen from the King. Difficulties about water supply were a constant worry. On 28 June 1331, the King confirmed the gift of Mariota Molle, late wife of Thomas Warewogyl, to the Friars Minor of Kaermerdy, of a spring in her park called '*Walter his Waseway* ' on the slope of Mount Berwyn, to make an aqueduct for their use, and freedom to dig and search for the 'veins of water' of such springs, and to collect and conduct these by under-ground passages to a certain place in her land where the Friars could erect a little house of stone, either round or square, as they pleased, ten feet long and as many broad.

In 1340 David Taverner, John Tredegolde, and Thomas Yonge had fled to the church of the Friars Minor of Carmarthen, and a thief, Thomas Sathavas, to the church of St Peter; when Gilbert Talbot, Justiciar of south Wales, whose headquarters were in Carmarthen castle, levied a fine of £20 on the burgesses for their failure to perform custody. The burgesses hotly objected and sent a complaint to the King claiming that they could not be held responsible. On 4 April King Edward directed the Justiciar to enquire into who should be responsible. On 7 August 1340 Rhys ap Griffith, found that those responsible for the custody of robbers fleeing to churches outside the walls of Carmarthen town, were the communities of Elfed and Widigada. It was they who should answer to the King for the escape of the said felons.

The friars had some difference of opinion with other religious houses and with clergy. The question of mortuaries led to a serious quarrel between the Prior of Carmarthen and the friars.

The Priory of St John, situated at the eastern end of the town, was a much older foundation and according to a grant by Henry II in 1180, the Prior was the ruler of 'Old' Carmarthen, outside the town walls. The dispute was settled on 1 December 1391, when Walter Taymer the Prior, John de Tyssynton, Minister of the Order of Friars Minor of Carmarthen, agreed that the remains of all parishioners of St Peter's, dying in the parish and desiring burial by the Friars should have a mass in St Peter's church before being carried to the house of the Friars.

A record from the early fifteenth century suggests that there were occasional lapses from the standards normally associated with the Order. In February 1411, the Pope issued a Mandate to the Bishop of Exeter to enquire into a petition he had received on behalf of Henry, donzel, (a page or esquire, sometimes a youth or young man), eldest son and heir of John Witberi of the diocese of Exeter. This petition stated that when the boy was eleven years old, his father handed him against his will to the Friars Minor in the suburbs of Exeter, in order to exclude him from his paternal inheritance. Fearing his father, Henry took the habit and tonsure of the friars before he was twelve. The friars, suspecting that he intended to escape, took him about the country for over six months in order to confuse him. They took him to remote places until at length *'they brought him against his will to Wales and placed him in the Friars Minor's house at Keymerthyn in the diocese of St Davids. Thus amongst unknown friars, and in a foreign land he asked the Warden to restore his secular garments and let him return to the world, or at least permit him to depart naked,'* but *'the Warden, a Welshman, moved with anger, caused him to be kept close,'* and at the end of the year urged him to make his regular profession, which he declined to do, repeating his request to be allowed to return to the world. *'The Warden threatened him with formidable punishments (cruciatibus) if he did not remain in the Order, and caused him to be kept more diligently, and strove by threats and threats and terrors to extort by some means or other his said profession. When in his fifteenth year, by formidable threats of prison and corporal punishment, and various other penalties, compelled him to take the order of sub-deacon, and occasionally to minister therein.'* Finally he managed to escape. The Pope ordered the Bishop to examine the matter, and, if true, to declare that it had been lawful for Henry to return to the world, and that he could contract marriage.

The religious houses were a source of recruitment of clergy men for the Welsh dioceses. Friars left the convent to become priests. In 1401 the Bishop of St Davids ordained four friars minor, David Sylly, Thomas Golld, John Rok, and Richard Flory as acolytes; in 1486 William Court *'of the Order of Minors, Carmarthen,'* was admitted by the Bishop on the title of letters by the Guardian of the Friary; in 1490 Hugh Richardes, *'friar of the Order of Minors, Carmarthen'* was admitted Deacon, and Priest in the following year; in 1491 Friar John Thomas *'of the Order of Minors, Carmarthen,'* was admitted sub-deacon, and subsequently deacon; in 1496 Lewis ap Rees of the same order was admitted acolyte; in 1502 John Lewis *'of the Order of Friars Minor, Carmarthen,'* and Friar Abraham Ugge *'of the Order of the Preachers of Carmarthen,'* were admitted priests. On 3 November 1490 in *'the house of Friars Minor of Carmarthen'* the Bishop collated Lewis ap Jankyn, chaplain, to the living of Aberyscir in Breconshire, and on the following day collated William Clement to Pencarreg, and Hugh ap Thomas, chaplain, to Llanybydder.16

The Friars received many gifts from the community. William Maliphant of Tenby, in his will dated 26 February 1344, bequeathed the sum of one shilling to the Minorite brothers of Carmarthen to pray for his soul. By a codicil to his will, dated 14 June 1531, Sir Mathew Cradock of Swansea bequeathed 20 shillings to the Grey Friars of Carmarthen. Griffith David Ddu, a west Wales priest, by his will dated 28 September 1537, proved in London 26 March 1538, made these bequests:

> To the grey friars of Carmarthen 20 shillings, they 'to keep my father, mother, and brother Llewys ap Reynall is obite solemphye by note the next Lent' in the presence of my friend Thomas Bruyn: and to a friar observant at Karmerdin 53 shillings and 4 pence to sing masses daily for my soul.

This was one of the very last bequests to the house as it was surrendered in the following year.

Many distinguished people who were buried in the church made gifts for the upkeep of the fabric and for masses for the dead. Among them was William de Valence, son of Earl of Pembroke, killed near Llandilo on 17 July 1282, and Edmund Tudor, Earl of Richmond, 'father and brother to kings' who died in November 1456, and was buried in the middle of the choir. After he ascended the Throne, Henry VII made a grant of £8 yearly to the Carmarthen Friars for keeping a daily mass and perpetual anniversary for his father's soul, and for his own soul after death. Also buried there were Sir Thomas Rede and Sir Rhys ap Griffith who died at Carmarthen on 10 May 1356. Griffith ap Nicholas, who died c.1456–8, was *buried in a Tombe of Allabastre before ye image of St Francis*; Griffith's son and grandson, Rhys ap Griffith and Sir Rhys ap Thomas; Sir Rhys's mother, Elizabeth, daughter and heiress of Sir John Griffith of Abermarlais; Sir Rhys himself in 1525 and his wife Janet, daughter of Thomas Mathew of Radyr in Glamorgan, who died at Picton Castle, Pembrokeshire, on 5 February 1535; and an ancestor of Sir Rhys' mother, Sir Rhys ap Griffith of Abermarlais, who died at Carmarthen on 10 May 1356.

Sir Rhys ap Thomas, in his 70th year, suffered a fatal illness and came to live for his remaining days die with the monks. He made a will on 3 February 1525, in which he stipulated that he wanted

> in the chauncell of the gray freres of Kermerdyn whereas my
> mother lyeth, and whensoever it please God to call my wife out of
> this transitory lyfe my will is that she be buried by me.

and bequeathed £20 to the:

> Freres of Kermerden; and I will that fyve pounds of lands be surely
> founded to the Gray Freres of Kermerdyn for a chauntry there, to
> fynde two priests to pray for me and my wife for ever.

The first witness to the will was *Doctour David Mothvey,
wardeyn of the gray freres of Kermerdyn*. Sir Rhys died on Thursday,
9 February 1525, and his body lay in state until it was placed in a
grave in the quire on Friday, the 24 February. He had been patron
of the bard, Tudur Aled, who died at the Friary in 1526, and was
buried in the churchyard in the habit of a grey friar which he also
had taken to wearing in his final days.

Another who stayed at the Friary was William Egwad
(1450–1500). He was from the parish of Llanegwad and composed
a poem of praise to *Cwrt y Brodyr, Caerfyrddin*, (The Brothers'
Court, Carmarthen). He names a *Syr Rhys Griffith* as the builder of
the Friars' house, maker of the chancel, and friend of St Francis,
who died in 1356 and was buried in the church (see above). The
bard also mentions *gwely Emwnt* – the tomb of Edmund Tudor.

Among the manuscripts of the Grey Friars was a vellum roll of
arms dating from about 1340 and now known as 'Cooke's
Ordinary.' On the back were words written in the sixteenth
century:

> *Rowch honn y gwrtt brodyr Kaer Verdinn*

(Give this (roll) to the Court of the brothers of Carmarthen).

The roll had been repaired with a piece of vellum stuck to the
back, which turned out to be a fragment cut from the fifteenth
century accounts of Villa de Drusselyn (Dryslwyn) and Villa de
Kerm'd.

During the period when Henry VIII attempted to divorce his

wife, he had been opposed by three friars, Peto, Elstowe, and Forest, two of whom he had thrown into prison. When Henry had broken with Rome and made himself supreme head of the Church in England the religious houses were closed but as the Grey Friars were a preaching Order, continuously moving about the country, with little property to lose anyway, they were considered to be more dangerous than the monastic and secular clergy. In 1535 the friars of Carmarthen had to leave and all their goods handed over to the Crown. They themselves were turned out and made homeless.

The instrument of surrender dated 30 August 1538 lists all the property of the Carmarthen Friary which included vestments and sacred vessels. Carmarthen Friary was the richest of the Welsh Franciscan houses. The roof of the choir and part of the church and chapel was covered with lead, and all of which had gutters and conduits. There was a leaded pane in a window of the cloister. The Sacristy contained a large number of beautiful vestments, among them a *sute of blake welvit purpulleid with the apostelles on the backe, a sute of redde welvit with redde offeras (orphreys) of flowers, and a paule of clothe of tussey for the Erle of Richemuntes tumbe.* The Choir contained Mass hooks, crosses, candle-sticks, *a goodly tumbe for Sir Ryse ap Thomas, with a grate of yron abowt him, a stremar banner of hys armys with his cote armor and helmit,* and many other items. The Chirche (*nave*) contained five altar tables of alabaster, two sacry bells, and a *frame of iron thorow all the chirche, before the auterys for taberys (tapers).* In the stepill (*steeple*) was a clock and two bells.

The King's Chamber had a featherbed, bolster, blankets, sheets, and coverings, and other bedroom furniture: then the Inner Chamber, the Chamber next to the *Laverys*, and the Chamber next to the parlour door. These were bedrooms, containing featherbeds. Then in the kitchen was a *gret range of iron to make in fyer,* the Brewhouse, the Buttery, the Hall (refectory) *iron to make in fyer*, the Brewhouse, the Buttery, the Hall (refectory) with two tables, forms, and trestles for the friars, and *a gret chayer of timber for the Warden*.

Not all the furniture and goods were in the convent. Some had been loaned to various people in the town, and among the items *abrode* were three brass pans and a brass pot, a coffer, while a vestment and two altar-cloths were on loan to the chapel in Carmarthen castle.

Despite its wealth the Friary had found it difficult to make both ends meet. The King's visitor noticed the following articles had been pawned – the Cross (for £20), a bason, ewer, and best chalice (£14), beside other plate; and recorded a claim of twenty marks for the table of the high altar, and six copes. These, the Visitor redeemed.

Nevertheless the Visitor netted a fair haul – a goodly *cross with Mary and John*, two chalices all gilt, a bason, and ewer, three cruets, a pax, a paten of a chalice, other pieces of a cross, a pyx all gilt and with a crystal. The Friars had lost some articles through burglary, and the Visitor left a cope to satisfy the losers. The Visitor also left the food in the house and 6s. 8d in money for a poor friar that lay sick.

The inventory was signed by the Bishop of St Davids, Thomas Prichard, Vicar of St Peters, and Martyn Davy, Mayor of the town. The Friars then put their names on the document – John Trahern, S.T.B., Warden, Lewis Richard, Richard Gr(iffith), Morgan David, Richard Ph(ilip), Thomas Makesfyld, Res Ord, Evan Phylyp, William David, Henry Morgan, Bernardin Blackburne, John Geffre, and John Brygon. Then the Visitor *gave every freere 12 pence and their own stuffe, & so departeid.* and sent them out into the world.

The real property of the friaries was usually placed in the hands of men called firmarii (farmers) or computators, responsible for collecting rents for the Crown. In charge of the Carmarthen house was John Lloyd, and his accounts at the end of the year immediately following the surrender show that the tenants were all in arrears with their rents. His account for the year ending Michaelmas 1539 shows that the property was held as follows:

i. by himself, the site of the friary and demesne, garden, cemetery, stable, and other buildings, attached, at 5 shillings a year, the Great Park (about 3 acres), at 10 shillings, a small close called Park Cyrill (about 1 acre) at 4 shillings, a small close called the little Park (about half an acre) at 2 shillings.

ii. by Lewis Hopkyn, a burgage in Kaystrete outside the walls of the New Town, at 5 shillings.

iii. by James Williams, a tenement next to the door of the friary, at 3 shillings and 10 pence. The house of the Friars was then vacant.

At the time of the Dissolution, or very soon afterwards, the remains of Sir Rhys ap Thomas and his lady were transferred to the church of St Peter, Carmarthen, and those of Edmund Tudor to St Davids Cathedral. The tomb of Sir Rhys, despite much restoration and repairs still retains many of its original features. It may have been the work of the Italian sculptor Mazzoni or perhaps Torregiano, both of whom were concerned with the design and execution of the monument of Henry VII and his Queen in Westminster Abbey. Sir Rhys' tomb was placed in the north side of the Chancel of St Peter, and remained there until 1865 when it was moved to its present site and restored at the costs of Lord Dynevor. On the covering slab lies the effigy of Sir Rhys, dressed in plate armour marked with his heraldic cognizance, his sword, and cloak of knighthood; above his head is the helmet and torce. At his side is the effigy of his lady. A number of sketches made by John Carter in 1803, and a description by Donovan in 1805 show what the monument had buildings were left empty. Bishop Barlow, who disapproved of St Davids as the seat of his diocese, tried to establish it in a more central spot, and saw the Carmarthen Friary as an ideal place. In 1536 he petitioned the authorities and wrote from Carmarthen to Thomas Cromwell on 31 March 1536, praying that a grant be made to him *of the Grey Friars place at Kermerddyn* where the King's grandfather lay buried, and where the collegians and canons could be accommodated and do much more good than *in a desolate corner at St David*.

The Bishop received no response to his plea, but the Precentor of St Davids, Thomas Lloyd was more successful in his attempt to obtain help and permission to open a grammar school in the town. On 30 January 1543, the King decreed that the school to be known as *The King's Scole of Carmarden of Thomas Lloyd's fundacion*. It was to be kept in the former house of the Friars and a master and an usher were appointed. The school flourished until a few years after the founder's death in 1547.

By 1632 the Friary buildings belonged to Mr Walton. On 24 November of that year, Lewis Walton of the city of Worcester, saddler, and Anne his wife, granted to the Rt. Hon. Richard Vaughan, Knight of the Bath, Lord Vaughan, of Golden Grove, in consideration of £595, *all that the scite and precincks of the late dissolved Monastry and howse called by the name of Gray Ffryers near Gelstreete also Gerstreete, alias Lama Streete, and all houses, edifices, buildings, orchards, gardens, barns, stables, pigeon houses, hedges, and ditches, adjoining the said premises; also that close, park, and parcell of lands called* The Greate Parke *alias* Parke y Skeebor *with a barn built thereon; and park and parcel of lands called the* Park Hill *alias* Parke yr hill *a close or park called* Parke y Clomendy; *and a close, called* the Little Parke *alias* the ffryers Parke; *all then in the tenure and occupation of Henry Vaughan, esquire, his assigns or undertenants.* The property remained part of the Golden Grove estate until 1912 when it was sold to a local doctor.

From 1634 onwards the Friary had a succession of tenants. The older buildings disappeared and the dwelling house was adapted so much that no features of the original structure are recognizable today.

The church was still standing in the early half of the eighteenth century, when Archdeacon Yardley commented:

to this Priory (read Friary) Church it was that Bishop Barlow attempted ye Removing ye See, the' but a small Building of a single Isle, and without a Steeple or Pillars; it is in length about 70 or 80 feet, and in breadth 30 feet.

The steeple, mentioned in 1538, had been taken down by 1700 or so. Buck's view of Carmarthen from the south east, engraved in 1748, shows Friars Park on a long slope with some trees growing on the Lammas Street side, and some buildings, details of which are obscure. According to Spruill, writing in 1879, the remains of the monastery *were to be seen in Friars'-park*. The tower of the church was also pulled down.

The burial ground was immediately to the east of the church, and occupied an area now cultivated as a garden. Human remains are said to have been found on the site, and the spot where a Warden – alleged to have broken his neck by falling down some stairs-lies buried, is on the southwest side of the present house.

Two plans of the town were made in 1786 by Thomas Lewis, land surveyor, one of which shows the property of John Morgan, the other the property of John Vaughan of Golden Grove. The Morgan plan shows only the outline area of Friars Park, while the Vaughan plan contains details of the actual fields and buildings. On the plans the land owned by the friars amounted to only some 4½ to 5 acres and was in the immediate vicinity of the Friary.

Friars Park House has always been a superior residence,

4½ to 5 acres and was in the immediate vicinity of the Friary.

Friars Park House has always been a superior residence, situated in a charming spot, sheltered by good timber, and enjoying an attractive southerly prospect. Towards the end of the eighteenth century, when the Reverend Peter Williams, of *Peter Williams' Bible* fame, was expelled from the Methodist Association in 1791 the Society conducted its meetings in Friars Park. Towards the middle of the nineteenth century Friars Park was the home of Dr John Morgan Hopkins, M.D. On 4 May 1894, Earl Cawdor granted a lease of The Friary with the three cottages and gardens adjoining, and also a garden and field, to Thomas Jenkins of Lammas Street a corn merchant, for twenty one years. This lease was later assigned to Dr Lloyd Middleton Bowen Jones, a medical officer of health.

Further Reading

Carmarthen and its Neighbourhood. W. Spurrell.

Monastic Wales http://www.monasticwales.org

The Grey Friars of Carmarthen. F. Jones. 1966.

Transactions Carm. 1917–18.

West Wales Historical Records, VII.

Name:	**LLANFAES FRIARY**
	RESTING PLACE FOR A KING'S DAUGHTER
Order:	**Franciscan**
Location:	**Fryars (private), Llanfaes Beaumaris, Anglesey**
OS Map Ref.:	**SH 608773**

Llanfaes was a royal township in the commote of Dindaethwy in Anglesey during the twelfth and thirteenth centuries. It is situated one mile north of Beaumaris. Amongst the most important buildings of the township were the royal halls and other buildings of the *llys* (royal court). The Llanfaes ferry, working across the Menai Strait was amongst the most important of the ferries plying backwards and forwards from Anglesey to Caernarfonshire. It had a safe anchorage in Llanfaes Bay. The fairs and markets of Llanfaes were full with stalls of brewers, butchers, bakers, clothes makers and shoemakers. Taxes were levied. Tolls had to be paid. Llanfaes became the centre of commerce for Dindaethwy. It was a busy village rapidly growing to town status, growing to be the centre of commerce for Gwynedd. Due to its importance as a market town and port, in 1254 Llanfaes church was the richest on Anglesey.

Looking at Llanfaes today, one would have difficulty in imagining such a place as it now a quiet halmet on the edge of the castle town of Beaumaris.

In 1283 the war of Llywelyn ap Gruffudd and Edward I was concluded with the death of Llywelyn and his brother Dafydd and the conquest of Gwynedd. Injustices in the newly established administration gave rise to a revolt, instigated by Madog ap Llywelyn. Damage was done at Llanfaes and the town never recovered. Edward I's response was to build a new castle named Beaumaris. Edward removed the population of Llanfaes to Rhosyr, in the commote of Menai, today known as *Niwbwrch* (Newborough). By 1240 Llywelyn ap Iorwerth and the Bishop of Bangor, who had consecrated the friary, were both dead. Franciscan friars usually settled in urban rather than rural areas as there was a larger congregation in towns and alms were easier to come by but as Llanfaes' slipped into obscurity, the friary lost a great deal of its importance and wealth.

Llanfaes' importance waned at the expense of Beaumaris' growth. The church remained, but its congregation had left. The friary also continued to exist. Joan, daughter of King John and

England, and a woman named Clemence Pinel. She spent her childhood in France, until when 1205 her father decided that she would marry Llywelyn, Lord of Snowdon (*Arglwydd Eryri* and who was known as Llywelyn the Great or *Llywelyn Fawr*) as a means of restoring peace with Wales. In May 1206 at the age of 15, Joan was taken to Chester to marry Llywelyn. She betrayed Llywelyn with William de Braose (*Gwilym Brewys* or *Gwilym Ddu* – Welsh for Black William), a Norman Marcher lord, the tenth Baron of Abergavenny, who was detested by the Welsh. In 1228 he was captured by Llywelyn's men in the commote of Ceri, Montgomery. He was later ransomed for £2,000 and later came to an agreement with Llywelyn, allowing his daughter Isabella de Braose to marry Llywelyn's only legitimate son, Dafydd. However, in Easter 1230, he was found with Joan in her bedchamber.

William de Braose was hanged in a field behind the palace of Garth Celyn in Abergwyngegyn, Gwynedd. Llywelyn had Joan imprisoned in a tower at Garth Celyn for twelve months. Afterwards she was forgiven for her adultery and taken back as Llywelyn's wife.

Joan died in February 1237. Llywelyn founded a Franciscan Friary near to the shore of Llanfaes, where Joan had been buried. The Friary was consecrated in 1240, just a few months before Llywelyn's death in April of the same year. Llywelyn was not buried with his wife, but at Aberconwy Abbey, to where he had retired during the last few years of his life. Joan's Friary at Llanfaes was destroyed in 1537 as part of Henry VIII's Dissolution of the Monasteries and her tomb was desecrated by the English army. The whereabouts of the coffin was unknown until it was found in the town of Beaumaris where it had been used as an animal drinking trough for almost 200 years. Today Joan's stone coffin lies in the porch at Beaumaris Church.

Llanfaes friary remained the burial place of many local

worthies including Dafydd ab Ieuan ap Hywel of Llwydiarth who was killed in a brawl in Beaumaris and Angharad his wife, who died of shock on hearing of her husband's death. (This is confirmed in poems by Guto'r Glyn, Hywel Cilan and Tudur Penllyn); Eleanor de Monfort, wife of Llywelyn ap Gruffudd died in childbirth in 1282 and was buried in Llanfaes Friary; Goronwy ap Tudur drowned in Kent on 11th December 1331 and his body was brought home to Anglesey to be buried in Llanfaes. Iolo Goch, poet, mentions the burial of Goronwy ap Tudor of Penmynydd at Llanfaes – the half-naked friar; Gwilym ap Gruffudd ap Tudur left the friary £2 in his will in 1375 and was buried there. In 1400 Cynwrig ab Ieuan ap Llywelyn of Rhosyr left 2/- to the friary of his old home town. Gwilym ap Gruffudd of Penmynydd, in 1431, expressed his desire to be buried in Llanfaes. Bishop John Cliderow left £1 each to the friars of Llanfaes in his will, dated 1435. Hugh Stretton of Beaumaris left the friary a cow in his 1491 will. Lleucu ferch Iolyn of Llanfair Dyffryn Clwyd left the friary 6/8d in her will, drawn out in 1494.

The church and township was burned during the Madog Revolt of 1294 and left in ruins but the friary and the priory at nearby Penmon were compensated for the damage done to the buildings.

The Bible of Brother Gervase of Bangor is an interesting relic from the thirteenth century. It is a 'pocket' Bible – written in small script in two columns on very fine parchment. This style of Bible is typical of a style developed in Paris, most likely for the use of Dominicans who needed to have a portable copy. An inscription c.1300 states that this Bible belonged to Brother Gervase of Bangor, a member of the Dominican house; and that following his death it should be bequeathed to the Franciscan house at Llanfaes, Anglesey.

The friary suffered during the troubles at the beginning of the

Llanfaes, Anglesey.

The friary suffered during the troubles at the beginning of the fifteenth century and was said to have been deserted as a result of their suport of the Owain Glyndŵr Rebellion; the friars were dispersed as rebels in January 1401 but the friary was reconstituted in 1414 when the king ordered that eight friars be settled there. Out of the eight, two were to have been Welsh speakers. Before that, all the friars were Welsh.

An inventory from the time of the suppression in 1538 gives a list of its belongings including the friary church, choir and vestry, a brew-house with a furnace and brewing vat, a yard with carts and various outbuildings including one with racks for cheese; another with beds, pillows and bolsters; a kitchen; a hall with table and trestles and a store house; agricultural produce, grain, cattle and twenty two sheep, two copies of a Mass book, a feather bed and standing corn worth £1 6s., land with a rent value of £3 1s 10d. The four remaining friars had left by 19 August of that year.

Richard Bulkeley, Baron Hill, Beaumaris offered Cromwell 100 marks for the friary to turn it into a dwelling house. In 1539 Thomas Bulkeley was granted a lease of the friary lands and proceeded to demolish its buildings. Loads of good stone were removed to Beaumaris for building and repairing the quay and town walls. In 1563, the lease passed to Ellis Wynne. The friary church survived as a barn until the nineteenth century. Later in 1623, Rowland Whyte built the first secular house at Fryars.

The Nave at Llanfaes was 51 feet by 28 feet and had a triplet of lancet-lights in the west wall and in the south wall a large arch, 17 feet wide, with a doorway to the east of it, both opening into a large transeptal chapel or chapels and corresponding very closely to the arrangement at Buttevant, Multi-fernam, Muckross (Irrelach) and many other Irish friaries. West of the large arch and in the transept, was a recess, probably for a tomb. To the east of the nave was a division (21 feet by 26 feet) opening to the east and west by segmental arches, which are said to have been of 'Perpendicular' character. This was no doubt the 'walking-place' between the friars' quire and the nave, and above it was the steeple.

In the north wall was a doorway, which was probably the only entrance from the cloister to the friars' quire. Marks in the turf were noted, in 1855, indicating a destroyed building extending 18 feet further east. This was the friars' quire, which in the first church, perhaps included the space under the steeple and making a total length of 41 f feet. When the fifteenth-century arches were inserted the quire must have been lengthened towards the east. This alteration may have been part of the reconstruction indicated in the charter of Henry V, dated 1414. As to the domestic buildings, they must have stood on the side of the church opposite to that of the transept, namely the north side, but there is no further evidence concerning them. An unusually fine tomb-slab, with the half effigy of a lady, and elaborate foliage, is now preserved in Beaumaris parish church. The effigy has been ascribed to Joan, daughter of King John and wife of the founder, and appears to date from the middle of the thirteenth century.

The inventory of goods taken at the dissolution, mentions the quire with a fair table of alabaster over the high altar, four tables of alabaster in the church, a bell in the steeple, the vestry, brew-house, kitchen, hall, store-house and cloister. The term 'church' included the transeptal chapels.

Further Reading
Crwydro Môn. Bobi Jones. Llyfrau'r Dryw. 1957.

Medieval Anglesey. A. D. Carr. Anglesey Antiquarian Society. 1982.
Monastic Wales http://www.monasticwales.org
The Architectural Remains Of The Mendicant Orders In Wales. A. W. Clapham.

PREMONSTRATERIANS

An order known as 'White Canons', monks of this order were followers of Norbert of Prémontré. The order was founded in 1126 and the mother house located at Prémontré, near Laon in France. Their life was one of prayer and working as parish priests and bishops. They also ran hospitals. Talyllychau (Talley) Abbey was their only foothold in Wales.

Name:	**TALYLLLYCHAU (TALLEY) ABBEY**
	THE ONLY ONE OF ITS KIND
Order:	**Premonstratensian**
Location:	**Talyllychau, Carmarthenshire SA19**
OS Map Ref.:	**SN 633229**

When it was decided that a visit to an abbey would facilitate my knowledge and understanding of a 'House of God' in preparation for this volume, all the planning consisted of was an early morning message to be ready at the appointed hour of nine o'clock. All instructions were obeyed and the sixty-five mile journey commenced on the hour and our target abbey (Valle Crucis) was duly reached by 10.45 a.m. All that needed to be done had been completed by mid-afternoon and we were home again by 5 p.m. in time for tea. Were we members of the Cardiganshire Antiquarian Society in 1909, our visit to Talley Abbey, the only Premonstratensian abbey in Wales, would have entailed much more planning and hours on the road. The Aberystwyth contingent of the said society:

> started by the 8.10a.m. GWR motor and by the time Tregaron was reached this was comfortably full of members of the Society. At Lampeter the party had increased in numbers so much that it was with difficulty that sufficient accommodation could be found for all in the conveyances provided. The journey of fifteen miles from Lampeter to Talley was accomplished in four well-appointed breaks.

On reaching Pumsaint, they were taken to see the grounds of Dolaucothi before resuming their journey (or was it a pilgrimage by then?) and reached Talley at about 1.30 p.m. to have lunch at the Edwinsford Arms.

On the return journey,

> The drive was continued to Alltmynydd Sanatorium, where a splendid concert was held. At seven o'clock, the journey was continued to Lampeter, where at 8.30, the party sat down to dinner at the Black Lion Hotel.

Goodness only knows when they eventually made it back home to bed, to dream perhaps of the tower of the ruined abbey:

> Guardian and monitor for all our days
> Like fortress stern, thou bad'st men hope and dare.
> Thy bells as angel-voices word on word
> Chiming with sweetest music in the air
> Called up men's hearts to Heaven, that they might praise
> The tower of hope eternal-Christ the Lord.

One can only admire their persistence as one admires the monks who built the original abbey.

Talley Abbey stands between two small streams, one of which flows north towards the lakes (*llychau*) that give the area its name and the other which flows south to join the Tywi. H. W. Owen and R Morgan believe that the original meaning of the name could be *end of the stone slabs* which could refer to *a causeway providing end of the stone slabs* which could refer to *a causeway providing access to the abbey between the two fishponds.* Colonised by a small group of canons from the house of St John at Amiens in north-east France, Talley Abbey was the only Premonstratensian abbey to be established in Wales, it was founded by Lord Rhys c.1185.

Troubles soon multiplied for the canons because of language differences, problems with planning a new church and difficult neighbours. Money was also scarce which meant that plans for a large eight bay nave church had to be abandoned and they had to make do with a smaller, four bays church. There was no north nave aisle, and lower grade building materials were used to complete the buildings.

Talley Abbey became one of the first victims of Edward I's Welsh conquests, and this was the start of a prolonged battle between the English and the Welsh over the paternal rights of the abbey. War brought more insecurity and financial difficulties leading to plans for other monsatic building work having to be forgotten.

On 17 August 1271, Rhys Fychan died at his castle of Dinefwr. He was buried in the abbey of Talyllychau to which he had been a benefactor, confirming the gifts of his great grandfather, the Lord Rhys, and his grandfather, Rhys Gryg.

The abbot of Talley, either Rees ap David or Rees ap Jevan, used a great deal of the abbey's money in 1381 and as a result, the abbey was reduced to poverty. In 1391 the king ordered his officials at Carmarthen to administer the lands at Talley and take them into his protection, allowing the abbot sufficient moneys to meet his needs.

There were eight cannons at Talley at the time of The Dissolution and most of the lands of Talley were leased to Richard Dauncey, a member of the king's household. Most of the buildings were destroyed, but the abbey church was used by the parish until 1772. In 1773, a Mr Hodgkinson of Rhydodin persuaded the parishioners to take down the chief part of the old abbey church, which until then been used for Divine worship. The material from the demolition was used to build a new church. The expense of the work was met by the sale of the great bell of the abbey to the authorities at Exeter Cathedral.

By the middle of the 19th century the whole site had collapsed into decay and became buried under later constructions. In 1845 a considerable part of the building fell during a very severe winter. Fortunately, a Victorian engineer with a great enthusiasm for monastic archaeology, initiated an excavation programme at Talley Abbey, and more extensive excavations were undertaken during the 1930s which revealed the ground plan of the abbey. The state of the ruins caused The Royal Commission on Ancient Monuments much worry in 1923 because so many visitors were carrying away fragments of the corner stones from the north transept! Today, the remains of the central crossing tower still rise to a height of 85ft (25.7m), completely dominating the site and the surrounding area. Other than this, there is little left to see apart from a few low walls, the rubble stone bases of the rectangular piers, and evidence of where the altars were positioned.

But beware! There are other things that have been seen such as the Ghosts of Talley Abbey. When the abbey was closed, the locals believed that the spirits of the dead monks would follow the remains wherever they went and as much of the stone work was recycled and used in the building of many local houses, it was only natural that they were followed and seen. Another story from deepest Carmarthenshire is that a tunnel exists between the oldest house in the village and the abbey which is also inhabited by ghosts. Such things have to be seen to be believed!

Further Reading

A Tour of the Abbeys, Priories and Cathedrals of Wales. D. S. Yerburgh. Yerburgh. 1999.

Dictionary of the Place Names of Wales. H. W. Owen & R. Morgan. Gomer Press. 2007.

Monastic Wales http://www.monasticwales.org

The Round Table. Megan Ellis. October 1934

Visit to Talley Abbey. Transactions and Archaeological Record. Cardiganshire Antiquarian Society. 1911.

TIRONENSIANS

Founded by St Bernard, who gave up his life as a solitary to start a new community and a new order at Tiron in 1109. His ideas about living a religious life were very similar to the Cistercians. Tironensian monks were used to manual work and gave much attention to all the arts and crafts. The order became established in Wales in 1115.

Name:	**CALDEY ISLAND PRIORY**
	CELTIC, CATHOLIC, CHRISTIAN and CISTERCIAN
Order:	**Tironensian**
Location:	**off south east coast of Tenby, Pembrokeshire**
OS Map Ref.:	**SS 140963**

Caldey Island, three miles off the coast of Tenby, Pembrokeshire is a private island and a religious site run by Cistercian monks. Much of the mile and a half long by three quarters of a mile wide island is uninhabited. In prehistoric times, it was joined to the mainland by a low marshy area. The monks who went to the island wanted peace so it can only be reached by boat, even today. Before the monks, prehistoric man lived on the island, and remains have been found. Caldey has been a place of worship for monks for 1500 years. Caldey's original Welsh name was Ynys Pyr, named after the first abbot whilst the name Caldey comes from the Viking period of the tenth century.

The island was a gift by by Henry I to Robert Fitzmartin but in 1113 he handed it over to his mother Geva, who was also the founder of the Abbey of St Dogmael's, who in 1136 presented it to Benedictine monks from France. They built an abbey on the site of the monastic settlement of St Pyro. A small corn mill was also established on the island.

It has always been a small religious community with only one monk in the late twelfth century, four in 1402 and six in 1504. In the priory is a sixth century stone with an Ogham and a Latin inscription referring to Dubracunas, who had consecrated St Sampson as abbot of the monastery in 550. He had followed in the footsteps of Pyro, the first abbot. Sampson left to found a monastery in Dol, Brittany.

The Benedictines were forced to leave when Henry VIII dissolved the monasteries when the annual income was only £5 and only the one monk in residence. The domestic buildings became a farm and still stand in a remarkably good condition.

The island then passed through a number of hands. In 1786 the owner Thomas Kynaston, built a mansion in the priory grounds and a number of farm buildings. Limestone was quarried on the island. In 1866 James Hawkesley purchased the island and encouraged market gardening. He also built greenhouses. The island was purchased by the Reverend Done Bushell in 1897, who renovated the priory and St Illtud and St David's churches. He is the person responsible for bringing monks back to the island. Under the leadership of Benjamin (later Abbot Aelred) Carlyle the island was purchased in 1906 and a monastery built. The abbey was built in 1910 and further restoration of other buildings took island was purchased in 1906 and a monastery built. The abbey was built in 1910 and further restoration of other buildings took place. In 1926 the island was sold to the Reformed Cistercians. It was purchased from an Anglo Catholic community in 1928. In 1940 a fire burned the south wing and abbey church.

The reformed or Trappist Cistercian monks of Caldey Island make perfumes and chocolate from imported ingredients.

The church has a presbytery and a sanctuary at the east end and a small tower at the west end. On the north side of the church is a small eight square metre cloister whilst on the west wing is a gatehouse with a guest room above. On the eastern side is the dormitory, over the kitchen. There is also a Prior's tower still standing, and apart from the refectory and parts of the west wing, all other remains are from the thirteen or fourteenth century. Only the church, though, is open to the public.

> *The tower of the priory church, surmounted by a stoe spire, is yet standing, and many of the conventual buoldiongs have been converted into offices, and attached to a handsome modern edifice, the seat of the present owner.*

> *Wales Illustrated.* Jones & Co. 1830

The present day abbey is a building put up by Anglican Benedictines but has been used for many years by Roman Catholic Cistercians.

St Anna (born c.AD 445) was a younger daughter of Vortimer Fendigaid, the King of Gwerthefyriwg, Gwent. She married her first husband, *Cynyr Ceinfarfog* (the Fair Bearded), Lord of Caer-Goch in Dyfed. St Ann's Head, west of Milford Haven, is probably named after her. The two had at least six children together, the eldest of whom was the famous Arthurian warrior, *Cai Hir* (the Tall), and another was Non, the mother of St David. Following *Myrddin* (alias Merlin)'s agreement with the King Uther that his son should be brought up in secret, the family was expanded by the addition of a foster-son, the future King Arthur.

Anna was probably the mother of St Samson, who was also from Gwent. Some time after Arthur became king, Cynyr died and Anna married Prince *Amon Ddu* (the Black) of Brittany. After they married, Amon made his home in Dyfed and became a high-ranking official at the Royal Court. They had at least three children, Samson, Tydecho and Tegfedd, all of whom lived a religious life. Samson became an influential bishop and eventually persuaded his parents to enter the church. Amon became a monk at *Ynys Byr* (Caldey Island), whilst Anna moved back to her native Gwent.

In a battle of 'democracy over bureaucracy', the monks and residents of Caldey Island fought to protect their right to independence in 2009, amid fears they could become part of Tenby, Pembrokeshire. The island, a religious retreat for more than 1,000 years and with an electorate of 28, was to be united with Tenby's town council but the islanders, including the semi-trappist brothers of the Reformed Cistercian Order, said the move would be a costly one for them with no additional benefit. With only a few hundred yards of road, no crime, and self-sufficiency dating back generations, there was nothing that Tenby town council could offer them. They were determined not to relinquish a right to independence granted to them in a Royal Charter dating back to Henry VIII.

The island is unanimous. We feel very strongly about it. It's purely a bureaucratic exercise, which makes no sense.

said retired pharmacist Herbert Moore, 94, who had lived on Caldey Island for more than 30 years.

minutes depending on weather and sea conditions. The island is closed to visitors on Sundays.

Further Reading

Abbeys and Priories in England and Wales. B. Little. Batsford Books. 1979.

Abbeys and Priories of Wales. R. Cooper. Christopher Davies. 1992.

Abbeys, Priories and Cathedrals of Wales. M. Salter. Folly Publications. 2012.

A Tour of the Abbeys, Priories and Cathedrals of Wales. D. S. Yerburgh. Yerburgh. 1999.

Early British Kingdoms. David Nash Ford. Nash Ford Publishing. 2001. Monastic Wales http://www.monasticwales.org

Name:	**PILL PRIORY**
	A PRIVATE PLACE
Order:	**Tironensian**
Location:	**in a private garden, Hubberston, north of Milford Haven, Pembrokeshire SA73**
OS Map Ref.:	**SM 902073**

Situated at the head of Hubberston Pill (pill=a tidal inlet) near Milford Haven, Pill Priory was a daughter house of St Dogmael's Abbey, as was Caldey Island priory. It was established as a Tironensian house by the Roche family, especially Adam de la Roche. Married to Blandina, he was the first to hold Roche Castle, Pembrokeshire. The date of its founding is uncertain but has been calculated as sometime between 1160 and 1190. When completed, the priory was dedicated to the Blessed Virgin Mary and St Budoc.

Pill Priory was a small community but had over 1,300 acres to its name in 1291 and was valued at £21. During the mid-fourteenth century, the prior complained that a descendant of the founder had done great damage to the priory and convent. In 1403, the prior-Walter Robjoy was accused of keeping a married woman as his mistress and of keeping the priory's assets, which included a small ship, to himself and for his own use. A report of a visitation in 1504, reported everything in good condition with a prior, five monks and a small convent working well. The chancel of the church, which had been reported in a bad condition, had been restored and the priory free of debt but it was poor enough to be excused payment of clerical subsidies in 113 and 1517.

There were only five monks in residence 1534 and four in 1536. Its lands and possessions included five orchards, a wood, a meadow at Pill, the priory mill and at least two churches – St Bidoc's and Steynton. All the buildings and holding were let on a lease by the Crown to John Wogan in 1536–37 and John Doune in 1544. At the time of the Dissolution of the Monasteries in 1536 it was recorded that Pill Priory had an annual value of £65 15s 3d. In 1546, the site was sold to Roger and Thomas Barlow, landowners of Slebech.

The priory church was a cruciform structure, at least 40 meters from east to west, with an aisleless nave and chancel. Today it is a private property, reputedly the oldest full time inhabited ruin in Wales. In the garden are what remains there are of the priory church including the chancel arch and parts of the south trancept which were built of local Old Red Sandstone and Carboniferous Limestone.

Further Reading

Abbeys and Priories of Wales. R. Cooper. Christopher Davies. 1992.
Abbeys, Priories and Cathedrals of Wales. M. Salter. Folly Publications. 2012.
Monastic Wales http://www.monasticwales.org

Name:	**ST DOGMAELS ABBEY**
	A TIRONENSIAN TREASURE
Order:	**Tironensian**
Location:	**Church Street, St Dogmael's, Pembrokeshire**
	SA43
OS Map Ref.:	**SN 164458**

Situated on the banks of the river Teifi near to its estuary to the Irish Sea, St Dogmaels was the only Tironensian abbey to be founded in Wales or England.

The first Dogmael of whom any account is found was the son of Cunedda Wledig. His grand-nephew, Dogmael the Saint, after whom the borough of St Dogmaels was named, was the son of Ithael, the son of Ceredig. St Dogmael lived between 450 and 500 A.D. His festival is celebrated on June 14th. He lived on the left bank of the river Teifi, in Pembrokeshire, where he founded a religious house in the field now called '*Yr Hen Fynachlog*' (The Old Monastery), about a mile from the ruins of St Dogmaels Abbey. It was probably here that Robert Fitzmartin brought his first thirteen monks from Tiron, in 1113, before he built the Abbey of St Dogmaels, Cemais, in 1118, when he incorporated the old religious house of St Dogmael with the Abbey, keeping up the name of the first founder.

St Dogmael was a hardy, clean man. One of the rules he made was that his monks were to bathe daily in the waters of the river, both in winter as well as the rest of the year.

St Dogmaels Abbey was originally founded as a priory by Robert fitz Martin on the site of a pre-Norman monastery around 1115. He came to Wales from northern France with a group of twelve monks of the Order of Tiron. It was raised to the status of an abbey in 1120, by which time there were two dozen monks in residence. It remained under the rule of Tiron until its dissolution in 1536.

The church was built on a steep slope which may be the reason why there is no west doorway entrance nor are there any windows in the north wall of the nave. In the floor are large areas of original fifteenth century tiles, still in place. Although domestic dwellings were soon established, the abbey church was not completed until the mid-thirteenth century. This was a time of prosperity for the monks, but the fortunes of the abbey were soon on the wane. In 1402, when the Bishop of St David's visited, St Dogmaels was suffering from a serious financial crisis. The plague had reduced its numbers, and only four monks remained, living a life of drinking in local taverns and carousing with women. The bishop was none too pleased.

The abbey was restored after much damage was done during the Irish invasion of 1138. In 1118 there were twenty six monks, an abbot and many lay brothers at the abbey. It was enlarged and improved from time to time and the ruins show Norman and Perpendicular architecture. The refectory remained standing but was used as a barn.

Life was peaceful at St Dogmaels until 1504, when Henry VII paid a visit and found that the abbey was a very prosperous one indeed. It had enough in its coffers to pay for fan vaulted ceilings during the early years of Henry VIII's reign.

Tironensian monks were skilled craftsmen, having mastered such crafts as carpentry and blacksmithing but lived according to rule of St Benedict. Most of their daily life was taken up by prayer and devotional activities. The monks of St Dogmaels were also renowned fishermen using the seive net or '*shot fawr*' to catch salmon and sewin.

St Dogmaels Abbey was dissolved on 30 July 1534 and the

the Bradshaw family, one of whom presided at the trial of Charles I.

The ruins of St Dogmaels abbey are set apart in a quiet corner of the village of the same name. Very little of the abbey buildings remain. The north nave wall of the abbey church is still standing along with much of the north transept, as is the infirmary and some of the chapter house. An interesting feature is the remains of an unusually placed crypt at the east end of the church, behind and below the presbytery, which it's believed may have housed the relics of St Dogmael.

There were two chapels belonging to the Abbey in St Dogmaels, 'Chappell Cranok' and 'Chappell Degwel'. These two chapels were 'pilgrimage chapels' and were also used for solemn processions on holy days.

The following list of Abbots contains all that are so far traceable:

Fulchardus: (first abbot) from about 1120. Abbot William of Tiron travelled to attend Fulchard's ordination; as did Bishop Bernard of St David's.

Hubert.

Andrew: abbot in the early thirteenth century.

Walter: abbot in 1198, 1202 and 1203.

John: abbot in December 1302.

John Le Rede: abbot before 1330 but died before March 1330.

Phillip: abbot in October 1399, January 1402, 1403, 1404, 1406, 1408, 1415.

Walter.

Lewis Barron.

John Wogan.

William Hire (last abbot) 1520–1536.

If we may judge by the few fine specimens of arches and

ornamental mouldings in the existing remnants of the choir, as well as foundations and other fragments of buildings everywhere to be traced for a great compass, St Dogmael's was a splendid building, and must have covered a very considerable space of ground.

A Historical tour through Pembrokeshire. R. Fenton. 1811

Further Reading

A Tour of the Abbeys, Priories and Cathedrals of Wales. D. S. Yerburgh. Yerburgh. 1999.

Monastic Wales http://www.monasticwales.org

St Dogmaels Abbey Together With Her Cells, Pill, Caldey And Glascareg. E. M. Pritchard. Blades, East & Blades. 1907.

Name: **GOGARTH ABBEY, LLANDUDNO**
          GONE BUT NOT FORGOTTEN
Location: **Unknown**

The exact site of the Abbey is not known but it is supposed to have been some distance from the place where the present (old) church stands on the Great Orme (*Trwyn Gogarth*). It is said to have been built in the sixth century and must have been a very large establishment, as the land between Gogarth and Anglesey had not then been submerged by the sea. It belonged to the Bishops of Bangor but was in ruins before Leland's time. He wrote: *'Ther is by Conway an arme like a peninsula called Gogarth, lying against Priestholine, and ther be the Ruines of a Place of the Bishops of Bangor.'*

Name:	**SINGLETON ABBEY**
	THE ABBEY THAT NEVER WAS
Location:	**Singleton, Swansea SA2**
OS Map Ref.:	**SS 630923**

Having been a student myself, I would be loath to permit students to hold their Summer Ball in an abbey, knowing full well what they can, sometimes, get up to! On reading that Swansea University's Summer Ball was held in Singleton Abbey in 2008, should one have worried that an abbey of all places was chosen to host such an event? Not at all. The main reason being that Singleton Abbey is a complete misnomer and is, anyway, by now part of the University of Wales Swansea and houses the University's administrative offices. One wonders if the students took the advice of Vernon Watkins (1906–1967), who in his Ode to Swansea, wrote about Singleton Park:

Pray, while the starry midnight
Broods over Singleton's elms and swans.

Singleton Abbey was never an abbey and has no ecclesiastical connections! In fact, it is has more connections with the city's copper industry and *Copperopolis* era of Swansea's history than anything else. Interestingly, the 'abbey' stands on land in the manor of St John's, also known as Millwood, which was at one time an estate of the knights of the Hospital of St John of Jerusalem, an order which supported pilgrims on their way to the Holy Land.

The name Singleton has Swansea connections going back to the fourteenth century when a 'de Sengeltone' or 'de Sengleton' family lived in the area. Robert de Sengeltone was a land owner at Bryn y Meiscyl in Millswood. By 1634 a mansion named at Bryn y Meiscyl in Millswood. By 1634 a mansion named 'Singleton' had been built above the shoreline in western Swansea on an estate of thirty two acres of land. It had once been the property of Ellis Price but was leased by David Jones in 1634. The land and house changed hands more than once and in the 1750's was the property of the Bevan family. Not only did the estate change hands but the house, by then, had a new name – Tir-y-Powell.

A new house was built on the site in 1784, one which was nearer the sea to take advantage of the sights to either side of the Bristol Channel and Swansea Bay. It was called Marino. The building of a *curious octagonal shape* was built by Edward King (1750–1819), a Swansea Customs collector. The architect was William Jernegan, from the Channel Islands. King and his wife lived in Marino until 1810, when his wife died, after which he moved to bath in retirement. In 1816, Marino was bought by the Vivian family.

The Vivians were just one of several Swansea's copper industry influential dynasties who owned the Hafod, Tai Bach and White Rock Copper Works and had been partners in the Penclawdd Works. Originally from Truro in Cornwall, John Vivian was an entrepreneur and an industrialist who had interests in all branches of the copper industry including mining, smelting, banking, buying and selling. John wanted his sons to gain control of the British copper market. Thomas, the youngest died in 1821; Richard Hussey became a soldier. This left John Henry to concentrate on business affairs and that is what he did with much success. So much so that John senior went back to Cornwall to live and work.

John Henry gave all of his time and energy to his work in running the family enterprises. He married Sarah Jones in October 1816 and the young couple moved into Marino to begin their married life. It was in an ideal position; near to the Hafod Copper Works but not troubled by the engulfing, poisonous smoke from the copper smelters. John Henry had the lease on the house transferred the lease into his name and very soon in 1818 began work on altering the shape and size of the house. He had paid £2,887 for the freehold and thought that this was to be his Swansea 'palace'. By 1823 the work was completed, two wings on each side of the front of the house facing the sea added making it one of the finest houses in Swansea. An ambitious man, John Henry did not rest on his laurels and in twenty years he had completely rebuilt the house in a late medieval or early Tudor style. In 1829, he had also bought a 42 acre farm owned originally by the Singletons and Marino was renamed Singleton, Singleton Hall, Singleton Park, Singleton Lodge or the one that stuck – Singleton Abbey.

The architect/designer of the new house was Peter Frederick Robinson who had a reputation for Tudor imitations and Gothic facades. His designs were meant to impress and they certainly did but when twentieth century builders were set to work on Singleton Abbey they dismissed much of his work as 'jerry building'. Stables and the stable yards were moved to give an even better view down to Swansea bay and the south Wales coast from the front of the house. Robinson published a book of his designs in 1837 – *Domestic Architecture in the Tudor Style*, which included most of his designs and plans for Singleton Abbey.

Flower gardens and lawns were another addition with fountains and statues; an orangery and a conservatory built to be filled with Himalayan plants. All this for the Vivian family, who were sitting at the top of Swansea's social hierarchy. John Henry had been granted a coat of arms in 1826; he had been High Sheriff of Glamorgan in 1827 and wanted his house to be fit for a queen. Princess Victoria and her mother, the Duchess of Kent were invited to Singleton. Unfortunately on 20 June 1837, Victoria's uncle – William IV died and she became queen. She never made it to Singleton. Some other famous visitors did visit the house including William Ewart Gladstone, British prime minister and his wife who spent five nights there in 1887 and both of whom were most impressed with a stunning display of rhododendrons, as was James Callaghan, a former British prime minister, in 1987.

The house was a family home, filled with children and antiques and reflected the success and wealth of the family. The eldest son – Henry Hussey Vivian moved into Singleton Abbey after the death of Sarah Vivian in 1886 (John Henry had died in 1855) but moved out after the death of his first wife.

After Henry Hussey's death in 1894, the family connections with Singleton Abbey began to wane and the house suffered. It suffered the most after a serious fire in February 1896 when ten rooms were destroyed and it was only by the dog barking that Lady Swansea and her daughters were saved. Some rebuilding was done following the fire but the house never recovered its previous elegance. Some of the family moved to Cae'r Beris, Builth Wells to live, where Richard Glynn, Henry Hussey's third brother composed an acrostic poem '*in memory*' of Singleton.

So sad, so silent art thou, dear old Hall,
In which in childhood I so oft have played –
No voice to answer, none to hear me call!
Gone are they all! Some in the grave are laid!
Lingering voices seem to ring around,
Echoes from each long-past familiar sound, –
The tones of loved and lost ones gone before!
On this sad earth they will be heard no more,
Never ah never, never, never more.

After a number of years during which the house was left to decay, the whole estate was bought in 1919 by Swansea

Corporation. In 1920 it was rented out and in 1923 sold to University College of Swansea.

Further Reading

King Copper – South Wales and the Copper Trade 1584–1895. R. Rees. University of Wales Press. 2000.

Singleton Abbey and the Vivians of Swansea. R. A. Griffiths. Gomer. 1988.

FRIARS

In the thirteenth century a new religious revival swept through Europe and many wanted to follow Christ as members of the different orders of friars that were formed:

Franciscan Friars – dedicated to following the example of St Francis of Assisi and were formed in 1209 and lived a life of poverty. They moved from place to place and lived by preaching and begging. Many became teachers and helped set up universities. The Franciscans came to England in 1224 and were known as the 'grey friars'. In Wales they were *Y Brodyr Llwydion* because of the coarse garment with a pointed hood of the same material, and a short cloak which they wore. Around their waist was a knotted cord – the cordeliére – and they went barefoot. Llanfaes, Anglesey became the most well-known Franciscan friary in Wales but they also settled in Cardiff and Cardigan.

Dominican Friars – led by St Dominic, a Spaniard. Known as the Order of Preachers which was recognised by the Pope in 1217. They wore a white habit of a woollen material but for their manual work, for preaching and in the choir in winter, wore a black cloak and hood. They were known as the 'black friars'. In Wales, Dominican houses were founded in Brecon, Cardiff and Haverfordwest.

Depending on which Order of monks they belonged to, the habit which monks wore was made of a particular colour of coarse wool cloth: black for Benedictines and Cluniacs (called 'black monks'), undyed, unbleached natural wool for Carthusians and Cistercians (often called 'white monks'). The underwear for Benedictines consisted of a natural linen shirt reaching almost to the knees, with long, tight sleeves. Underpants were only issued to monks leaving the monastery on some errand, otherwise they were not worn – they were called *braies* and were long, baggy and made of linen.

Shoes were of black or tan leather (sandals were not worn by monks, despite the popular cartoon version of history) and socks were permitted in cold climates, as were fur undergarments called *pelices*.

The habit reached almost to the ground and the sleeves were made very wide and far too long – they had to be turned back or bunched up the arm. At certain times the sleeves were allowed to fall to their full length, hiding the hands completely. A hood could be attached directly to the habit, or to an overgarment known as a cowl. The hood had to be worn at specific times. When doing manual work, monks put on a protective garment called a *scapular*. This was a long rectangular piece of wool cloth with a hole in the middle for the head, falling over the habit front and back to keep it clean. Belts could be of leather, tied in a knot at the front, or of linen cord (without the three knots worn by friars).

The obvious mark of the monk was not any kind of wooden cross but his haircut, which left a bald patch at the crown of the head, known as the Roman tonsure, which symbolised the Crown of Thorns worn by Jesus. This was performed for the first time before a monk took his vows in the church and subsequent shaving occurred in the cloister about nine times a year. Combined with the black or white habit this instantly marked him

9. OTHER ESTABLISHMENTS –
'designed to bring Heaven to men, and men to Heaven.'

The Welsh friaries included five Dominican houses in Bangor, Brecon, Cardiff, Haverfordwest and Rhuddlan; three Franciscan houses in Cardiff, Carmarthen and Llanfaes; one Carmelite house in Denbigh and one house of Austin Friars in Newport.

The name of 'mendicant friars' was given to several groups of 'begging friars' whose origins in Europe date to the 13th and 14th centuries. These friars, in contrast to the monks, moved about freely among the people, especially the poor, preaching the gospel. Recognized by their religious habits they were popularly referred to as Grey Friars (Franciscans), Black Friars (Dominicans), Austin Friars (Augustinians) and White Friars (Carmelites).

BANGOR
The establishment dated from the middle of the thirteenth century is first mentioned in 1251. The remains indicated a small establishment with a cloister 62 feet from east to west, and lying on the north side of the church. Of the church itself there were remains of an aisleless building (26 feet wide), probably the quire, with traces of the start of a wider building, probably the nave, to the west. Walls found to the east of the eastern range served to indicate that a chapter-house projected in this direction, as two carved stone coffin-lids were found within its area. Two other carved coffin-lids were also discovered, one with a curious heraldic checked design, with the silver indicated by lead run into the alternate squares.

Name: **BRECON FRIARY**
Order: **Dominican**
Location: **Brecon, Powys**
OS Map Ref.: **SO 042298**

The Black Friars' house at Brecon was founded about the middle of the thirteenth century and is first mentioned as being in existance in 1269. Its remains were, early in the twentieth century, the most extensive and important of all the Welsh friaries, their partial preservation being due to the founding or refounding of a school there by Henry VIII. The remains consist of the quire of the church, dedicated to St Nicholas, with a north aisle and some indications of the position of the cloister, dorter and sacristy and a detached group of buildings to the south.

The Quire (65 feet by 26 feet) is a mid-thirteenth century building, with a large east window consisting of five lancet-lights of unequal width, and all incorporated under a two-centred outer order or head. The north wall has a series of eleven lancet windows divided by attached shafts with moulded capitals and bases and having moulded rear-arches; below the third window from the east end is a recess in the wall with a moulded segmental-pointed arch, probably the founder's tomb. The eastern part of the south wall has four lancet windows uniform with those opposite; below them and set in a projection are the double piscina and sedilia of four bays. At the back of the piscina and in the westernmost bay of the sedilia are squints form communicating with the sacristy, which was entered by a doorway further west.

The quire is closed at the west end by an inserted cross-wall from the fourteenth century, pierced by a two centred archway. This wall was inserted to support a bell-tower or a bell-cote, replacing the original structure which was probably of timber.

The Nave measured 95 feet by 26 feet. The whole structure appears to have been rebuilt and perhaps extended in the fourteenth century. The north wall had an arcade, opening into the aisle, and probably of five bays. East of the arcade is a pointed doorway, opening into the north chapel. The south wall has, at the east end, traces of the blocked doorway from the cloister; further west is a second doorway, of fourteenth-century material. Of the two other doorways in the western part of this wall, the eastern is modern but the second is of the fourteenth century. Intruding into the south-west angle of the church is a rounded projection of post-reformation date. In the west wall of the nave the bases of the splays of a large west window still remain. Across the east end of the nave is a modern wall, enclosing the existing vestibule, which may represent an ancient feature, together with the west wall of the quire perhaps supported a steeple.

The north Aisle (12 feet wide) has a chapel at the east end, which is still in use. It has much restored windows in the east and north walls and a double piscina in the south wall. The chapel is closed in on the west by a modern wall. West of this chapel only a short length of fourteenth-century walls survives, with the splay of one window; beyond this point the wall is a reconstruction of uncertain date, incorporating, towards its western end, a reset fourteenth century archway.

The Cloister has been entirely destroyed.

The range, on the eastern side of the cloister, contained the Dorter on the first floor, as there is in the south wall of the quire, a fifteenth-century doorway, now blocked, which led to the night-stairs from the dorter.

The detached group of buildings, standing 170 feet to the south of the nave of the church consisted of two halls at right angles to one another. This group of buildings was from the fourteenth century although the windows are of a later date. Both halls have large fireplaces and retain much of their original roof-construction; the roof of the western hall is of a more ornate style. The two stone fireplaces have heavy hoods from the fourteenth century.

At the time of the Dissolution, it had about six acres of land and a small garden.

CARDIFF (Blackfriars)

The house of the Black Friars of Cardiff was founded before the year 1269, on a site outside the west gate of the town. Though nothing was standing above ground its remains were completely excavated by the Marquis of Bute in 1887. The church was burnt by Owain Glyndŵr in 1404 and again destroyed in 1414. The inventory from the time of its closure mentions the vestry, high altar, Lady altar, a pair of organs and the kitchen.

CARDIFF (Greyfriars)

The date of the foundation of the Grey Friars at Cardiff is uncertain, but the house is first mentioned in 1399. The remains were excavated in 1896 by the Marquis of Bute.

Further excavations were carried out in 1925 by Mr J. P. Grant, F.S.A. His plan showed the walls uncovered in the excavations. The domestic buildings were largely built over by a mansion of the Herbert family. The remains of the nave arcades of the church, discovered during the excavations, show that they were erected about 1300, but provided no explanation of the extra width of both the east and west bays. Perhaps this was a legacy from an earlier building. This house was spared by Owain Glyndŵr in 1404, because of his well-known favour for the Franciscan Order. The suppression inventory mentions the quire with a table of alabaster, a pair of organs, five tables of alabaster in the 'church' (nave), a bell in the steeple, the vestry, kitchen, hall and a new chamber, also a grate of iron that stood in the quire.

HAVERFORDWEST

The date of the settlement of the Black Friars at Haverfordwest is unknown, but they were established there in 1246 and according to Leland the site was changed in 1256. The buildings stood on the east side of Bridge Street, between it and the river, on the site now occupied by the Black Horse Inn, a foundry and other premises. These buildings are mainly constructed of rubble, but there is no recognisable fragment of pre-Reformation work, now visible, though lead coffins and a stone coffin are said to have been found on the site. A letter from Edmund Yardley to Browne Willis, about 1739 says that there were then little or no remains, but that two effigies had been dug up.

The inventory of goods, taken at the dissolution mentions the 'Candllbemys' and a table of alabaster as they stood in the church and in the quire, a table at the high altar, the new stalls, the hall and two bells in the steeple.

Name:	**RHUDDLAN FRIARY**
Order:	**Dominican**
Location:	**Rhuddlan, Denbighshire**
OS Map Ref.:	**SJ 029774**

The Black Friars were established at Rhuddlan at about the middle of the thirteenth century and began their buildings soon afterwards. In 1283 there were twenty-three friars, but at its dissolution in 1538 this had dropped to three. The outbuildings of the farm, called Plas Newydd, surround a square yard which may represent the cloister. No trace is left of the church or of the eastern range but it was standing when the brothers Buck made a drawing in 1742 which shows not only some highly interesting details but also indicates that the buildings at Rhuddlan were on a much more ambitious scale that was usual among the lesser or smaller friaries. The whole length of the building was occupied by the dorter on the first floor and at its north end is indication of the junction with the church. Projecting eastwards from the range is a gabled structure, with three lancet-windows in the east end and three in the south return wall; this, most likely, was the chapter-house with a room above it. Further south, in the main range, is the archway of a passage from the cloister, and still further south a chimney-stack, probably that of the fireplace in the warming-house. At the south end of the range is a large doorway, at the dorter-level, leading to the rere-dorter, the ruins of which, with its connecting bridge, are also shown.

Of the southern range of the cloister court, the eastern part of the inner or north wall is still standing and contains four small square-headed windows of red Chester stone, set high in the wall, above a string-course which probably marked the level of the cloister-roof. The rest of the range seems to have been rebuilt, but the south side of it is shown in steep perspective in Buck's view. The only other ancient portion of the existing buildings is the northern portion of the outer wall of an outbuilding on the west of the yard. It appears to have projected westward from the original western range, as there is a return angle at the south end. It contains two pointed windows, probably of the fourteenth century, and blocked with ashlar. The rest of this range contains other pointed windows, but they appear not to be original and the walls themselves to be of post-suppression date.

Built into the garden-wall, to the north of the yard, are portions of a moulded and cusped arch of early fourteenth-century date and probably part of a tomb recess. Various funeral monuments built into the walls of the buildings round the yard include:

On the east side of the yard:

(a) effigy of a civilian in hood with flap, belt with skirt of gown

(a) effigy of a civilian in hood with flap, belt with skirt of gown tucked into it and holding in both hands a mace, probably fourteenth-century;

(b) part of a coffin-lid with inscription.

On south side of yard:

(a) slab with cross, head in a quatrefoil, sword at side and inscription to Robert, son of Robert de Bridelton, early fourteenth-century.

On west side of yard: coffin-lid with elaborate cross; on stem an incomplete inscription Hic jacet Snaisii, the rest destroyed, thirteenth-century.

The inventory of goods at the suppression lists the quire with a table of alabaster on the altar and new stalls, two bells in the steeple and the kitchen.

Further reading

Religious Houses of England and Wales. D. Knowles & R. N. Hadcock. Longman. 1971.

The towns of medieval Wales. I. Soulsby. Phillimore. 1983.

NEWPORT

The only house of the Austin Friars in Wales was established at Newport in 1377 and was situated between Church Street and the river Usk. In 1800 it was described as the remains of a friary and consisting of several detached buildings, including a sizeable hall with Gothic windows, the dilapidated body of the church and a small but elegant north transept. By 1859, all the remains had been destroyed and demolished. There is now nothing recognisable on the site.

Name: 'TRAWSCOED' (Cantref Selyf) ABBEY
Order:
Location: Llandefalle, Powys

Land in Cantref Selyf, formerly belonging to William de Foria, was presented to Dore Abbey for the foundation of a monastery by Walter de Clifford of Bronllys, between 1172 and 1174. It was associated with the monastic grange of Trawscoed, (to the north of the valley of the river Dulas) by *Giraldus Cambrensis* who stated that the mother house of Dore Abbey had reduced Trawscoed from a convent to a dependant grange in the early 13th century. He also mentioned a visit to the abbey by Abbot Canawg of Cwmhir. A possible reason for the suppression of the abbey was that it never became of the size hoped for.

There are no monastic building at Trawscoed as whatever was originally built were only temporary buildings and the plans for an abbey never came to fruition. There is, at Lower Trawscoed, a blocked hood-moulded window, of an early date but no other stonework to suggest an abbey.

Further reading

The location and siting of Cistercian Houses in Wales and the West'. J. Bond. Archaeologia Cambrensis, 154. 2007.

Medieval Religious Houses. D. Knowles & R. N. Hadcock. 1971. Longmans. 1971.

Name: TŶ FAENOR ABBEY
Order: Cistercian
Location: Powys

This is believed to be the site of a Cistercian foundation in 1143 valley. This belief was instigated the Royal Commission in 1913, but there is very little evidence to support the claim.

Cwmhir is said to have had two foundation dates, one in 1143 and another in 1176 but its connections with Tŷ Faenor can only be guessed at and by now the truth has probably evaded all researchers.

Further reading
Abbeys and Priories of Wales. R. N. Cooper. Christopher Davies Ltd. 1992.
Religious Houses of England and Wales. D. Knowles & R. N. Hadcock. Longman. 1971.

Name:	**RHAYADER FRIARY**
Order:	**Dominican**
Location:	**Powys**

Apart from one brief comment by historian Jonathan Williams, little evidence exists of the existence of Rhaeader Friary. A map of circa.1770 is said to show an abode and small field on the east bank of the river Black Friars, but it is not known where the said map can be found in 2014.

Further reading
The Friars in Wales. R. C. Easterling. Archaeologia Cambrensis 14, 350 1914.

Monkton Priory Church Pembroke Pembrokeshire
Cardigan Benedictine Priory Cardigan Ceredigion
Ruthin Friary, Denbighshire

Llandrudion Hospice; Parc Croes, St David's And The Cathedral

Close, Pembrokeshire
Llawhaden Hospice Llawhaden Pembrokeshire
Keeston Hospice Camrose Pembrokeshire
St Davids Hospice, Whitewell Hospice, St Davids And The
Cathedral Close, Pembrokeshire
St Mary's Hospice, Spittal, Pembrokeshire

Llansantffraed in Elvel Nunnery, Powys (Radnorshire)

Cardigan Priory
Gwenddwr Priory, Powys (Breconshire)
Llanbadarn Fawr, nr, Aberystwyth, Cardiganshire
Llanfair Priory, nr. Llandovery Priory
Llangua, Monmouthshire
Malpas Priory, nr. Newport, Monmouthshire
St Kynemark, nr. Chepstow
St Tudwal's, island off the coast at Abersoch, Gwynedd
Snead Priory, Powys (Montgomeryshire)

Further Reading

The Architectural Remains of the Mendicant Orders in Wales. A. W.
    Clapham, F.S.A. Archaeological Journal, 84. 1927.

10. THE END OF AN ERA – *'THE KING'S 'other' GREAT MATTER'*

By the fourteenth century, many monasteries were beginning to show that their religious zeal was waning. Factors that contributed to this state of affairs included the Black Death. In England, the Black Death killed 1.5 million people out of a total population of 4 million people between 1348 and 1350. It was to strike England another six times before the end of the century. The Black Death was the name given to a deadly plague (often called bubonic plague). It was to have an impact on England's social structure. Many monks had other responsibilities forced upon them that took them away from their religious work. Some sat in the House of Lords. Smaller abbeys found it very difficult to continue.

By the time Henry VIII came to the throne, he and his ministers saw that all was not well. Not only that but Henry had other problems to deal with. As a young and inexperienced king, Henry VIII left the governing of his realm to his ministers. At the time he had little interest in such things and much preferred sports and music, horse-riding and hunting but there was a serious side to his character and another of his hobbies was a study of the Christian faith. At the beginning of his reign England was a Catholic country and the English Church ruled by the Pope from the Vatican in Rome. When a German reformer named Martin Luther spoke out against the Catholic Church, Henry wrote a book condemning him. The Pope, Clement VII, was so pleased with Henry's response, that he gave him the title of *Fidei Defensor* (Defender of the Faith) in 1521.

One of Henry's chief ministers was Thomas Wolsey, a butcher's son who, during his term of office between 1514 and 1529, became a very ambitious man. By 1515 Wolsey was chief minister, Lord Chancellor, leader of the King's Council, chief judge, Bishop of London and Archbishop of Canterbury. He was also appointed a cardinal by the Pope and was his special ambassador. He was the most powerful man in England, apart from the king himself and became very rich. Hampton Court on the banks of the Thames was his palace. Cardinal Wolsey closed twenty one religious houses so that he could endow a grammar school in his home town of Ipswich and a new college (Christ Church) at Oxford but for religious houses in general, this was but a shadow of what was to come.

Wolsey was also a vain and greedy character and very unpopular amongst the ordinary people who had to pay the taxes he levied to pay for wars against France and Scotland. His downfall was his inability, in 1529, to help solve *the King's great matter*.

Henry was married to Catherine of Aragon, his brother Arthur's widow. Special permission had been granted by the Pope for the marriage to go ahead in 1509. In 1511, Catherine gave birth to a son but he died two months later. By 1525 Catherine had given birth to four other sons who had all died shortly after their birth. Henry desperately wanted a son as his heir to preserve the Tudor dynasty but his only surviving child from Catherine was Mary (1516-1558). Catherine became too old to bear any more children and by 1526 Henry had met and fallen in love with Anne Boleyn. He wanted to marry and have children with her but firstly he had other problems to deal with.

Anne Boleyn would give herself entirely to him only if he would give himself entirely to her.

Henry was also worried by a passage from the Bible, Leviticus XVIII,

And if a man shall take his brother's wife, it is an unclean thing. They shall be childless.

Wolsey was ordered to arrange for the marriage to be annulled so that after a divorce Henry could marry Anne but the Pope refused to allow such a thing. It was decided by the Pope that the matter would be discussed in a special church court in London but after convening the court in 1529, he changed his mind and insisted the hearing take place in Rome. Henry refused to attend or even agree to such a change, seeing it as an affront to his position and power. Henry blamed Wolsey for the failures of the visit to England of Cardinal Campeggio, who was sent by the Pope. There was nothing Wolsey could do as the Pope did not want to grant Henry a divorce as he (the Pope) was under the control of Charles V, the Holy Roman Emperor, who also happened to be Catherine's nephew.

Wolsey fell from grace and was replaced as Lord Chancellor by Sir Thomas Moore, a lawyer and a scholar but more importantly, a devout Catholic. He could not agree to Henry's plans for a divorce and his profound faith led him to resign in 1532. In 1535 he refused to acknowledge Henry as Supreme Head of the Church of England and was executed. His final words from the scaffold were,

I die loyal to God and the King, but to God first of all.

Another new chief minister was appointed. Thomas Cromwell, a Protestant with a dislike for monasteries, was far more prepared to do as his king asked and his solution to '*the King's great matter'* was a simple one-that Henry become head of the English Church. It was thought that by a change of leadership, the king's divorce would be a mere formality. Thomas Cranmer, the new Archbishop of Canterbury quickly agreed to the divorce. Many Acts of Parliament were passed between 1532 and 1534 to end the Pope's authority and make Henry VIII Supreme Head of the Church of England. If Henry and Anne Boleyn were to have children, it was decreed that they, rather than Catherine's offspring, would inherit the throne. Such new laws were unacceptable to Thomas Moore and that is why he was executed.

(As it happened, it was Henry's third wife-Jane Seymour, who bore him the son and heir that he so wanted and it was he who was crowned after his father's death and reigned as Edward VI (1547-1553), followed by Catherine's daughter Mary who reigned between 1553 and 1558 and lastly Anne Boleyn's daughter Elizabeth who reigned between 1558 and 1603.)

When Henry VIII became head of the Church of England he appointed Thomas Cromwell (once described as being *as clever as a bag of snakes*)as his Vicar General. Priests at this time were unpopular, as was the church itself, with nobles and peasants. Having to pay taxes did not go down well especially paying a tithe-one tenth of a person's income or produce to the church as it owned about one-third of all land. Henry decided to reform the Church and as head, to take all the Church's wealth for himself. The monasteries were a stronghold of the Pope's power in England. Monks and nuns recognised him as the head of the Church in England. This was a situation that Henry could not tolerate. In 1530, Parliament accused the priests of showing more loyalty to the Pope than to Henry. Though it was they who had provided charity, education, hospitals and shelter for many, the wealth they had collected had made many of them greedy, lazy and rich. In 1532, Henry demanded that all priests swear loyalty to him. Many refused. Henry needed their wealth as he had spent most of the money left to him by his father by becoming involved with wars and living a very lavish lifestyle. If he broke away from Rome and if he could get his hands on the monasteries' wealth, he could, and did, become the enemy of Spain and France and catholic Europe and would need to prepare for war.

Cromwell and his deputies visited all the abbeys and religious houses and decided that those with an annual income of less than two hundred pounds would be closed or dissolved. An inventory of all their holdings was compiled and published in July 1535 in a book called '*Valor Ecclesiasticus*' (Value of Church Property). This showed that land held by the monasteries was valued at £100,000 a year and that they were also worth £25,000 from other means. Another visitation was arranged by Commissioners to investigate rumours about the monks' behaviour. The report on this visit showed that they were idle, corrupt and useless. More favourable reports were changed and re-written to include condemning clauses such as '*manifest sin, vicious, carnal and abominable living is daily used and committed amongst the little and small abbeys*'. Such comments more or less sealed their fate, whether they were true or not. But the revenue secured by closing them and selling their treasures went straight into government coffers.

More than one abbot had read *between the lines* of the *Valor Ecclesiasticus* and had anticipated what was coming. Efforts were made to raise more income or to line the pockets of those facing an enforced retirement. They leased and sold land to individuals and families so as to increase their income and hopefully, keep their abbey safe from dissolution. The abbot of Aberconwy was careful to provide for himself and others in case the abbey should be dissolved. Thomas Pennant, the penultimate abbot of Basingwerk Abbey, transferred lands to members of his family as did his son Nicholas, last abbot of Basingwerk. *He had an intelligent anticipation of coming events and provided generously for his family and friends at the expense of the abbey*. Neath Abbey leased out many properties and fishing rights to raise more money. When a new abbot was appointed to Grace Dieu Abbey, the old allowed the new one a generous pension to live on for the rest of his natural life. Some valuables were hidden for future use and a mid-twentieth century search found a horde of gold coins dating from the reign of Edward IV to 1536/7 on land belonging to Grace Dieu Abbey, hidden in anticipation of a future *rainy day*. A thirteenth century chalice and paten were discovered at Cymer in 1890, hidden quite probably for the same reasons.

An Act of Parliament was passed in 1536 which permitted the dissolution of the lesser monasteries with an income of less than £200 a year. Money and valuable treasures were sent to the King's 'Counting House'. Buildings were destroyed. It was a loss that had long lasting effects. Rebellions broke out in Lincolnshire and Yorkshire. Fifty Lincolnshire rebels were executed. Robert Aske, a Lincolnshire lawyer led an army of 30,000 on the Pilgrimage of Grace in Yorkshire which, by 24 October 1536, had captured York and had been joined by the Archbishop of York and Thomas Darcy, a powerful local leader. The Pilgrimage of Grace was meant to be a peaceful protest march. The rebels or pilgrims as they preferred to call themselves presented their demands to the king who, at first, appeared to be agreeable to them but in reality he had no intention of keeping his word. As the leader of the Pilgrimage of Faith, Aske had paid tribute to the work of the abbeys and monks of northern England.

> *The abbeys in the north parts gave great alms to poor men and laudably served God. By occasion of the suppression, the divine service of almighty God is much diminished. Many of the abbeys were in the mountains and desert places, where the people be rude of condition and not well taught the law of God, and when the abbeys stood the said people had not only worldly refreshing in their bodies but also spiritual refuge. None was in these parts denied so that the people were greatly refreshed by the said abbeys, where they now have no such succour. Also the abbeys were one of the beauties of this realm to all men and strangers passing through. Such abbeys as were near the sea were great maintainers of sea walls and dykes.*

But Aske was captured, imprisoned for six months and

executed together with more than two hundred others. The pilgrimage achieved nothing only giving Henry the excuse, if he needed one, to continue with his plans to dissolve the larger monasteries. Between 1537 and 1540 the 645 larger monasteries were dissolved, the last being Waltham Abbey in 1540. Abbots who resisted these moves were executed and hanged at the gates of their own monastery. The buildings were stripped of doors, glass, lead and timber, art and literature, gold plate, silver, gold and jewellery. Livestock was seized. Land was sold to the wealthy. Buildings were bought to be turned into mansion houses. Stones were sold to repair other buildings. All of which meant that Henry had increased his wealth to the extent of an extra £140,000 a year (worth over £43,058,400.00 in 2013) between 1536 and 1547. (His normal income at that time was £100,000 a year.)

The total number of suppressed monasteries amounted to 645. The abbots of twenty three had seats in Parliament. Ninety colleges were dissolved, 2,374 churches and free chapels and 110 hospitals or fraternities, also shared the same fate. The total new income to the King amounted to £161,000. Many of the magnificent churches and monasteries were simply stripped of their roofs and were soon in a ruinous condition.

The poorer inhabitants of the country were the ones who suffered mostly from the dissolution and suppression of the larger establishments, as not only did the monks administer to their religious wants, they also attended to their physical ailments and needs. In another way its effects told disastrously on the nobility and gentry, who often provided for their younger sons, or friends and relations, by placing them in the various monastic institutions. In some cases the monastic lands were bought by land-jobbers, who threw them out of cultivation, and so deprived many labourers of work. All this created bad feeling against the 'reformers'. The monks founded schools, drained marshes, cleared the thick forests, and were invaluable members of society in many ways. Some of the monasteries near the sea coast were strongly fortified, and were often attacked by Danish marauders.

Much of the money was spent on armaments, defence and building a new navy. War with France broke out in 1543 and by 1547 Henry was more or less bankrupt again. (He had been paying the 7000 monks who had been displaced from the monasteries a pension which cost the Treasury £44,000 a year.) The whole country suffered architecturally, religiously and socially. Unemployment and poverty was on the increase. New landlords set themselves up as a powerful group who did not want a return to the Catholic faith. The Pope's influence in England became negligible and gave Henry complete control over the Church in England.

The Dissolution of the Monasteries had an undoubted effect but no new class of landlords was created as most of the land went into the hands of private, established families and landowners. No great army of begging monks appeared. No educational disaster was to follow.

But the break off of relations with Rome saw the beginning of a much bigger religious change in Europe. Today it is known as the Reformation because it tried to reform or change the Catholic Church. It did not succeed and a new type of church was formed—the Protestant or 'protesting' church which wanted churches to be better organised and worshiping to be made simpler. Henry was not a Protestant; he still held his Catholic beliefs but would not obey the Pope. Many leading Catholics turned against him and rebelled. Religious unrest was a prominent feature of future Tudor reigns. Henry's great matters had been resolved but at a price.

Level, level with the ground the towers do lie,
With their golden glittering tops pierced once to the sky!

Further Reading

Dissolution of the Monasteries. G. W. O. Woodward. Pitkin Guides. 1998.

Henry VIII. A. Langley. Heinemann. 1995.

Life in a Medieval Abbey. T. McAleavy. English Heritage. 1996.

The Tudors. A. Langley. Hamlyn. 1993.

The Welsh Cistercians. D. H. Williams. Hughes & Son, Ltd., Griffin Press. 1969.

11. MY STAFF OF FAITH TO WALK UPON –
THE CISTERCIAN WAY

'If we walk in the footsteps of the past with respect and humility, there will come a change of heart; we will travel more prudent paths in future'. according to Father Fahey (1883–1954). An opportunity to do so is available in Wales. If one was to ask what have Conwy, Cwmhir and Cymer; Llanllugan, Llantarnam and Llanllyr in common, how many would guess at the correct answer?

They are all important points on a 650 mile footpath in Wales. As there is another Cistercian Way for pilgrims and walkers, this one must be called the Welsh Cistercian Way. (The Cumbrian Cistercian Way is a route along the paths, tracks and byways of the limestone hills that fringe the northern shores of Morecambe Bay via woodlands to Hampsfell and Cartmel Priory to Cark and Holker Hall. The route continues over the sands of the Leven Estuary, but as this is dangerous it should only be attempted with the recognised Sand Pilot. Otherwise the train should be caught to Ulverston where the Way continues by Dalton to Furness Abbey and the coast.)

The Cistercians were a religious order of great importance in the history of Wales who believed in the ethic of hard work. They were farmers who cleared much of the upland farming landscape of Wales.

The Cistercian abbeys were well known for their hospitality to pilgrims, poets and writers. It was the Cistercians who wrote to the Pope in support of the Welsh kings Llywelyn ap Iorwerth (1174–1240) prince of Gwynedd and ruler of most of Wales, and Llywelyn ap Gruffudd (also known as Llywelyn ein Llyw Olaf (Llywelyn our Last Leader) (c.1223–1282) last prince of Wales and the only one to be recognized by the English as Prince of Wales, and who backed Owain Glyndŵr (1349-1416), leader of a revolt against the English crown between 1400-1409 and was the last claimant of the independent title of Prince of Wales, in his bid to regain Welsh independence. The Cistercians looked after important pilgrimage shrines like Penrhys-one of the holiest places in Wales, a place where pilgrims came 'over land and sea' (according to the poets) to worship at the shrine of the Virgin Mary. The shrine had a miraculous statue of Jesus and his mother. Tradition states that the statue had appeared in an oak tree and a team of oxen had been unable to drag it from its place so a chapel and a hostel for the pilgrims were built there. The site belonged to the monks of Llantarnam who provided hospitality and maintained roads and bridges to the shrine but the site was destroyed during the Dissolution of the Monasteries.

The ruins of the Cistercian abbeys are among the most beautiful and evocative places in the Welsh landscape.

In 1998 a group of walkers decided to celebrate 900 years of the Cistercian Order by walking along a route, a pilgrimage route, to all the Cistercian abbeys in Wales. They followed a circular, clockwise route, which means that it can be started at any point, calling at all the sixteen medieval Cistercian houses in Wales, including Caldey Island and Whitland. Research began in 1997 and the route was walked for the first time in the summer of 1998.

Bishop Anthony Crockett (Bishop of Bangor 2004-2008) believed that travel broadens the mind, and at the same time broadening the spirit as well. This route offers an opportunity to exercise the mind and body through many varied experiences for Christians, Cistercians, pilgrims and walkers alike through many different areas of Wales. It can be tackled as a challenging footpath or as a personal pilgrimage. It can be completed in one go (though quite an effort would be needed!) or in stages.

According to Maddy Gray, lecturer in history at the University of Wales, the long-term aim, is to define the principal route and have it way marked. The parallel objective is to encourage links, loops and alternative routes, to provide a choice between challenging upland paths or easier, flatter options, while always following a Cistercian theme.

The seventeen different stages include:

1.   Llantarnam to Penrhys.
2.   Penrhys to Margam.
3.   Margam to Neath.
4.   Neath to Tenby.
5.   Tenby to Whitland.
6.   Whitland to Llanllyr.
7.   Llanllyr to Strata Florida.
8.   Strata Florida to Cymer.
9.   Cymer to Conwy.
10. Conwy to Basingwerk.

(There is on offer a high level alternative route from Cymer to Basingwerk.)

11. Basingwerk to Valle Crucis.
12. Valle Crucis to Strata Marcella.
13. Strata Marcella to Llanllugan.
14. Llanllugan to Cwmhir.
15. Cwmhir to Grace Dieu.
16. Grace Dieu to Tintern.
17. Tintern to Llantarnam.

The route also links many of Wales's other long-distance paths such as the Coed Morgannwg Way and the St Illtyd Way, the Knights' Way and the Landsker Borderland Trail, the Cambrian Way, the North Wales Coast Path, the Offa's Dyke Path near Holywell. It is much more than a long-distance path, for as well as exploring the abbeys of the Cistercian order, one can see and visit small parish churches and holy wells along the way, study the geology of the Pembrokeshire coast, Stone Age burial mounds, medieval castles and sheep-farms, landscaped gardens and the industrial heritage of the nineteenth and twentieth centuries. It takes the walker onto Roman roads, medieval pilgrimage routes and nineteenth-century canal towpaths.

The whole route was walked in 2005 taking from 29 May to 2 September with a break for tired feet from 6 June to 17 July. It has since been walked by groups, individuals, clergy and lay people, Welsh and other nationalities.

12. GLOSSARY

WHO'S WHO?

Abbot/Abbess – man or woman in charge of an abbey

Almoner – abbey official responsible for looking after the poor.

> *He shall take great pains to discover where may lie those sick and weakly persons who are without means of sustenance. Entering a house he shall speak kindly and comfort the sick man, and offer him the best of what he has.*
>
> *(From a Guide to Monastic Life written by Lanfranc, Archbishop of Canterbury in the late eleventh century.)*

Barber Surgeon – the monk who shaved the faces and tonsures of the monk and even performed surgery when necessary

Canon – a member of a body of churchmen serving a cathedral and living a life similar to monks

Cellarer – in charge of food and drink in an abbey. He also tested the drink of the abbey. His store rooms usually occupied the west wing.

> *He shall provide utensils for the cellar and the kitchen, and flagons and tankards and other vessels for the refectory. He should be the father of the whole community and should have a care for the sound and still more for the sick.*

Chamberlain – in charge of housekeeping in an abbey, for all the monks clothing (a rough fabric cloak, or habit, a rope belt and sometimes a pair of sandals) and supervised the bedding, bathing and shaving.

> *He sees to the glazing and repairing of the dormitory windows. To brethren about to go on a journey he shall give capes, gaiters and spurs. Once a year he causes straw to be removed in all the beds.*

Choir monks – also known as cloister monks. They did not have the same responsibilities as an Obedientary who could be absent, with permission, from services. Choir monks had to be present to carry out the full round of prayers and services.

Circator – monks who ensured that all monks were obeying abbey rules

Conversi – another term for lay brothers (see below)

Corrodians – ones who spent their retirement years at an abbey

Fraterer – in charge of the refectory and responsible for table linen, crockery, and lavatorium where monks washed their hands before eating

Guest-Master – supervisor of the guest house and responsible for offering hospitality to visitors.

The brother who is appointed to receive guests should have ready in the guest-house beds, chairs, tables, towels, cloths, tankards, plates, spoons, basins and suchlike. Whoever wishes to speak with the abbot, prior or any monk shall use the guest-master as his ambassador.

His duty is to show the buildings to those who want to see them, taking care that the community is not then sitting in the cloister. He shall not introduce into the cloister under any circumstances anyone wearing riding-boots or spurs, nor anyone who goes barefoot or only has drawers on his legs.

Infirmarion – who looked after the infirmary or sick-house. He was the house doctor and had authority to relax the dietary rule for the sick and infirm.

Every day after Compline he shall sprinkle holy water over all the beds of the sick. He himself shall place before the sick brethren all the dishes prepared for them.

Kitchener – cook and distributor of food

Lay brothers – men who lived within the abbey, took monastic vows but undertook to carry out more of the manual labour and less of the devotional aspects of abbey life

Lay servants – workers at a monastery who were paid for their labours

Master of Novices – responsible for all new recruits, Made sure that they learnt Latin prayers off by heart. Also in charge of maintaining discipline

Novices – new recruits.

> *The older boys shall sit apart from one another. In the afternoon they shall not read or write or do any work but shall simply rest. If necessity causes them to rise at night, they shall first rouse their masters, and then lighting a candle, they shall go with them to relieve themselves. They shall not speak with one another unless a master is present to hear what is being said.*

Obedientary – an office bearer beneath the abbot and prior. A deputy

Precentor or Cantor – in charge of church services. Also responsible for the library and the scholarly work of the monks.

> *Whenever anyone has to read or chant anything in the church the cantor shall, if need be, hear him go over his task before he performs it in public. He takes care of all the books of the house and has them in his keeping.*

Prior – second in command to the abbot or his deputy. Also in charge of discipline.

> *Saving the reverence due to the abbot, the prior is to be honoured above the other servants of God's house. He takes precedence in the choir and chapter and refectory. If the abbot be far away he may depose from office those whom he learns to be handling their business in a way contrary to the profit of the monastery. When he enters the chapter house all rise and stand.*

Roundsmen – see Circator above

Sacrist – responsible for all the church furnishings, vestments, ornaments and lighting. He also took charge of any building work.

> *His task is to ring the bells, or to instruct others how they are to be*

rung. He distributes candles. He takes charge of burials. It is his task twice a week to wash the chalice.

Scribe – someone whose job was to copy documents and books before printing was invented. One who does calligraphy (putting words on paper), illumination, (arts used to decorate the page) or both

Synod – a formal meeting of church leaders. A group of church leaders who are in charge of making decisions and laws related to the church

WHAT'S WHAT?

Abbey – a senior monastic church ruled by an abbot or abbes

Aisle – part of a church on either side of the nave or chancel

Alien – a religious establishment whose mother house was based in France

Arcade – a line or row of arches

Bracile – a leather belt or girdle used during the day, large enough to serve as a receptacle, instead of pockets

Buttery – a room for storing food and drink

Calefactory – the warming room where monks could warm up

Caligas – solid working boots

Chalice – Communion cup

Chancel – the eastern part of the church for the use of priests and choristers

Chapter – the governing body of an abbey (or cathedral)

Chapter house – meeting room in an abbey

Choir/Quire – the area between the nave and sanctuary in a church or cathedral

Cloak – usually a semi-circle, fastened at the throat by a pin, button or brooch and provided with a hood

Cloister – a square courtyard with a garden around which lay all the domestic accommodation in an abbey

Cowl – hood worn by monks

Cresset – an oil lamp

Crucis – cross

Cultellus – a knife that was hung from the belt

Daughter house – a cell or an offshoot of a bigger establishment

Dorter – a dormitory in a monastery. Term also applied to single bedrooms or other sleeping quarters

Femoralia – (*breeches*) Trousers or drawers extending to or just below the knee. Described as 'clothing for the thighs'

Florida – flowery

Frater – another word for the dining area

Friary – a religious house similar to an abbey but not separate from the world; friars went out and preached to communities

Garth – the cloister garden

Grange – an abbey farm

Habit – tunic worn by monks and nuns

Herbularius – a monastery herb garden

Hood – a covering attached to a cloak or cowl worn over the head when travelling

Hospice – building or chapel used to care for the sick or poor

Lancet – a long, narrow window with a pointed head

Lavatorium – area for washing hands before entering the refectory

Mantle – a loose sleeveless cloak

Mappula (Mappa) – a handkerchief, kept tucked in the belt

Mass – celebration of Holy Communion

Mendicant – begging or relying on charitable donations

Misericord – a small ledge on the seat in the monks' choir area of the church, which the monks could rest against

Nave – the central aisle of the abbey church

Necessarium – toilet

Offices – church services

Opus Dei – the work of God

Papal Bull – a type of letter issued by the Pope and named after the lead seal (*bulla*) that was attached to the end. From the twelfth century, papal bulls have carried a lead seal with the heads of the apostles Saint Peter and Saint Paul on one side and the pope's signature on the other.

Pedules – stockings, socks or light indoor footwear

Pee pot – a clay chamber pot used by monks

Piscina – alcove in a church for washing vessels used in services

Plainsong – unaccompanied choral prayer

Priory – a monastery or nunnery headed by a Prior or Prioress and dependent on an abbey. Most priories were 'daughter houses', under the rule of an abbot from a 'mother house'.

Pulpitum – a stone or wooden screen separating the lay people from the monks in a church

Refectory – the dining area

Reliquary – container for 'relics' – bones of holy people

Reredorter – toilet area for monks

Presbytery – the easternmost end of the abbey church

Sacristy – the treasury, where the silver plate and garments used in church services were kept

Sandals – leather or cloth straps holding a protective sole in place

Scapular – an apron-like work garment worn on top of the habit

Scriptorium – room for writing and copying holy texts

Slype – a passage leading from the cloister through the east range where the rule of silence was usually relaxed

Strata – pavement/or street

Stoup – a container for holy water at the entrance of a church

Tithe – the tax payable by local churches to an abbey – a tenth of a person's income or produce

Tonsure – shaving of the head or a patch on the crown of the head

Transept – the 'cross arms' of the church, extending north and south of the nave

Valle – valley

Vestments – clothing worn during divine services

Vigil – a watch kept on the night before a religious feast with prayer or other devotions

Warming house – the only room in a monastery, apart from the kitchen, with a fireplace

Further Reading

Abbeys and Priories of Wales. R. Cooper. Christopher Davies. 1992.

Abbeys – An Introduction. R. Gillyard-Beer. HMSO. 1958.

Abbeys and Priories of Wales. R. Cooper. Christopher Davies. 1992.

Abbeys, Priories and Cathedrals of Wales. M. Salter. Folly Publications. 2012.

Cathedrals, Abbeys and Priories of England and Wales. H. Thorold. Collins.1986.

Investing Abbeys and Priories in Scotland. Heritage Scotland.

Medieval Manuscripts. Utah Museum of Fine Art. 1997.

Further General Reading

Abbeys-An Introduction. R. Gillyard-Beer. HMSO. 1958.

Abbeys and Priories in England and Wales. B. Little. Batsford Books. 1979.

Castles and Abbeys of Wales. D. J. Cathcart King. HMSO. 1975.

Cathedrals, Abbeys and Priories of England and Wales. H. Thorold. Collins. 1986.

Discovering Abbeys and Priories. G. N. Wright. Shire Publications. 2004.

Welsh Churches and their Heritage

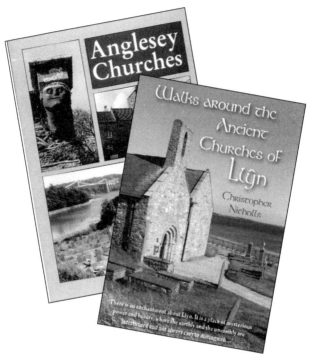

Visit our website for further information:
www.carreg-gwalch.com

Orders can be placed on our
On-line Shop

Heritage

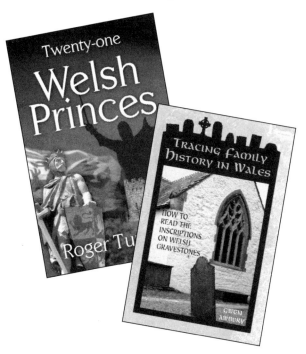

Visit our website for further information:
www.carreg-gwalch.com

Orders can be placed on our
On-line Shop

Welsh Churches and their Heritage

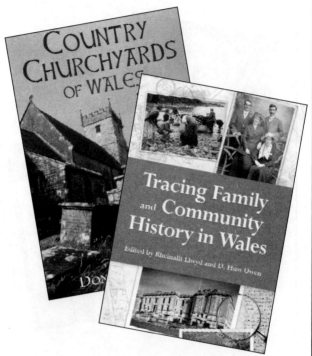

Visit our website for further information:
www.carreg-gwalch.com

Orders can be placed on our
On-line Shop